free yourself

TEN

LIFE-CHANGING POWERS OF YOUR WISE HEART

Carolyn Hobbs

Foreword by James Baraz

WISDOM PUBLICATIONS • BOSTON

Wisdom Publications
199 Elm Street
Somerville, MA 02144 USA
www.wisdompubs.org

Library of Congress Cataloging-in-Publication Data
Hobbs, Carolyn.
  Free yourself : 10 life-changing powers of your wise heart / Carolyn Hobbs ; foreword by James Baraz.
       pages cm
  Includes bibliographical references and index.
  ISBN 978-1-61429-081-0—ISBN 1-61429-081-4 (pbk. : alk. paper)—ISBN 978-1-61429-100-8 (ebook)
  1. Self-actualization (Psychology) 2. Happiness. 3. Conduct of life. I. Title.
  BF637.S4H588 2014
  158—dc23

2014007278

ISBN 978-1-61429-081-0
Ebook ISBN 978-1-61429-100-8

18 17 16 15 14
5 4 3 2 1

Cover and interior design by Gopa&Ted2, Inc.
Set in ITC New Baskerville 10.5/15.6.

"The Friend" on page vii is used by permission of Devi Weisenberg.

Wisdom Publications' books are printed on acid-free paper and meet the guidelines for permanence and durability of the Production Guidelines for Book Longevity of the Council on Library Resources.

This book was produced with environmental mindfulness. We have elected to print this title on 30% PCW recycled paper. As a result, we have saved the following resources: 13 trees, 6 million BTUs of energy, 1,103 lbs. of greenhouse gases, 5,979 gallons of water, and 400 lbs. of solid waste. For more information, please visit our website, www.wisdompubs.org.

Printed in the United States of America.

MIX
Paper from responsible sources
FSC® C011935

Throughout this book I speak in generic composites about my work with therapy clients. All of their names and identifying details have been changed to protect their privacy and to honor client confidentiality. In addition, this book is not intended as a substitute for medical advice. If you believe that you are suffering from a serious psychological condition, please consult your doctor or primary health care provider. Neither the publisher nor I accept any responsibility for injury, illness, or loss sustained in connection with the exercises and instructions herein.

Free Yourself

To Jo Alexander, whose loving, supportive presence
held the silent space for me to drop deep into
our inherent heart wisdom and write about
kindness, gratitude, forgiveness, and compassion.

And to the hundreds of clients who, by courageously
facing their human struggles, help us all meet our
shared unconscious habits with courage
and loving compassion.

May all beings be happy, healthy, and free.
May all beings be free of fear and doubt, judgment and shame,
anger, resentment and self-delusion.
May all beings bask in the great, great happiness
devoid of unconscious suffering.
May all beings be free.

The Friend

Why settle for a cup of water
when you are the river?
You are the wetness in water.

Slide into the unknown,
The Beloved that knows you is waiting.

Climb down the rickety ladder
into the mystery cave
where your own quiet music plays.

Become the great Friend to yourself.

Tip your identity into the
empty bowl of Being.
Hold only space where you used to fill it.
A cup already strained can hold no more.

Escort people through you to the Beloved,
Loving them, teaching them, learning from them,
always returning to the solace of the Friend.

Hold your animal body tenderly,
caress the cheek of grief with presence.

You are a gateway, no beginning, no end,
a flame of living truth unfolding.
Become the great Friend to yourself.

—Devi Weisenberg

Table of Contents

Foreword

We live in extraordinary times. Never before has humanity faced the enormous challenges it does today. Unbridled consumption is so much the accepted norm that genuine connection and contentment with life can seem a rarity. We rely on smart phones and computer screens as substitutes for true intimacy and engagement with each other. And our disconnection from nature is so extreme that we can't see the consequences of actions that threaten all life on our planet, including our very survival as a species.

At the same time, never before has there been as much consciousness in human history. Our world is so interconnected that revolutionary ideas can go viral and inspire millions to rise up against oppression with a few keystrokes and the tap of a send button. Our knowledge of the human body is so advanced that we can crack genetic codes and cure diseases never before understood. Modern neuroscience has revealed subtle secrets of the brain to unlock its enormous potential, while psychological modalities have been developed for healing trauma like never before. Unprecedented sharing of perennial wisdom and mindfulness practices are leading many to discover true inner peace.

Whether we as a species continue in the direction of inevitable destruction or wake up to the possibility of unparalleled healing is the great question of our times. As one friend put it, "We live in a race between fear and consciousness."

That is why *Free Yourself: 10 Life-Changing Powers of Your Wise Heart* is such an important offering at this time. Drawing from her years of experience as a gifted healer, author Carolyn Hobbs offers teachings and practices to transform knots of contraction into well-being and wholeness. Having taught meditation and centering techniques for many years, I've seen the power of applying the principles contained in this book in my own life.

Presenting deep teachings in accessible, practical ways, *Free Yourself* is a map of transformation that will benefit anyone who clearly intends to develop well-being and joy. Because of her many years as a skilled psychologist and body-centered healer, Carolyn not only understands the wisdom of the teachings, but she also shows the reader how to embody them and live with a free and open heart. The great discovery is that we have everything we need right inside us, not only for personal fulfillment but to really make a difference in the world.

The teachings in these pages are more than merely concepts; if practiced with sincerity, they will come to life. Going through personal inner transformation affects everyone in your life. Compassion, love, kindness, gratitude, and joy are contagious. As you take in the wisdom of this book and strengthen those beautiful qualities life has gifted to you, I hope you welcome your process as a gift to everyone you know and to the world. We all benefit from the love, caring, and wisdom you have to offer.

James Baraz
Berkeley, California

Introduction

May I and all beings be free.

Every day for the past twenty years, midway through my morning hike, I've stood overlooking a cliff on a narrow dirt trail I share with elk, deer, and coyote and said this lovingkindness phrase: *May I and all beings be free.*

Whether traveling or at home, I say it every morning in my personal effort to call freedom into this world.

I first heard the phrase at a weekend meditation retreat in Santa Rosa, California, in 1983. At that time, thirty years ago, I needed something to quiet my fear and grief over several endings: a five-year relationship, my full-time counseling job in Napa, California, and my thirteen-year-long love affair with the San Francisco Bay Area. My U-Haul sat in the retreat center parking lot holding all my belongings. I was stepping into the unknown to live on forty acres I bought with two friends in Northern California.

At that time I had no clue the lengths we humans unconsciously go to in order to hold freedom away. At thirty-three, I had so much to learn about how we, including myself, unknowingly imprison ourselves in fear, doubt, judgment, guilt, and shame. Back then, in my ignorance, I told myself, "Yes, if only I felt relief from this heart-wrenching grief, then I could be free. And if only I knew securely where my next paycheck was coming from, then I could be free. And if only I stopped doubting my choice to leave the Bay Area, then I could be free." I had no idea what true freedom was.

Thirty years later, I share the freedom that comes from knowing who we really are.

Over 2,500 years ago, Buddha taught that, underneath our thoughts and feelings, we are all born with unlimited joy, loving-kindness, compassion, and inner peace.

In this book, I share teachings I have adapted from Buddha's wisdom and honed into practical tools that are useful regardless of your belief system or spiritual leanings.

As a therapist, author, workshop leader, and visiting professor, I have shared the powerful heart choices in this book with thousands of clients, students, and workshop participants. Whether we are Christian, Jewish, Buddhist, Muslim, Wiccan, agnostic, or atheist, we can all benefit from the practical, unorthodox heart tools in this book—which will never attempt to convert you away from your religious preferences.

This book is your invitation to wake up free of unconscious ego habits.

This book is an invitation for busy people of all faiths to find inner peace.

This book is an invitation to see that freedom is a real place in your heart.

In order to wake up free, we must first understand what we need to wake up from. Few of us realize that, at birth, we inherited a common misunderstanding about who we humans are, which we then ingested as our reality. Buddha calls this our *unconscious human conditioning*. Everyone around us, including Mom and Dad, Grandpa Fred and Aunt Alice, all reinforced this detour from reality because they never knew any different. The problem is that ignorance, no matter how well intentioned, no matter how much the person may love us, causes suffering.)In the thick cloud of human misunderstanding, we shortchange ourselves.

We believe we are our name, our body, our family history, and our achievements. We believe we are our thoughts, feelings, body sensations, and beliefs. And in the narrow world of our ego—which Webster defines as that part of our psyche that organizes thoughts rationally and governs action, and which Buddhism defines as that pervasive self-important "I" thought that personalizes everything—this is true. But who we are in our heart is lifetimes more than this. If we force ourselves to live inside ego's tight shoe, we waste precious years looking for freedom in the wrong places.

Who we really are is *conscious, loving, compassionate awareness.* Inside our wise heart, we tap into the same universal knowing and ancient wisdom that keeps our heart beating and lungs breathing. From this spacious place, we see unconscious thoughts, feelings, and beliefs—but we stop identifying with them. From our new eagle's nest view of life, we become loving awareness that *notices* thoughts, fears, feelings, and reactions, our own or others, and lets them go. We still eat, sleep, parent, exercise, work, and make love like usual. But in shifting out of our small ego-identity into our heart's unlimited joy, compassion, kindness, and awareness, we feel free.

For instance, my client Lois struggled with depression for years. Antidepressants failed her. Labeling her thoughts "thinking" in meditation failed to dislodge her depression. But after locating her depression *in her body* as a tight fist in her belly, she breathed into the center of the knot. "By breathing directly into my grief," she said, "the memory of a miscarriage years ago popped into my mind. At the time, when the miscarriage happened, I stayed busy with work to avoid the grief. Recently I let myself cry until my body was done crying. Later the tight fist melted into a peaceful, spacious feeling I'd never known." Once Lois located her grief directly in her body—not an overwhelming story too large to address—she was able to free herself of it.

Two distinct voices speak to us simultaneously all the time: our ego and our heart. To hear the gentle wisdom of our kind heart, we must first identify ego's loud, demanding, judgmental, shaming voice inside our head as "ego," not "me." We have listened to ego's voice for decades, since we learned how to talk. We assume its voice is our voice. But ego is only one small part of who we are.

Ego is Latin for "I," which sounds innocent enough. But this "I" thought multiplies so fast inside our head that within seconds millions of complex thoughts abound for us to organize, analyze, and somehow make sense out of. As we grow and mature, a simple thought like "I am this body" multiplies into "I am this fear, this anxiety, this despair, this guilt, this regret, this pain; I am my swollen joints; I am my cancer," ad infinitum until we spend our daily lives confused and filled with doubt. In no time flat, ego becomes the root of our self-hatred and increased suffering by reacting personally to every little thing.

In meditation, labeling thoughts "thinking" takes care of hundreds of the ups and downs of daily life. But when worry, anxiety, despair, or grief come knocking in our daily lives, our heart's capacity to detour obsessive thoughts and soothe feelings by locating them in our body brings welcome relief. Once awareness sets ego's ranting aside, we can hear the soft voice of our wise heart.

A quiet revolution in human consciousness is underfoot, one that takes place one moment, one breath, one heartbeat at a time as each of us recommits daily to waking up. Each time we meet anger or fear with compassion, world consciousness takes a step forward.

Recognizing the voice of our wise heart and inner awareness frees us to consciously choose each moment between suffering and joy, fear and love, anxiety and inner peace. The first five heart choices—trust, curiosity, awareness, resourcefulness, and compassion—

offer freedom from unconscious thoughts, fears, habits, and reactions. The last five—kindness, gratitude, forgiveness, integrity, and inner peace—help challenges feel workable and cultivate freedom in our relationships and in our world.

With its uncanny ability to remain peaceful amid chaos, our heart makes such unorthodox choices as loving fear when it arrives or trusting the wisdom of unexpected changes. Each time we consciously choose to respond to our own grief with kindness, we relinquish centuries of unconscious human conditioning. Each time we respond to another's sadness with compassion, we step into the freedom, joy, and inner peace that are always present inside our heart.

This book is your passport into the inner sanctuary of your wise, loving, compassionate heart. Keep it safe and handy. Conscious choice brings awareness. Awareness brings freedom.

How I Came to Trust These Ten Heart Choices

When I was ten, my mother suffered from depression, which lit a flame inside me to understand human happiness and unhappiness. This is why I became a therapist, and this is why I spent my adult life practicing insight meditation while understanding body awareness. In my twenties and thirties, I immersed myself in meditation, Bioenergetics, Body-Centered Therapy, and Feldenkrais work, all to further plumb the connection between our minds and our bodies, our hearts and our unconscious ego habits.

By blending meditative wisdom with body awareness into my therapy practice, I've seen life-changing results; I've watched countless individuals and couples in my therapy practice rave about the freedom they felt after labeling ego's story "thinking" (drawn from insight meditation) and breathing directly into their fear, anxiety, grief, or despair (culled from body-centered therapies). Regardless of whether the physical ailment was major or minor, after locating the feeling in their body and releasing it with their breath, the vast majority of clients followed sadness, pain, or tension with "I feel more spacious, peaceful, free, or happy."

Tools from both these powerful practices are woven throughout this book.

For years now, in addition to watching my own thoughts, fears, and feelings in meditation, I've sat in a room with clients' deepest pain. Year after year, I witnessed how true and useful Buddha's wisdom still is today: suffering is part of life, and we have the power to reduce our own suffering each time we stop unconsciously resisting what is true. Buddha's teachings offer practical life skills for coping with dilemmas and understanding how to make friends with feelings.

One April morning in 2005, at the end of a peaceful meditation, my life changed. From this spacious place opened up by the meditation, I thought, "I'd like to bring more heart qualities into my daily life." I decided to spend a month or two on each of the following ten heart choices: presence, curiosity, awareness, resourcefulness, compassion, kindness, gratitude, forgiveness, integrity, and inner peace. I chose kindness first, whispering to myself at the end of each morning meditation, "Today I cultivate kindness."

Some days went smoothly, which I expected since I had meditated for years. But when a driver cut me off, or a workshop got canceled, or someone hurt my feelings, kindness between gritted teeth took effort, presence, and awareness. Yet I kept my intention and at times kept my mouth shut until I could respond with kindness. My intention to be kind, coupled with meditative awareness, proved a powerful combo.

The next three months, I practiced presence, curiosity, and awareness with similar surprising results. Heart choices helped carry the awareness I felt in meditation over into my daily life. With each new heart choice, joy and lightness became the norm. That fall, during a health crisis, I chose compassion for myself. This quieted those lifelong loyalties to ego that had still seduced me in moments of tiredness and worry. As I held my fear, sorrow, pain, and anger in loving compassion, my quality of life changed forever. No longer able to cling to fear and resentment for hours, I watched them slide through my hands. As I met others' judgments with compassion, my need to react personally fell away. I still spent time lost in thought, but awareness came to the rescue more often.

My deep intention is to share these powerful heart choices with you. Whether you meditate, pray, attend the church of your faith, or turn to nature, these ten heart choices are your birthright. Since we never received them in school, please accept them now. Clients have taught me the pain we cause ourselves by severely limiting our sense of self. I have witnessed scores of clients wake up out of ego's illusions into the freedom and inner peace that changes their quality of life forever. I now share this with you.

When we stand tall as a ponderosa pine or redwood tree in the truth and stillness of our being and respond to ourselves, our loved ones, and our lives from this inner strength, we invite others to stand tall in their being.

How to Derive the Most Value from This Book

Each of the ten chapters offers one heart quality essential to meeting life's challenges with confidence. They are written in a language that many different people can understand. The first, "Your Trusting Heart," lays a foundation. Each subsequent chapter deepens awareness to prepare you for the next heart choice, so it is wise to let each chapter lay the groundwork for the next.

Since we humans require time to change old habits, ideally you will spend at least one whole month on each chapter, and if compassion or forgiveness requires more time, please gift yourself with the time it takes. One month affords you countless situations in which to practice presence, curiosity, awareness, or gratitude. But if you can't spend ten months with this book, at least spend one full week with each chapter and practice each heart choice for as long as you need under a variety of experiences.

At the end of each chapter, I provide four heart tools to help you bring resourcefulness, gratitude, forgiveness, or whichever quality you're working on to specific life situations. Most heart tools are brief, to fit easily into a ten-minute morning commute, into your workout routine, or at the end of your meditation.

As you get the hang of asking such questions as "Which ego story am I running now?" and "How am I causing suffering by my reaction?" you free yourself to hear the soft, kind wisdom of your loving heart. Like a good lover, your heart gently reminds you to let go of ego's incessant thoughts and bask in the freedom and inner peace that is always present. We spent decades practicing our unconscious conditioning—our ancestors practiced for centuries!—so we should all be able to afford ten or twenty minutes in a busy day to wake up free. The reward is priceless.

Hopefully we will practice trust, curiosity, awareness, resourcefulness, compassion, kindness, gratitude, forgiveness, integrity, and peacefulness—in some form or another—every day for the rest of our lives. These ten heart choices stand alone as the gateway to who we really are. And they prove a powerful adjunct to any meditation, prayer, spiritual, or yoga practice.

Together we embrace this silent evolution in consciousness. In the privacy of our own home and heart, with our own family and loved ones, we join together to change human consciousness one choice, one moment, one breath at a time.

PART I
Freedom from Sabotaging Ego Habits

Freedom and inner peace live right here, in this moment, inside our heart.

We hold in the palm of our hand all the tools we need to release ourselves from fear's brigade of troops: from judgment, doubt, anxiety, and despair. Whenever we indulge anger or resentment, hopelessness or fear, whenever we lose heart and declare this moment too hard, we cover over the brilliance of our trustworthy heart. Despite our parents' best intentions, we all inherited—as our parents inherited from their parents—an unquestioned loyalty to ego's clever thoughts, schemes, stories, and reactions, as if these were our best bet in tough times.

Our job is to shift loyalties to the unorthodox compassion and generosity of our heart. In the blink of an eye, in a second of conscious awareness, we can lift the blindfolds of our ancestors and see all fear, all worry as mere thoughts with no more importance than "I want a stick of chewing gum." Seeing judgment, doubt, anxiety, and fear as thoughts—not who we are—brings choice. We are all born with the power to consciously choose between fear's compelling story or inner peace. Either we can postpone our freedom by repeating "I'll be free after I retire or after I find love" or we can accept and speak our deepest truth: "I am free." It comes down to moment-to-moment choices.

These first five heart choices hand us the keys to freedom and inner peace. How we use them is always our choice.

4. Your Trusting Heart

The Power of Conscious Choice

When the struggle stopped, a quiet presence opened up that I knew was home. And with that I had a sense of peace, of trusting who I really am. —TARA BRACH

I lie on the living room couch exhausted, two weeks before Christmas. Luckily, after years of coming back into the present, I know how to switch channels. I shift focus—away from racing thoughts about cards and packages I need to mail, toward my trustworthy anchor: my breath. As I watch my inhalation and exhalation, my breath deepens, body relaxes, pulse slows. I reconnect with my heart, trusting what is.

From this deeper sense of self, my wise heart easily holds what I am thinking, feeling, seeing, hearing, and sensing. It holds it all in spacious awareness, taking none of it too seriously. Focused fully in the present, I now see the snow-laden ponderosa pine towering outside the back patio window and hear a black crow flapping her wings overhead. For a few seconds, my sacred connection with all living things floods my senses. I see how the ponderosa's huge presence—and my own trusting heart—accept and receive life on life's terms. A veil of inner peace descends over me.

Awakened with gratitude, Christmas chores all feel workable again.

Our heart trusts life. It trusts the present moment, where life happens, and where our heart always lives. It trusts the infinite wisdom and truth that unfold in the everyday details of ordinary life. It delights in all the sights, sounds, thoughts, feelings, and experiences sharing this present moment without judging any of them.

When we join our trusting heart in the present moment, we too trust life.

Buddha had a knack for describing what makes us tick in terms we can understand. He taught that, in the big scheme of things, we humans resist what is. No matter what is true in any given moment, we want life to somehow be different, easier, more in our favor. Unknowingly, our thoughts drift into anxiety, fear, doubt, and judgment out of habit. Whether living in Europe, Asia, Africa, North or South America, we are all born into a binding, blinding molasses-type substance called *unconscious conditioning*. Until we spend some minutes each day making these unconscious habits conscious, they will rule our life.

While we go about the business of our lives, we spend the lion's share of our time letting thoughts, fears, doubts, and judgments captivate every waking minute—as if these are who we are. Of course we don't wake up declaring, "Today I'll waste every moment lost in thoughts." No, such habits occur unconsciously. Like subliminal advertising, they grab our attention while we are driving, working, eating, playing, and generally living our lives. Soon, without realizing it, we've slid down the slippery slope into fear, doubt, and judgment.

The grand prize for waking up out of our unconscious conditioning is better than a brand new Mercedes or free trip to Paris. Buddha taught that—underneath all thoughts and fears, feelings and sensations—we are all born with an unlimited capacity for joy, loving-kindness, compassion, and inner peace. This is our pot of gold. Inner peace and freedom live right here, right now always, inside our trusting heart.

For instance, when my friend Jan's husband died suddenly of a heart attack at sixty-two, she felt enraged, then sad, then hopeless, like she had no reason to live. But a seasoned meditator for years, as Jan watched her incessant thoughts—"This should never have happened this way, how will I ever recover?"—she began to focus on the present. "All my thoughts terrified me, Carolyn, but I trusted my body to know what to do even now. It relaxed into sobbing for all the sadness I've ever experienced in my whole life. Afterward, inner peace washed over me, inspiring me to keep honoring my waves of grief."

Shifting from unconscious habits into freedom takes work and conscious choice.

Uncovering Our Real Daily Practice

Many of us already practice yoga, meditation, or prayer and set good intentions daily. But this book addresses our real practice: the other twenty-three hours a day. Every minute we indulge anger or judgment (however justified), we postpone freedom. Every hour we take a ride with fear's story about losing our lover, job, home, savings, or health, we cultivate fear. Every week we resist what is true and tell ourselves that life should be different, more in our favor, we perpetuate a false belief we should have questioned years ago: "If I'm clever enough, I shouldn't have to suffer ever again."

Lucky for us, Buddha saw right through our most common human fallacies. He saw that suffering is woven into the fabric of life, and he taught us to reduce our suffering by accepting—not resisting—this truth. Buddha further described how three human propensities perpetuate suffering: craving, aversion, and ignorance. When we constantly crave more love, more money, bigger homes, sex, or the latest cell phones, we create a petri dish of restless dissatisfaction, never satisfied with what is true.

When we spend hours trying to avoid the imperfection, loss, and sadness that come with being human, we waste time trying to avoid the unavoidable. When we bury our head in the sand, uninterested in how unconscious thoughts, feelings, and beliefs sabotage our lives, we let ignorance rule. Such craving to acquire and achieve more, coupled with avoiding dislikes and ignoring what is, only perpetuates a gnawing feeling that who we are and what we do is never good enough.

Our new practice begins by honestly asking, "What is my real daily practice? Am I proving myself right today at the expense of proving a loved one wrong? Am I strengthening skills of worry, anger, or hopelessness by indulging them again? Have I spent hours lost in a fear fantasy of losing my lover or child?"

My client Jenna's aversion to ever feeling lonely held her stuck in a marriage ten years after it had died. "Fear of never finding true love kept me swirling in confusion and indecision," Jenna said. "One day at the end of meditation, when I asked myself, 'What is my real practice?' I saw fear's claws digging into me, keeping me imprisoned. I filed for divorce the next day. Now, five years later, we both found people we really love."

My favorite question for calling myself into the present is "Am I here now?" When I take ten seconds to stop and come back into the present, I often laugh out loud. I'm amazed at how my wild mind bounces all over the place: from last night's gluten-free linguine, to Grandma's homemade spaghetti, to the night she died on the dance floor at seventy-two, to how she swore by chiropractors, to how I need one for my back pain.

Mindful, deliberate questions shine a light on unconscious patterns and return us to the present. Chapter 2, "Your Curious Heart," details the power of questions in depth.

Being present redirects our focus from unconscious to conscious thoughts. It names thoughts "thinking" and lets them go. It gives us courage to face grief and anxiety, or stop fantasizing about the future and instead feel gratitude for what is true. It invites us into the present again and again to bask in the joy and inner peace right here.

For example, my client Charlotte felt consumed with jealous rage. "When my husband went on nightshift with a female security guard, I felt insanely jealous," she said. "I called my doctor for antianxiety drugs, and we joked about a lobotomy to quiet my thoughts. But each time I sit by the river in my car, breathe deeply, and name the thoughts 'thinking,' I find peace of mind. Some days I spend hours naming thoughts, but it's way better than believing those images of my husband with another woman."

Coming back into the present frees us from identifying with the unconscious prison of fear, doubt, anxiety, and judgment we inherit at birth. It puts us back in the driver's seat, stopping the runaway train of thoughts. By returning to the present, we stop reliving that same old disappointment story. We wake up out of the dream of unconscious thought and become who we are—awareness, watching thoughts.

Being present offers a new foundation under our feet. Rather than stay loyal to the suffering, dissatisfaction, and feeling not good enough of old unconscious habits, we stand grounded in the present, embracing our trusting heart.

Adopting the Power of Conscious Choice

Being present introduces the power of conscious choice. Every second of every day, whenever we notice thoughts as thoughts, we have a choice: We can let that despair drag us around by the nose like it has for years—or choose joy. We can stay lost for hours in a fear trance about losing our income—or we can choose presence. We can stress all night about our teenager breaking curfew—or we can choose freedom. Being present in joy and freedom is always our moment-to-moment choice.

Presence brings conscious choice. Conscious choice brings freedom.

However, we humans don't surrender our timeworn strategies for avoiding discomfort easily. More often than we care to admit, we kick and scream, begging life to fit our mental picture of how it should be. Since thoughts (planning, strategizing, and organizing) promise freedom from suffering, we trust thoughts far more than the simple truths revealed in daily life. With that big carrot—freedom from pain—dangling in front of us, just out of reach, we stay lost too long in the clever fantasies that promise an escape. By the time we finally wake up out of this stupor, thoughts have exhausted our patience and exposed their ineptness. It's time for a run, a glass of wine, or bed.

But it is precisely at this juncture where our trusting heart becomes our new hero. Equipped beyond imagination for handling overwhelming feelings, our heart lays down a new brilliant blueprint for feeling happy, peaceful, and free again—one that works. It whispers an illogical but very effective strategy in our ear: "Try holding your fears about money or health or loneliness in loving compassion. What is there to lose?"

Our heart may even welcome fear like an old friend, saying, "Hello, fear. I was expecting you. Sorry to rush off but I'm having too much fun creating joy in my life to visit." When our trusting heart discovers us lost in fear, it chooses freedom. It reminds us that all we need to do to dissolve fear is love the fear just as it is.

Being present occurs in a few seconds. The problem: we must keep consciously choosing it moment by moment. Three quick practices show how easy this is:

1. Our breath lives in the present, so it offers an easy entry point. If we only have a few seconds in the grocery line or at a red light, we can pause and say "yes" to what is. Or we can notice a fear story in our head, such as losing our job,

take a deep belly breath, and on the exhalation, replace that story with "I am free," "I choose inner peace," or "I let go of every thing unlike love." The second we say any of these phrases, our unconscious fear story dissolves.

2. If we have two minutes, we can ask ourselves, "What do I long to hear now? Would I love to hear that I have plenty of time, or that I am safe, or that everything will be okay?" Then we can whisper these loving words to ourselves, rather than waiting for anyone else to do so.

3. If we have ten or twenty minutes, we can sit erect in a chair, close our eyes, and focus on the breath in our belly. This practice teaches how the mind works by showing us how we can anchor our awareness by watching our belly rise and fall with our inhalation and exhalation. Regardless of religious preferences, we all breathe. So we can all sneak in five, ten, twenty, or thirty minutes a day to watch our breath—and watch our thoughts slip-slide into plans and memories, fears and doubts, judgments and regrets. Returning to our anchor, the breath, calls us back into the present.

That Small Part of Us That Resists Everything, Including the Present

To practice conscious choice, we must first become aware of the habits of our ego.

Most of us let ego run our lives without realizing it. Few of us know how deeply our ego—the less mature, defensive part of us that reacts personally to every little thing—sabotages us by resisting what is. Whether its voice is loud and demanding or soft and seductive, our ego convinces us that we have much more important things to worry about and plan and do than waste our time in the silly, boring present. It obsessively pulls our attention into past mistakes, which we cannot change, or potential opportunities (and mistakes) in the future, which we cannot always control. Because ego focuses solely on survival, it has no use for the present moment. Underneath all this busyness and bravado, ego treats the present like a life-threatening plague.)

Ego's job is keeping us safe at all costs, and it takes this job very seriously. It can't help itself. But ego is near-sighted; it cannot decipher between fear and reality. If it convinces itself that our lover might possibly hurt us, ego does everything in its power to destroy our relationship, even if in truth our partner is devoted to us.

Remember, safety (not happiness or love) is ego's single goal. It pulls out all the stops when helping us avoid possible hurt, discomfort, illness, suffering, or pain—especially a broken heart. All day long, ego crams our head with incessant thoughts, memories, fantasies, fears, regrets, plans, worries, hopelessness—anything to distract us. Ego is so focused on the past and future, it has no time to waste on the present.

Besides Grandma's wedding ring and Dad's gold watch, we also inherited an unquestioned loyalty to ego's shenanigans. When it labels our current experience as "good" or "bad," we buy its judgment. When it devotes hours to analyzing past hurts in a futile attempt to avoid future hurts, we swallow its conclusions whole. When ego captivates us with juicy stories about *my* thoughts, *my* feelings, *my* wants—knowing how susceptible we are to stories about ourselves—we ride the big wave.

Ego does all this below our awareness, counting on our ignorance.

Now is the time to question our undying loyalty to this one small part of who we are. One scratch below the surface reveals how ego acts and thinks like a five-year-old. It hides under the bed at the whiff of any unfamiliar, unpredictable, unexpected things that *might* cause discomfort, often creating more suffering for us in its wake. If our goal is freedom and joy, we need to see through ego's clever antics.

Some deep excavating is in order. Ego mastered its games centuries ago and fine-tunes them every time it captures our attention. First, we need to replace ego's shaming falsehood—"If you just get it right next time, you'll never have to feel hurt, disappointed, scared, or rejected again"—with the deeper truth: "Suffering comes with life." We can smile and nod at ego's compelling stories, instead hearing our trusting heart whisper softly, "You're safe to feel the fear or doubt directly, let it be, and let it go."

Sue and Sarah both demonstrate how wise it is to shift into the present. When Sue's life partner of twenty years left for a younger woman, Sue struggled to get out of bed most mornings. "My mind kept going over and over the past, judging me for every time I told her what to do. I couldn't stop finding the 'one thing' I did wrong. But I kept dropping into my trusting heart, coming back into the present, and naming all those thoughts 'thinking,' even if obsessive thoughts returned in a second or two. With time I focused directly on the real culprit—an old, persistent fear that I would lose my home and have to live on the streets—and faced my fear directly. My equilibrium returned when I put both hands over my heart and reassured myself, 'You'll be okay, Sue. You'll get through this.'"

When Sarah faced breast cancer, her ego feared that lolling around in the present would lock her into a death sentence. But her trusting heart revealed the healing powers of presence: "My whole life, I prided myself on my smarts. I denied the cancer was real, staying busy helping others. But my resistance gave ego a heyday; it pummeled me constantly with thoughts about dying and pictures of caskets. When I shifted focus onto my trusting heart, I saw all the precious beauty of my child's eyes, my husband's smile, and my home cluttered with shoes and toys. Whether I die next month or fifty years from now, my heart taught me to smile at fear's great imagination. When I label it 'fear' and let it go, I remember that fear doesn't know any more than I do."

We can't stop fear, doubt, or judgment. Ego's thoughts arrive before we have time to think about them. But we can consciously choose how to respond. Stepping into the present is a gift we can give ourselves anytime, anywhere, any moment. When we choose presence, our inner compass navigates our direction toward inner peace and freedom.

Our journey into waking up free begins with the following steps:

- Notice ego's seductive strategies to resist life and react personally—and label them "thinking."
- Notice ego's compulsion to make our reality different, better, easier—and embrace the present.
- Notice ego's chronic like/dislike reaction to what is true—and let it go.
- Notice ego's obsession with past and future thoughts— and let them go.

Right now, if we pinch ourselves, we might wake up out of the sleepwalking story playing in our head and stay present for a few seconds. But shortly the next thought will drag us into ego's never-never land of past memories, future fantasies, and countless regrets of how life, love, and this moment could have been better.

Floating in and out of conscious and unconscious thought frustrates us—until we realize that the process of waking up free is a lifelong process. Each time we catch ourselves lost in judgment, doubt, or fear, we need to pause and celebrate. We can jump for joy or give ourselves a special treat—until the next moment we get lost in thought.

With each passing day, as we label thoughts and let them go, we find ourselves living in the present more often while moments of staying lost in anger, jealousy, or worry last much less time. Our true nature—our unlimited joy, kindness, compassion, and inner peace—patiently awaits our arrival in the present.

Trusting Bare Attention as Our Primary Source

Buddha first directed our gaze toward ego's stories with a tool called *bare attention*: resting in the facts of this moment without letting ego embellish them endlessly with who did what and how wrong it was. In other words, without letting ego create a mental story that consumes our attention for hours.

Right now, my bare attention is this: It is 10:48 on the morning of Monday, October 5. Yellow aspen leaves outside my window sway in the breeze. My left knee aches after Sunday's six-hour hike. I feel relief seeing this morning's clear sky, after numerous lightning storms the previous month. Today's thirty-six-degree high temperature signals an early winter. Twenty-five grosbeaks line the back deck railing as they gorge on sunflower seeds before migrating south. I feel excited to write.

Externally, trusting bare attention brings our full awareness to our sensations; it focuses on what our eyes are seeing, our ears are hearing, our nose is sniffing, and our hands are touching in the present. It sticks to the facts, just the facts, without indulging ego's personal preferences, judgments, reactions, or stories. In other words, it dismisses ego's snobbish opinions about what is wrong with our current experience and how life could be more perfect if this had never happened.

Internally, trusting bare attention names our inner sensations: contraction, pain, tightness, numbness, and tingling. It also names inner feelings that are passing through, such as fear, joy, sadness, hurt, guilt, or resentment, without judgment. This is to say: presence notices what is without needing to get rid of any sensation or feeling.

The problem is, we humans have great trouble sticking to the facts. We all love a juicy story, especially our own. And ego joins in by planning our next great scheme to gain pleasure and avoid discomfort. It's a deeply ingrained habit. We routinely go off on some tangent about how we like or dislike, love or hate what is happening now with a passion—or a vengeance. Several times a day, without any prodding from the peanut gallery, we launch into elaborate details about what happened, who did what to us, and how it should have never happened.

For instance, Sharon entered my office in tears. "We're losing our home!" she said. "With Tom not working, our three rentals are our only income. And with two of them vacant, we can't cover our mortgage this month. I'll have to go back to work."

"I hear how scared you feel," I replied. "I'd like to use this opportunity to help you feel fear without getting lost in it. If you're willing, I'd like you to try a great tool: bare attention. Try stating only the facts without elaborating on what might possibly happen."

"We have two vacancies, and we're losing our home," Sharon repeated.

"The facts are the two vacancies and Tom's lack of work. The rest is conjecture based on fear. Instead of buying into fear, what would you love to tell yourself instead?"

Sharon paused to focus on her breath. "I'd love to notice fear as fear, trust the truth of these vacancies, and picture new, good tenants—as my higher, wiser choice."

The following week, Sharon arrived grinning. "Last Friday I signed a one-year lease with a single guy from Denver who transferred here for his new job. We still have one vacancy remaining, but my hope is back. I like this 'bare attention' stuff."

When we trust the present we relax into what is, whatever it is.

Checking In with Our Breath

Whether we call the process "meditation," "meditative awareness," or "watching our breath," our heart loves nothing more than to bask in the present, free from ego's thoughts, judgments, and fears. It finds freedom whenever we focus on our breath.

There is just one tiny hiccup. The more we watch our breath and come back to the present, the more we notice zillions of distracting thoughts racing through our mind. Even with a strong intention to stay present, ego's lifelong obsession with thinking, thinking, thinking remains deeply entrenched.

Addressing this unconscious habit requires focus and attention.

Often beginners to meditation mistakenly believe that thoughts will stop if they name them "thinking" and let them go. But no matter how committed we are, and how many minutes we watch our breath daily for years, we still think a lot. Thoughts come with being human. What does change is the type of thoughts we infuse with our attention. By labeling thoughts "thinking" and coming back to the present, to the inhalation and exhalation of our breath, we waste less moments staying lost in thoughts of fear, doubt, and judgment. This frees up many more moments of open space in a day to focus attention on kindness, compassion, joy, or whatever we want to create. Such fresh, conscious, spacious moments add up to peacefulness inside.

When we finally realize that the part of us lost in anxiety, worry, or despair for hours, days, or years is our immature ego—not us— we feel tremendous relief.

The truth is this: no thought, no matter how overwhelming, possesses more importance than "I want a stick of chewing gum." We are the ones who infuse thoughts with passion and meaning. Out of unconscious habit, we give negative, scary thoughts top billing. The more often we repeat a fear, such as "If I lose my job, I'll lose everything," the more real and terrifying it feels. No one knows what will happen next, not even fear.

Whether we realize it or not, we step into the unknown every day. No matter which thoughts hold our attention, we face the unknown every day. If we think about it long enough, we'll see that nothing in life turns out the way we (or fear) thought it would—not childhood nor college, not loving nor parenting, not aging nor dying. Nothing.

This is where our trusting heart steps in. When we pull attention away from ego's compelling stories, we feel more space around thoughts inside. Issues feel more workable. Focusing on our breath in the present makes us start to wonder, "If I'm *not* my thoughts and fears, who am I? And who notices thoughts come and go?"

On a recent morning hike, I was lost in thought. I obsessed about a young couple coping with a recent affair. Fears about them breaking up swarmed in my head—until I remembered to focus on my breath. Instantly I labeled the fears "thinking" and shifted channels to what my eyes were seeing and my ears were hearing.

The next hillside stood ablaze with red, burnt orange, and yellow leaves as the oak brush delivered its fall performance. When I redirected my attention, my belly took a deep breath. Ego's story about the affair took a backseat to being present.

Two weeks later, I shared this story with the young couple while teaching about presence. I invited them to label their fear thoughts "thinking" and look deeply into each other's eyes in the present. Tears flowed down their cheeks, and their hearts shifted into compassion and forgiveness. In the end, despite what fear said, the affair brought them closer.

Day in and day out, when back pain or illness strikes, when the stock market plummets or life disappoints, our heart helps us see *even this* is an opportunity to say "yes" to what is. Being present allows us to see thoughts as thoughts, feelings as feelings, and fears as fears. In the open space that follows, we wake up and consciously choose which thoughts deserve our focus, time, and attention.

When we stop resisting what is true, stop arguing with reality, we are free to choose presence. The more often we hold fear in compassion, the more safe we begin to feel in our body, despite what is happening around us. By stepping away from ego's tyranny, we flow easily toward our heart's unlimited capacity for joy, kindness, compassion, and love that live in the present, with our breath.

Being present helps our eyes and heart open to the hidden mysteries of life. With trust, we accept that we are having the life lessons we need to have right now to mature. Over the years, as life and love stretch us beyond ego's comfort zone, we respond to our feelings, our heart, and our life with acceptance and compassion.

In those precious moments when we bask in the silent present, everything stops. Worry stops. Anxiety stops. Fear stops. Despair stops. And in the quiet stillness, we see what has been true all along—that life moves through us in its own timing, own changes, and own unparalleled wisdom. Our job is to witness it.

Resting in and trusting life's timeless wisdom helps our body feel more peaceful.

Checking In with Our Body

We may exercise, feed, and dress our body, even take it to the doctor for a pap smear or colonoscopy. But how often do we stop to listen to our body? Nowadays, we push and push our bodies to exercise daily, work hard on too little sleep, sit still at a computer for endless hours, digest everything we stuff in our mouth, and starve for days on a fad diet. We get mad when our adrenals collapse from sheer exhaustion. And when illness or injury erupts, we pop pills to silence our body's alarm system.

Being present in our body is a two-way street. Since the body lives in the present, like our breath, it delivers loving messages to us every day. These arrive nonverbally, through symptoms, pain, and illness, all designed to paint the short path back to balance, freedom, and inner peace. If fear lodges in our lower back, it begs, "Please, please let me dance or swim or run or walk to move this ache, this worry, out of my body." When digestive pain persists, our body coaxes us in a loving way to meditate or do yoga to address that hurt or sadness that is stuck in our belly. Rather than silencing our pain with pills, we need to focus on our body and ask, "What are you trying to tell me?" This question permits us to accept what is true and respond with respect.

For instance, Clare struggled with migraines for years—until she realized the headaches gave her body exactly what it needed in that moment. When Clare paid close attention to her tiredness and voluntarily rested in a dark room, the migraines lost their job. As she listened intently, her body no longer needed to press the issue.

We may try to eat healthy foods, exercise daily, and practice Pilates, qi gong, or yoga regularly. But making friends with our body is respecting when it speaks to us through symptoms—and hearing its loving message. It is taking five minutes each morning to close our eyes, scan our body from head to toe, and welcome any tightness, pain, tiredness, pressure, or symptoms into our awareness without wishing they were different. The key is being present with what is—no matter what it is.

At sixty-two, Beth woke up each morning scared of losing her retirement savings. But once she replaced fear with checking in with her body, she found peace again. "The second I wake up, my mind races with the same old fear thoughts. But I name it 'thinking' and take ten deep breaths. After focusing on my right and left leg, my right and left arm, and the breath inside my ribcage, I feel fully present in my body. Then, as a kind of dessert, I whisper 'yes' to any tension, pain, anxiety, or tightness, which brings a silky spaciousness to my whole body. By the time I get to work, I feel and look so great that all my coworkers tease me that I must have had great sex that morning. I just smile."

Making friends is including our body in our daily life by asking it sincerely, "What do you need today?" and patiently listening for an image, feeling-sense, or word—the way our intuition speaks to us. If we hear that our body needs a walk in nature, a massage, a rest, or to dance to African drum music, we create time for it. For more on deciphering the messages of body symptoms, check out chapter 2, "Your Curious Heart."

Respecting our body's intelligence allows it to guide us toward inner peace. Since pain and symptoms are often fueled by unexpressed hurt, fear, grief, or rage, making friends with our body leads to being present with our feelings.

Checking In with Our Feelings

Feelings are so misunderstood. Mostly, we try to avoid them—the negative ones, that is. We long for joy, love, happiness, hot sex, and freedom; we strain to hold on to these as long as we can, feeling cheated when they disappear. But too often we try to medicate, avoid, or at least postpone sadness, anxiety, disappointment, loneliness, and despair.

Perhaps we avoid negative feelings because we don't know how to express them. We might feel we have only two black-and-white options: Raging Drama Queen or Stoic Silent Type. Maybe we watched our parents vacillate between these two and don't want to emulate their example, so we choose to avoid bad feelings altogether. Or we naively choose one option and pay dearly when a relationship or career suffers. When we indulge or repress feelings, loved ones leave us either because we are too angry and moody, or too shut down and unemotional. We can't win.

But being present has nothing to do with acting out, repressing, analyzing, or interpreting feelings. Being present is locating where we feel sadness, anxiety, fear, or despair *in our body* and focusing directly on that feeling, free of ego's juicy story about what happened and how it should have happened differently. It is pausing to ask inside, "What feeling is moving through me now?" without getting lost in the feeling. It is breathing directly into feelings to discover the best-kept secret: negative feelings, given our full expression, can lead directly to freedom and inner peace.

For instance, forty-year-old Judy came to therapy so depressed she was afraid she might hurt herself. In our third session, I had her close her eyes and locate where she felt depressed inside. She described a tight knot in her belly. "I thought I was over this," Judy said, "But I'm remembering Bill, the love of my life. Both eighteen, we were going to marry in July. We had so much fun together, laughing and doing crazy things. But he was in a head-on crash with a drunk driver on June 16 and was killed." She gasped as her throat clamped shut. I invited her to take several deep breaths and breathe into that tight knot. Tears poured out. "I had no idea I was sitting on all this sadness." Judy had plenty more grief work to do to heal completely, but her stomach pain stopped.

Direct experience permits us to accept, and love, all feelings as they are. In chapter 3, "Your Aware Heart," we'll discuss focusing on feelings to heal.

Feelings are like children. Once a feeling receives our full attention for a moment or two, it moves to the next thing. It is the *story* about feelings, not the actual feelings, that holds us prisoner for hours or days, even years. The antidote is to acknowledge whatever feeling is present. Five times a day, we can pause and check in: "I feel tired, rested, happy, sad, worried, joyful, frustrated, contented, disappointed, calm, lonely, clear, guilty, peaceful, ashamed, discouraged, excited..." To grow familiar with feelings, it helps to list fifty possible feelings on a piece of paper and carry it in our pocket.

The instant we name a feeling, we put space around that feeling— as if we jumped to the outskirts to watch the feeling rather than stay overwhelmed by it. Spaciousness drops the story and reminds us, "I'm not my feeling; I'm presence, noticing the feeling."

Rather than becoming frustrated by or carried away with feelings, befriending them allows our trusting heart to hold them in spacious, loving compassion.

Checking In with Our Heart

The poet Rumi said, "Out beyond our ideas of right and wrong, there is a field. I'll meet you there." When we stay present in our heart, we step through an inner keyhole to a real place inside that few of us even know exists. It changes us forever.

When we drop beneath ego's incessant planning, remembering, thinking, and worrying, we touch the joy and magic of being alive. From this new vantage point, worry, fear, and despair do still visit us routinely. We still feel unhappy and disappointed. But we respond differently. Our trusting heart reassures that scared, younger part of us that we are safe and loved, even now. No longer enthralled by thoughts and distractions, we turn our fresh attention to the best game in town: harnessing that unlimited joy, love, kindness, and compassion pulsating inside our heart.

Inside the naked silence of this newfound place, the present, where ego's voice fails to penetrate, our heart whispers kind, loving words in our ear. It gently invites us to abandon all thoughts and receive the pleasure and joy abounding in this moment. It tugs at us to pause and notice the pair of black crows traversing the crisp January sky. It reminds us that we are good enough, always, and that we are kind, loving, gentle, compassionate beings deep inside, just as we are. It nudges us to rest when we are tired, connect with loved ones when we feel lonely, and trust life now.

When we listen sincerely, deep heart truths embrace us:

- Our heart lives in unlimited kindness, joy, compassion, and inner peace. It invites us to do the same.
- Our heart holds both good and bad in gratitude. It invites us to do the same.

- Our heart lets go of everything unlike love. It invites us to do the same.
- Our heart feels connected with all life forms. It invites us to do the same.
- Our heart loves our humanness unconditionally. It invites us to do the same.
- Our heart remembers the loving presence we are. It invites us to do the same.
- Our heart sees us and the world through loving eyes. It invites us to do the same.

A clear example helps our understanding. Douglas lost sleep, hope, and twenty pounds when the love of his life moved in with him. "Ten years of meditation doesn't stop me from reacting defensively whenever Sue asks me to talk about my despair. I learned years ago, between a critical dad and workaholic mom, that sharing vulnerable stuff brings hurt. Instead, I stomp out and leave for hours to avoid conflict."

In therapy, Doug worked through his anger and underlying grief toward his folks. But he kept holding Sue at arm's length. Then one night at midnight as Doug lay awake, he found an open chamber to his tender heart and stepped inside.

"It felt like a loving voice inside me, one I'd never heard before. It began whispering the most kind words to me. It told me, 'You're safe now to let love in, Doug, your own and Sue's. And you're never alone. I'm always here with you.'

"Like applying salve to an open cut, my loneliness disappeared. I treasure those words so much. That night, I repeated them over and over until I fell fast asleep."

For the first time since he was a toddler, Doug reconnected with his unlimited loving-kindness. "I still notice the scared place inside that wants to leave. But when it arises, I put my hands over my heart and repeat, 'I love you, dude. I'm loving you now for being scared.' Afterward, peacefulness oozes into every cell."

Being present in our trusting heart is a gift we can give ourselves each morning. I do. I lie on my back with eyes closed and take ten deep belly breaths, noticing my thoughts race. I softly place both hands over the center of my chest and repeat the word "yes" to every feeling, every pain, every sensation that arises. Then I recall someone I love deeply. I collect all this love and shine it through my hands into my heart. As I breathe the love into my heart, a calm spaciousness descends on me.

Then I ask my heart directly: "What do you need today?" I breathe deeply and listen for an image, feeling sense, or picture. My heart may nudge me to write in my journal, dance, meditate, call a friend, sing on my morning hike, or read a spiritual passage— things that feed my soul and return my spirit to balance. When I have a powerful dream, I lie still in bed to ask, "What loving message is this dream bringing me?" Over the years, with practice, I have grown to deeply trust my wise, loving heart.

Unlike ego, our heart responds to questions slowly. It ponders its response like a wise grandmother, testing our patience. But when we keep listening patiently for a picture or feeling sense, we receive the most loving guidance imaginable. Over time, we come to count on the heart. It prods us to slow down and rest long before illness appears. It transfuses us with courage to pursue our dreams long before ego releases us from its countless "what if" fears. When we include our heart in daily life, we stay balanced, healthy, happy, and peaceful. We trust life.

Being present in our trusting heart is like hanging out with the best friend we could ever have. It loves us like a good mother, lover, and companion all rolled into one. Whether we face loss, pain, divorce, illness, or undesired change, our heart doles out reassurance and love at every corner, every heartbreak, every point of confusion. It puts everything in fresh perspective.

When we listen, we take ego with a grain of salt. And after we hear the words of reassurance, our heart holds us and our pain in a loving embrace for as long as we need. Since our heart welcomes all life equally, it teaches us to delight in every new experience.

This loving heart rests on our fingertips. Whether we stay lost in thought for ten minutes or ten years, our heart waits patiently for our return home to its embrace.

When we stop buying into fear, stop chasing after answers outside ourselves, we slow down enough to hear the wise words of reassurance, kindness, and compassion emanating from our heart. Always tender and loving, gentle and inviting, our trusting heart teaches us to greet each moment with love:

- When anxious, our heart is right with us, softly repeating, "You are safe, even now. Take some deep belly breaths and hold the scared you in loving-kindness."
- When lonely, our heart comforts us with "I'm here. You're not alone. Relax into this moment and feel all the love holding you and your loneliness in compassion."
- When ego scolds us for not having enough time to accomplish our obligations, our heart counters, "You have all the time you need, always. Now breathe and come back into the spacious present."
- When tired, our heart reassures us, "Rest first for an hour or two, reading something you love. Then you'll have plenty of energy to do everything later."

Being present is a gift we can consciously choose to give ourselves every day, every moment. It connects us with feeling awake, alive, and connected to all of life. Each time we step out of the prison of thoughts, fears, reactions, and stories, we return to pure, naked awareness. This is so simple that often we forget it is right here right now, inside, all the time. We still think, plan, remember, and pursue accomplishments, because that is what we humans do. But we do it awake rather than asleep. When we devote ten, twenty, or thirty minutes to being present daily, we feel the returns a hundredfold in vitality, good health, and a fresh ability to love.

Remembering to practice is key. One moment we are fully present and free; the next, we are imprisoned in thoughts, fears, memories, or reactions. But each time we come back into the present, we surrender to what is. We trust the wisdom of life.

Presence is our new habit. Freedom is our new goal. Trusting life is our heart's practice. Luckily, we have the rest of our lives to practice and enjoy.

Heart Tools for Trusting the Present

Spend two, five, ten, twenty, or thirty minutes each morning for a week or more practicing one of the following tools. But if a specific tool calls you to spend more time with it, give yourself another week, month, or as long as you need in order to heal. Doing one practice for seven to fourteen days will give you a tangible body experience of being present amid anger, hurt, fear—and the gamut of human reactions. Set the alarm fifteen minutes early; if you practice when you first wake up, your mind is fresh, your heart is soft, and ego is too groggy to start its "to do" list. If you can't do it in the morning, set aside time after work, at midday, or after dinner to practice.

1. *Being Present with Your Breath*
Our heart loves to bask in the present. But ego distracts us and prevents us with countless thoughts, memories, worries, fears, and stories. Upon waking each morning this week, take ten deep

belly breaths and focus attention on the inhalation and exhalation of your breath. Then set an intention to stay present today by saying, "The second I notice I'm lost in thoughts today, I name it 'thinking,' let it go, and return to the present." (Once we set an intention, this pops into our awareness during the day when we most need the reminder.)

As you go about your day, when you wake up and notice your focus is lost in fear, doubt, judgment, or thought, end the thought midsentence with "thinking," and focus on what you are seeing, hearing, touching, or feeling in the present. If a thought is persistent, be equally persistent in letting it go and focusing on your breath.

2. *Checking In with Your Body*

In week two, expand your morning practice by focusing inside your body. Upon waking, lie on your back, breathe deeply, and feel the life force in your body. First, focus on your left and right foot for one second each. Continue up your body, focusing on your left knee, right knee, left thigh, and right thigh. Notice your left hand, right hand, left arm, right arm, belly, and chest. Then ground yourself in your body by quickly scanning your feet, legs, hands, arms, and torso in one fell swoop. Now pause to feel the life energy in your breath and your body.

With eyes closed, scan your body and ask, inside, "What sensations am I noticing?" Ask, breathe deep, and patiently notice any pain, tension, discomfort, or numbness (ignore ego's compulsion to judge these as "bad"). Allow these sensations to be the truth in your body now. To relieve pain or tension, focus directly on the area where you feel pain or tension inside and imagine sending your breath directly into the center of it. Watch it slowly disappear as you bring your breath and loving awareness to it.

3. *Making Friends with Feelings*

Ego tells us we don't have time for feelings. But being present with a feeling for two, five, or ten minutes takes much less time than staying lost in a story of grief or fear for hours or days. Make friends with your feelings by sitting or lying down when a particular feeling is present. Close your eyes, place one hand over your belly and the other over your heart, take a few deep breaths to relax, and remind yourself that feelings are visitors that come and go. Then softly ask, "Where am I feeling this worry, anxiety, hurt, jealousy, anger, sadness, or despair *in my body?*"

By locating the feeling as a tightness or knot in your throat, chest, belly, diaphragm, or back, you can focus directly on the feeling. Once you locate it in your body, take a deep belly breath and imagine sending your exhalation directly into the center of that feeling. Do this for five, ten, or fifteen minutes—however long the feeling needs to express fully and return you to spacious stillness.

4. *Checking In with Your Trusting Heart*

This is best practiced after you've worked with the second tool, "Checking In with Your Body," and the third tool, "Making Friends with Feelings," one week each.

Upon waking, lie on your back with both hands over your heart. Take several deep breaths until your whole body feels spacious. Notice any tension, pressure, tingling, numbness, or feelings inside. If any feelings are present, take a few minutes to breathe into them, just allowing them to be.

Now begin a dialogue with your heart. Start with a simple question. Since the heart speaks to us through dream images, symptoms, feelings, and hunches, first ask, "What are you trying to tell me?" Ask, breathe deeply, and patiently listen for an image, feeling, or phrase to bubble up into awareness. Since our heart responds much slower than ego, patience is critical. Treat your heart like your new best friend. Gently ask, "What does my heart need now, given my recent experiences?" As the dialogue flows, get creative. Ask things you wonder about: "What is my life purpose?" "Is this new lover my soul mate?" "Should I have a child?" "Am I ready to start my new business?" When you feel depleted, lost, or out of balance, ask your heart, "What sounds good to heal my body, heart, and spirit right now?" Grow skilled at receiving the soft, loving, compassionate genius of your trusting heart. Discover new ways to integrate this wealth of wisdom into your daily life.

2. Your Curious Heart

The Power of Simple Questions

What happens when I feel I can't handle what's going on?
What are the stories I tell myself? What repels and what
    attracts me?
Where do I look for strength and in what do I place my trust?
—PEMA CHODRON

Spring arrived two months early in the southern Rockies. Traditionally, March is our snowiest month. Yet the snow that blankets the high mountainsides is melting into rushing creeks. Yellow crocuses and daffodils are sprouting on the lower slopes, unable to wait until May. And with seventy-degree days this first week of spring, townsfolk don t-shirts and shorts for their first evening bike rides.

But locals greet this unseasonably warm weather with elation *and* apprehension. After all, the Missionary Ridge fire a decade ago, which burned thousands of acres and forced hundreds to evacuate their homes, remains fresh in everyone's mind. In the high desert, a low amount of winter snow can easily be followed by June fires.

Reacting to weather—as to the rest of life—is what we humans do. We react. Or at least our ego does, instantly, with a like/dislike judgment or opinion to all those unexpected, unfamiliar, unwanted aspects of life. It secretly wishes the weather, and life's current moment, would stay predictable, within our comfort zone. Ego pressures us to anticipate the future by preparing for the worst and mistrusting our inner knowing.

Resisting or reacting is not our problem. Failing to see it as a reaction is.

Curiosity, untainted by ego's endless judgments, invites us to pull up a chair in the land of "don't know" and enjoy the entire show as life unfolds before us. As much as ego coaches us to avoid hurt and pain at all costs, we don't really know what youth or old age, love or parenting, illness or death will actually be like. We just think we do.

Simple Questions Contact Our Inner Genius

Curiosity is the best invention since blue jeans. Curiosity can be our new best friend, our inner therapist, if we allow it in. It brings the gifts of freedom and inner peace we never knew were missing—or possible. Curiosity gently takes us by the hand and brings us backstage, behind the wizard's curtain, to see just how immature and small that ego pulling all the levers and pushing the buttons really is. It removes ego's reactions that cloud over our joy, happiness, and inner peace.

Curiosity reminds us to freely *choose* where we wish to put our attention now.

Every situation, every conflict, every symptom and feeling holds a pearl of wisdom inside, if we respond with curiosity. Our job is to use our discomfort, despair, hopelessness, and pain to see ourselves, and our humanness, more clearly. Curiosity invites us to be fully present and unlock the secrets of life by asking questions. I call this *the power of simple questions.*

When we ask a question, ego's constant chatter takes a break. Our attention shifts into hearing our wise heart. Rather than staying on the surface, lost in guilt, anxiety, jealousy, or anger, we drop down into a deeper sense of self. The moment we ask one simple ques-

tion, such as "What story am I telling myself now?" we stop identifying with the *content* of our life: the stories, judgments, doubts, and
fears that dominate our waking life. The moment we pause to ask,
"How am I perpetuating this conflict?" we shift—from being lost in
ego's reactions to being the *space around* our thoughts, feelings, and
reactions. The instant this occurs, our sense of who we are sinks
down into the quiet, loving, spacious awareness in our core.

Curiosity brings awareness and choice. Choice changes our
experience of life.

Curiosity helps us notice which reactions are just passing
through, like radio waves, and which ones we should pay attention
to. It helps us to stay open and curious in *all* situations. It invites us
to ask, "What story do I tell myself when I feel overwhelmed?" or
"Where do I look for strength when I feel afraid?" Simple questions
put breathing room around our thoughts, feelings, and symptoms
so we can collect ourselves and ask, consciously, "How do I wish
to respond in this moment?" The more we know ourselves (and
understand ego), the more freedom we feel to choose wisely.

For example, my client Pete had to learn a lot when his fiancé
Wendy canceled their wedding. At first, Pete felt angry, embarrassed,
hurt, and confused. But his pain motivated him to see himself—
and his reactions—clearly. "I always twist her feelings into something I did wrong," he said, "so she never feels heard."

"Wendy, would you be willing to share how you feel right now?"
I asked, "Pete, as she shares, would you be willing to just listen quietly without a word? Recognize your feelings as *your* reactions, not
Wendy's, and use this opportunity to practice setting them down
so that you can really hear exactly what Wendy says. That is, step
back in your mind and notice how you habitually take her feelings
personally."

"I feel lost, lonely, and hopeless," Wendy said. "Whenever I try
telling you how I feel, you explode and make my feelings all about
you. I feel so unheard and unloved."

Pete's jaw clenched shut. His face turned crimson red. But he said nothing.

"Pete, rather than pouring out your reaction," I said, "notice your angry response and set it aside. Then tell Wendy what you heard her say, especially the 'feeling words,' with no personal input. In fact, I'm asking you to sit on your reaction for twenty-four hours. By 5 p.m. tomorrow, if you still feel strongly, you can share your personal input."

Pete took several deep breaths. "I hear you feel lost, lonely, and hopeless. I hear you experience no room for you in our relationship. I hear you feel unheard and unloved."

Wendy wiped her eyes. "That's all I ever wanted. I don't want to break up. When you hear my feelings and feed them back, like you just did, I do feel loved. I feel closer."

Two weeks later, after practicing daily, Wendy and Pete returned. "Wendy and I treat this curiosity thing like a new, exciting game," Pete said. "Since I don't have to take her feelings personally, I feel much freer. All I have to do is listen and hear her inner process. Some nights, when we start to fight, she's quick to ask how my reaction is causing suffering for both of us. I do the same for her. We both laugh and joke about it." They rescheduled the wedding for May 12, their second anniversary.

Recognizing that we are not our reactions and feelings feels unnerving at first, like someone pulled the rug out from under us—a rug that has supported us all our lives. But this shift in identity unleashes the inner joy, aliveness, and presence that are our birthright. We feel so much freer. We might play this new curiosity game, as Pete referred to it, with ourselves, calling it "Being a Human Being in a Body without Taking Life Personally." We might even teach it to our friends.

Like a TV remote, curiosity switches ego's channel. Instead of worrying for hours, curiosity brings gratitude for *every* life experience, the good and the bad, in a split second. How? It opens all the shutters, doors, and windows to notice ego's demanding voice, which pressures us to stay on top of things, stay in control, have all the answers. It reopens our childlike eyes to wonder: "What could this pain, headache, conflict, or disappointment be trying to teach me in this moment?"

Curiosity hands us our very own "stop" and "pause" buttons, with full permission to use anytime, anywhere, whenever any thought, misperception, or story distracts us from the present. This skill comes in handy when judgment, doubt, fear, or blame swoop in unannounced and try to hold us hostage for hours, days, even years at a time.

Curiosity does all this on a dime, with the power of simple questions.

The instant we ask ourselves, "How am I reacting?" we stop sleeping with the enemy: those same old reactions to worry and despair that we inherited as infants, those same unconscious habits that imprisoned our parents, grandparents, and every human being for centuries. With one simple question, we see our reaction as just a reaction, a visitor passing through our awareness—not who we are. This allows us to choose how we *want* to respond in this moment to fear, hurt, or sadness.

Questions free us to leap into bed with our curious heart—that vein of gold, jam-packed with timeless wisdom, patiently awaiting our attention. Immune to ego's thoughts and reactions, this new friend forms a bridge for us to walk, run, leap, or skip across in our awareness. It introduces us to the new "us" that, armored with clarity, responds to ego's reactions with "hmmm, very interesting," and moves on. This quantum shift from "I am my reaction" to "I am *awareness* watching my reaction" changes how we see ourselves, see loved ones, and see life itself, forever.

The vigilant knowing that sniffs out any whiff of ego reactivity, which I call our *inner genius*, now coaxes us to ask the next question in this curiosity game: "How do I and my loved ones suffer by my own personal reactions?" Once we see the confusion and frustration our angry, sullen, or defensive reactions cause, we free ourselves to consciously choose a more compassionate response.

The next question from our inner genius is "What mental story is this asking me to let go of?" If we never question ego's story, we risk living our whole lives assuming it's real. We trade in a direct relationship with life for manufactured stories ego weaves in our head, based on past hurt, disappointment, and trauma. Clueless about which hidden feelings feed our current story, we live disconnected from our heart.

Curiosity's playful inquisitiveness gets us out of some sticky places fraught with jealousy, fear, guilt, anxiety, or despair. For example, Sherry lived with a suitcase packed in her closet for three years. Ever since her husband Michael, a hotel manager, hired his new female assistant, jealousy consumed her every waking moment. "I picture him in bed with this young, sweet, thin coworker, kissing her face and neck, and my blood boils," she said in therapy. "Before work, I scour his emails and text messages while he's asleep from a late night. The minute I find evidence, I'm headed back to Texas for good."

"Has Michael ever cheated on you before?" I inquired.

"Not that I know! But everyone I love betrays me eventually. Mom let Grandma raise me while she got drunk and high with her latest boyfriend. Everyone blamed me when I got molested. When I stopped trusting anyone, I stopped being disappointed."

In therapy, Sherry worked every week to release her childhood rage, grief, and fear. At home, in between sessions, she spent a whole month choosing curiosity, asking herself, "What story am I telling myself now?" and "How am I suffering from it?"

"It's hard. Some days I spent the whole day watching jealousy stories propagate more by the minute. For a while, the jealousy story felt far more real than labeling thoughts 'thinking.' But the more I labeled the stories and let them go, the less time I spent believing them. Now, after spilling the beans to Michael about how I don't know how to trust anyone, he tells me every day that he loves me and would never cheat on me. With the jealousy absent, my heart can feel my love for him again. Last night, I took my bag out of the closet and unpacked it."

Curiosity investigates *all* stories, even those we have adopted as reality for years.

Hearing the Loving, Unorthodox Messages of Our Heart

To begin a lifelong dialogue with our greatest source of wisdom, our heart, we must drop below ego's aggressive voice in our head. First, we grow skilled at asking open-ended questions while dropping any preconceived notions about what the answer might be; we embrace curiosity. Next, we cultivate an open, willing, patient attitude so that we can hear our heart's unorthodox answers, despite ego's prohibition against answers outside of logic's narrow box.

In addition to yanking us out of the present every chance it gets, ego convinces us every day, every chance we give it, to avoid all pain, hurt, sadness, fear, disappointment, failure, and above all, a broken heart. This sounds perfectly logical. But it forces us to lump the vast array of life experiences into two limiting categories: safe or unsafe. When we step outside ego's logic, we free ourselves to once again remember the First Noble Truth that Buddha offered 2,500 years ago: suffering is woven into the fabric of life. If we resist, ignore, medicate, and lean away from pain that is an integral part of being a human in a body, we miss the hidden messages planted by our inner genius.

Curiosity quiets ego's distractions and opens our mind to hearing the silent, unorthodox language of our heart. Lacking a voice of its own, our heart speaks to us through those same body symptoms and feelings that ego avoids; these offer an excellent entry point for beginning a lifelong dialogue with our inner genius. Though ego judges illness and pain as "bad" and dashes to the medicine cabinet for the latest cure, our inner genius invites us to see pain as the voice of loving truth, tugging gently at our shirt sleeve and begging for a few moments of our undivided attention.

For instance, Frank tired of popping painkillers to deal with his chronic backache. Though skeptical of talking to this pain he hated, he finally agreed. Frank closed his eyes, focused directly on his back pain and asked, "What are you trying to tell me?" At first, nothing came. He grew bored and discouraged. But when he asked again, an image of himself lying on the couch popped into awareness. "It was as if the most loving voice deep inside whispered, 'Please stop pushing me and let me rest.' I'll never admit to the guys at work that I'm conversing with my back pain," he chuckled, "they'd laugh me out of the building. But if paying attention makes it disappear, I'm on board."

Once we view pain and symptoms as our loving heart trying to gain our attention, we can focus directly on it and listen for the loving nonverbal message inside. As we give ourselves what the symptom requires, the symptom is free to leave. Simple questions help us move beyond logic to hear the unorthodox messages hidden inside.

By the time Karen turned seventy, she had had two knee replacement surgeries, and the doctor was scheduling a hip surgery. A tomboy all her life, with all her relatives touting a "buck up" attitude, she laughed when I spoke about "listening to her body symptoms." "I don't want to wind up helpless my last ten years like Mom," she said, "But I'm not a touchy-feely sort. I hate sharing feelings; I hate being vulnerable."

"Humor me," I pleaded. "Focus on your hip pain and ask what it's saying to you."

"Only if it helps me avoid wasting my time on that post-surgery rubbish," she said. After dialoguing with her hip pain, she said,

"When I closed my eyes, I saw a picture of myself swimming. Before I grew obsessed with running marathons in my thirties and forties, I loved to swim in my twenties. It's so meditative."

Karen still avoids feelings. But she's enjoying a new affair with swimming.

I love curiosity. I love how it disappears anxiety, guilt, despair, and fear with its simple question: "What story am I telling myself now?" The instant I ask, I chuckle at the silly story hijacking my attention. Free of scolding, the question returns me instantly to the present, to what my eyes are seeing and ears are hearing. Its sister version, "Am I here now?" also reminds us that, on a deeper level, everything is story—those fears about money or love or health. Now that I'm in my sixties, I notice many more fears concerning cancer or death. This seems to come with the territory of aging.

I do not love the physical symptoms that come with aging. For three weeks recently, I suffered from nausea more days than not. I tried antacids, peppermint tea, kefir, ginger, and acupuncture to alleviate it. When nausea returned, my chiropractor adjusted my digestion valves, which usually works. But still the nausea returned, tugging at my shirtsleeve to say, "Psssst. I need to interrupt your routine. Something very wrong needs your immediate attention now."

Finally I carved a morning out of my busy schedule to focus directly on the nausea. I breathed deeply into my stomach, asking, "What can I not stomach? What am I having trouble digesting?" Immediately, tears poured out. Images of the ponderosa pine forest behind my home flooded my awareness. But instead of picturing the elk herd, bear cubs and moms, coyote, and deer I had shared the animal trails with for twenty years, I saw dead oak bushes and pine trees strewn in every direction. In two days, a giant bulldozer had destroyed what nature had taken decades to perfect. Mitigation, the term for wildfire prevention measures, had struck my sanctuary. I cried for the deer, who lost their shade in oak bushes on hot days, for the elk who sleep under pine trees on cold, wintry nights, and for the rabbits who tunnel through snow to shelter their families inside logs. And I cried for the world's rain forests, changed forever by bulldozers.

Persistent symptoms bring our unconscious feelings to awareness.

Curiosity Calls Feelings into Awareness

Feelings below our awareness trigger much more of our behavior than you might think. Curiosity is our get-out-of-jail-free card for ending those angry outbursts and sullen silences. It identifies which unconscious feelings and needs fuel our reactions.

Since our body cannot lie, our body has to act out all feelings we fail to identify and verbalize. It has no choice. Therefore, when we ask, "Which feeling is fueling this incessant story in my head?" we release the body from its continued need to call our attention to feelings. And when our inner genius calls the feelings into our awareness, relationships change for the better.

For instance, though Mark promised himself each morning "I won't dump my anger on my lover John today," he inevitably would and then would feel ashamed and discouraged for failing. A smart and successful man, his inability to stop pushing John away with anger perplexed him.

In therapy, Mark closed his eyes and asked his heart, "Which feeling feeds my anger?" He focused on his breath, listening patiently for an image or feeling sense. Finally a picture arose of himself at age seven by his mother's bedside. "Mom was depressed again and refused to take me to my baseball game as she'd promised. Enraged, I threw my glove on the floor and stormed out, declaring that people aren't trustworthy. It protected my heart from more disappointment by not expecting anything from Mom," Mark admitted. "But now, when John makes a loving request, I believe I can't trust him."

When Mark went home, he asked John for a half hour to share some feelings. "For years," he said, "I've felt a thick shield covering my heart, blocking your love. I felt too ashamed to say anything before, but now I so apologize for exploding in anger. As a boy, I had to shut down my heart to guard against disappointment. Based on Mom's broken promises, I didn't think I could trust anyone. But now, after shedding the tears of my boyhood, my shield has dissolved. My heart is open again to love you and feel your love. I agree to drop my imaginary story about you and trust you with my feelings." They held each other on the living room couch for a long time and wept together in silence.

Curiosity offers a safe, nonjudgmental way to stick our big toe in the yet-unexplored waters of the unconscious—those waters we were taught to avoid. It gently invites us to ask, "Which feeling is fueling my story now?" Just as naming thoughts "thinking" releases us back into the present, identifying feelings underneath stories gives us conscious choice. We can choose to set down ego's repeated reaction and ask, "How would I like to respond in this moment?" to whatever is troubling us. When we ask directly, we see that the answer is usually obvious. Most of us, once we realize we have a choice, prefer reassuring ourselves for two seconds than spending hours lost in fear.

From our inner genius's perspective, most fears stem from two basic sources: fear of losing what we have and fear of not getting what we want.

For example, Sandy found herself drinking too much wine while preparing the family dinner. Like her father before her, she dismissed all feelings as "silly." By age forty-seven, this ignoring habit kept her clueless about her feelings and needs. When she read about curiosity, she set down the second glass of wine and asked herself, "What am I feeling?" Inside she seethed with resentment just below the surface.

In therapy, Sandy said, "I had no idea I was drowning such resentment with wine. My father's needs always felt more important than my little-kid needs. But he was lousy at asking for help. Between his depression and his anger, we kids had to avoid him or figure out by ourselves what he needed. Now I'm doing it too."

"Have you asked your teenage son or daughter for help?" I inquired.

Sandy burst into tears. "No. I have a million rationales for putting their needs first. But between running my travel business and taxiing them both to soccer practice and all it takes to run a household as a single mom, I'm exhausted. I don't have the energy I used to. But when I think of asking, I minimize my needs and my throat chokes up."

"Sandy, if you dropped the judgment that your feelings and needs are silly," I asked, "how would you like to respond to your need for help?"

"I'd like to ask my oldest, my son, for help first, but I'm really afraid."

"So make an intention. 'I'm willing to ask my son for _____.' State your fear by adding 'and I'm afraid.' If we verbalize fear, we don't have to act it out."

"I'm willing to voice my needs to my son *and* I'm afraid," she grinned.

Between her father's angry depression and his belief that feelings are "silly," Sandy never practiced voicing her needs and feelings when she was growing up. This unconscious habit continued for years, manifesting itself in illness and reliance on alcohol. But by asking herself five times a day, "What am I feeling?" and "What do I need?" she reconnected with herself and practiced expressing them to her children, employees, and most of all her self. By voicing her needs, she teaches others to value them.

Whether lost in despair, worry, jealousy, guilt, or anger, one simple question, such as "How would I like to respond now?" changes our whole experience. Since our bodies cannot lie, stating feelings and needs directly stops the habit of forcing our bodies to act them out again and again in the old, unconscious ways.

Which Part of Me Feels Sad, Scared, Anxious, or Angry?

Our heart's loving nonverbal messages help us recognize all the parts of ourselves.

We tend to think of ourselves as one entity—"My name is Laura. I was born in Washington, DC, in 1981. I live and work in Boston. I'm raising two children."—as if we could summarize this precious gift of being human into a few biological facts. But many different mature and immature parts make up the whole of who we are.

First, as revealed in chapter 1, our ego judges, doubts, fears, and resists every little event and feeling, demanding that we merge with its countless positive or negative reactions to life. Our young self, on the other hand—that tender version of ourselves that we carry tucked inside—gets scared often and needs lots of reassurance. Focused on past hurt, loss, betrayal, and rejection suffered in childhood, scared it will happen again, it lacks the radar to discern who and what is trustworthy in this world now.

Luckily our wise heart, equipped with unlimited joy, compassion, loving-kindness, and inner peace, responds to our current dilemma *and* our symptoms, feelings, and stories with loving compassion. It remains steady as an ancient redwood tree, allowing the hurts and discomforts of life to blow through without taking any of it personally.

As our inner genius identifies which part of us is reacting, we can use that information to respond to the situation in a new way. For instance, Dave had suffered from panic attacks for years. Medication had reduced them, but when Dave's panic attack forced him to pull over on the freeway at seventy miles an hour, he knew he needed more help. In therapy, he worked on his childhood terror of hiding in the backseat while his drunken father raged down the freeways.

That week, he met his panic attack with reassurance. "It happened again on the freeway," Dave said, "while I headed to work. But this time, I felt the panic rising in my chest. This time I remembered to ask myself, 'Which part of me is panicking?' I knew it was young Dave, so I spoke to my mental picture of him at seven. 'It's okay. You're okay. You're scared, but I'm here with you, and you're safe.'" His panic soon subsided.

Improving Relationships by Naming Reactive Parts Out Loud

Curiosity transformed my therapy work. In my practice, I have patients stand up and move around the office, exaggerating a current fear, hurt, or anger by naming its "story" out loud. This helps them realize that they aren't their story, that they have a choice how to respond. Then curiosity helps them dig deeper: "How is this feeling familiar to you? What happened in your world the first time you felt this way?" As clients identify where they first felt hurt, scared, or angry when they were young, they are free to heal the root trauma from their original wound. Once this injury receives the focus, expression, and love it needs, we stop overreacting in similar situations.

This new ability to describe our ego and our young self to loved ones changes our relationships. Rather than acting out anger, hurt, rejection, and disappointment for the thousandth time, our curious heart witnesses our reactions, feelings, and stories—giving ourselves the option to describe rather than act out our inner process to loved ones. This stops our unconscious habit of blaming and projecting our personal reactions onto loved ones, inviting closeness and compassion rather than distance.

For instance, Sara and Jim hit a stalemate in the relationship.

After a passionate honeymoon phase discovering how much they loved nature, backpacking, sex, and travel, their communication filled with hopeless disappointment. A long-time student of Buddhist meditation, Sara responded with love to Jim's angry outbursts, triggered by anxiety around not feeling lovable, by holding him while he cried, sometimes for hours.

But his outbursts continued, making Sara question whether to stay in this relationship. In desperation, she invited Jim to witness his anxiety rather than dump anger on her. One night, paralyzed with fear, Jim lay on their bed describing the anxiety to Sara. "My chest feels so tight, it could explode. If I try to move at all, I feel like I'll disappear. If I don't explode in anger, I feel like I'll never stop crying."

Sara, filled with compassion for his pain, held Jim as he wept the tears of growing up with an alcoholic mother. Several days later Sara said, "I have unlimited tolerance for hearing your inner feelings, but zero tolerance for your angry outbursts toward me."

Jim, terrified of feeling abandoned again the way he was as a boy, mistrusts everyone. But as his heart witnessed his childhood feelings and identified the fears of his younger self, he found the courage to trust Sara with the tender words that described his inner hurt and sadness. As Sara, too, stopped projecting her feelings onto Jim and described them as her own, their romance flourished again. Teaching each other their inner processes and asking directly for their needs, a close tenderness they had never known entered their daily life together.

Curiosity spells freedom. By shining a spotlight on old unconscious reactions, and by recognizing that we have a choice to respond differently every second, curiosity opens countless doors of new possibility. The more we respond to ourselves differently, the more curiosity nudges us to remove ego's blinders to see loved ones, and even strangers, with compassion—as struggling human beings, just like us.

Living Life in Expanded Curiosity

Opening our hearts comes from the willingness to be curious, to ask simple and leading questions and patiently listen for our inner genius to respond with an image, feeling, or symptom. When we finally drop ego's storyline, dip below fear, and ask our heart sincerely, "How am *I* holding love away? How am *I* sabotaging the love I most long for?" we access the heart's eternal wisdom. Like a breath of fresh air, one good question puts space and breathing room around our reactions, fears, pain, and feelings.

Too often, when feeling overwhelmed, we look for strength in habits that actually weaken us: compulsive drinking, eating, smoking, working, exercising, reading, or "keeping ourselves busy." Curiosity cuts through these compulsions. It invites us to experience feelings, and life, directly. It returns that juicy spark of spontaneity that has been missing far too long in our relationship. It welcomes each new situation as an opportunity to pause and ask, "Where do I look for strength when I feel scared, lonely, unlovable, or lost?" Curiosity lets us love ourselves as we are and guide our choices.

As human beings in bodies, our task is to take ourselves—and especially our reactions—much less seriously. Whenever I wake up to the fact that I am struggling inside with ego's latest story, I set my reactive story down and ask, "What great lesson lies hidden inside this issue for me?" Asking is simple. Hearing is life changing.

Cultivating the art of curiosity is a shortcut to happiness available to everyone. It opens the golden gateway to our inner genius. It keeps us from sleepwalking through the rest of our lives. It is the escape hatch out of ego's incessant habits. Curiosity brings an inner peace and joy few of us have ever known. It allows us to welcome all of life, the good and bad, the pleasant and painful, equally as a gift. It helps us see ourselves (and our reactive egos) with humor, patience, and grace. As we release everything we thought we needed to be happy, we relax into the unlimited joy, loving-kindness, compassion, and inner peace of who we really are, in our wise heart.

With curiosity, no feelings need be resisted or feared. We are free to stand in the center of our human life, experiencing and savoring each precious moment directly.

Heart Tools for Being Curious

Practice each of these four heart tools for one week before moving on to the next one. If a specific tool calls you to spend more time with it, give yourself another week, month, or as long as you need in order to heal.

1. *Cultivate the Art of Curiosity*
Ask yourself several times a day, "How am I reacting now?" The instant you ask, you witness rather than stay lost in the reaction. Follow up with "How am I and loved ones suffering by my reaction?" During your commute to work, exercise routine, or morning meditation, just ask the question, breathe deep, and listen for an image, feeling-sense, or word. Listen compassionately, free of any judgment toward yourself or the answer. As you grow more familiar with your reactions, you will be better equipped to nip them in a few seconds.

2. *Deepen Curiosity with Simple Questions*
Ask, "Which unconscious feeling fuels my current story or reaction?" After you ask, pause while taking several deep breaths, and listen patiently. Other times, think of a situation when you typically react strongly, and peek underneath to name the feeling fueling it. When pain or illness arises, notice ego's first reaction, then ask, "How would I like to respond now to my symptom?" Invite answers free of judgment.

3. *Identify Which Part of You Is Reacting Personally*

Whenever strong feelings visit, ask, "Which part of me inside is afraid, sad, lonely, or scared of getting hurt again?" If ego pops up, notice its reaction and set it down. If your young self is reacting, offer loving reassurance without hiding under the bed with them. Consider yourself "in training" to stay open and curious without taking yourself, and your issues, too seriously. Such questions as "How does my ego react when I feel uncomfortable or out of control?" or "How is my young, immature, inner self sabotaging my love relationship?" or "What great lesson is my symptom teaching me here?" bring deeper awareness and choice. The more curiosity you bring to daily life, the more playful, flexible, and joyful you will feel.

4. *Practice the New Relationship Game, "Being a Human Being in a Body Without Reacting Personally," with Family and Friends*

Bring this "curiosity game" into your relationship. Set aside twenty minutes, and sit facing each other. Invite yourselves to close your eyes, choose an issue that repeatedly upsets you two, and then answer the following questions: "What story am I telling myself now?" After you confess your inner story to each other, ask, "How do I react?" "How does my reaction cause us suffering?" "What is this repeated issue asking me to accept or let go of?" Treat the vulnerable answers that arise with tenderness, free of judgment, teasing, or joking. Sharing inner feelings transfuses your relationship with fresh, vibrant joy and aliveness.

3. Your Aware Heart
The Power of Responsibility

True freedom and the end of suffering is living in such a
way as if you had completely chosen whatever you feel or
experience at this moment.
—ECKHART TOLLE, *Stillness Speaks*

Armed with presence, curiosity, and conscious choice, we
begin to find some breathing space around unwelcome feelings. Things feel more hopeful again. But we don't want
to make a common mistake: deciding that labeling thoughts "thinking" and asking simple questions will extinguish ego's perpetual
resistance to what is.

The truth is, ego reactions vie for attention our whole life. Rather
than eliminate ego (our first impulse), we achieve freedom by inviting its habits into conscious awareness.

When my client Dwayne first started daily meditation, he felt even
more confused. "I watched my breath twenty minutes every morning," he said in therapy, "but no matter how much I labeled my
anger 'thinking,' I stayed angry about the lack of sex in our marriage. I believed if my wife Suzie really loved me, she should welcome my advances.

"Nothing changed until I stopped blaming her and looked at

myself. One morning at the end of meditation, I inquired, 'How is my anger sabotaging our sex life?' Suddenly an image flooded my awareness: Suzie, acquiescing to sex just to please me. I was horrified that she might fear my moods to such an extent. That morning I apologized profusely to Suzie for all the times my anger muted her desire. I begged her to be honest, and, every day for a while, asked her what she needed to trust me enough to be close again. Slowly, with time and tenderness, our lovemaking returned. Once I saw the connection between my anger and her contracting, I stopped indulging anger."

Conscious awareness is not some heavenly hotel we arrive at, check in, and set up permanent residency. Our whole life, moment to moment, day after day, we move in and out of conscious and unconscious awareness. One moment, our aware heart sees a fear thought or ego story clearly, names it "thinking," and lets it go. But for the next several hours, ego may hold us hostage to some story of resentment, loneliness, or rejection.

Sometimes clients ask, "Why bother cultivating awareness if it slips through my fingers like sand? At least I feel justified momentarily when I blame loved ones or life when things go wrong." I often reply, "Because any form of complaining or playing victim, no matter how justified it feels, deems us powerless. Nothing changes. We lose vitality, hope, and joy. Awareness, like water over time, erodes away our unconscious habits of a lifetime. Awareness lays a strong foundation for happiness and inner peace."

Watching our thoughts in meditation and asking key questions do help to free us. But moments of awareness add up quicker if we set a morning intention, such as "I am willing to be aware of ego thoughts and personal reactions today." Then, during the day, whenever we find the story in our head stuck in resentment, our aware heart asks: "In this present moment, will I stay resentful, creating more angst for myself, or will I empower myself to drop the story and choose freedom?" Each moment we wake up out of illusion is cause to celebrate who we really are: conscious awareness.

For instance, Jessie sat quietly and practiced labeling her thoughts "thinking" thirty minutes each morning. But this failed to stop her depressing thoughts when her partner Tom disappointed her. Perplexed at how to overcome this obstacle, she agreed to set a new intention: "I'll watch my depression story rather than swallow it as gospel."

"That was *hard!*" she said the next week. "I found Tom pouring his heart out in emails to some woman at work. I felt justified to wring his neck. But just as my mouth snarled to launch an attack, I remembered my intention. I jumped up, ran into the bathroom, sat on the toilet, and took several deep breaths. Through gritted teeth, I asked, 'How might an aware person respond?' Dead silence until my heart whispered, 'Meet his unconsciousness with awareness.'

"I rolled my eyes; it sounded so cheesy. But I couldn't think of a better idea. Finally I went back into the kitchen and said, 'I know you hate to disappoint me with bad news. But I'd love to hear what motivated you to email that coworker, and I swear I won't react personally. I promise to listen and not interrupt.'

"Tom stared in disbelief, as if I'd hidden his real wife in the closet. Then he blurted out that his dad had colon cancer, and he'd been afraid to tell me, not knowing how I'd react. The woman at work had lost her husband to colon cancer last spring and understood what he was going through. Then he told me that he just needs me to stop talking all the time and listen, stop taking his feelings so damn personally."

"I took Tom in my arms while he wept. Later, he shared his fears about dying."

Conscious awareness changes how we respond in relationship, whether with our spouses or our coworkers. Of course, ego never misses an opportunity to insert itself into a conversation or embellish a big story—anything to distract us from feeling our feelings directly. But as long as we know this, we can smile as we welcome and then dismiss ego through the same revolving door.

With practice, by consciously choosing to stay present, curious, and aware, we can stay lost in ego's habits only for two minutes— instead of two days or twenty years.

Unconscious Human Conditioning: Ancient Ways Still in Vogue

For centuries, we humans—with ego's full support—have resisted, reacted, judged, doubted, and feared our way through life, fully believing that this is the smart way to survive. We all know the routine: hide tender feelings like hurt or sadness (even from ourselves), take everything personally, make up a story to avoid feeling our feelings, blame everyone else or life itself for all misunderstandings, then repeat ad nausea. When avoidance fails and a situation or relationship feels intolerable, bail.

We sabotage love relationships, blame others for our unhappiness, and perpetuate suffering for ourselves with endless reacting, judging, and resisting in the name of "this is how humans do reality"— until awareness turns the light switch on.

With generations of our ancestors refining what Buddha aptly named our *unconscious human conditioning*, these habits live deep in our bones, our blood, our DNA, and our cells. We rely on them to meet scary situations, meaning anything unfamiliar, new, or unexpected. Our conditioned habits are such deeply ingrained parts of us, like our right arm or left foot, we literally never think about them; they occur prethought. In fact, these habits occur so far below our awareness that, without questioning them at all, we deem these recurrences "reality."

In our youth, none of us escaped this indoctrination. The moment the doctor announced "It's a girl!" or "It's a boy!" to the delivery room, we began soaking up the misperceptions, mistaken beliefs, and ego reactions that form our family's special brand of unconscious human conditioning. Whether raised Catholic, Protestant, Jewish, Muslim, Buddhist, or atheist, we all began seeing, thinking, and reacting to life through certain culturally tinted filters. Whether born in Northern Europe, South America, the Middle East, or Kansas, we all struggle day in and day out with this human predicament: ego's fears and stories running our lives unconsciously.

Our unconscious reactions—not just the life events—cause us untold suffering.

Awareness of fear's familiar voice is our short path to freedom. Fear can sound so clever and seductive, so demanding and logical, we often mistake fear for truth. Its chorus of "never good enough" judging our every action holds us in self-doubt.

When ego denies fear's presence and brags, "I'm so over fear," fear runs our life unconsciously. It repeatedly holds us hostage to past mistakes and future what-ifs until we can't hear the soft voice of our aware heart. If we are thinking about having a baby or opening our own business, fear scolds, "Where will you ever find the money and time to do that?" After we do find love, fear tries to sabotage it with "They will leave too, like the others, once they see who you really are." Over time, consumed with doubt, we feel afraid to care, afraid to trust, afraid to believe in ourselves.

Cutting right through fear's countless disguises, awareness saves the day. In fact, during any major transition—graduating, getting married, raising children, advancing a career, traveling, retiring— awareness lessens fear's impact. By disarming fear's element of surprise, which it counts on to catch us off guard, awareness responds instead with "Hello, I was expecting you."

Simple questions call unconscious habitual fears into conscious awareness. When we ask "What is fear telling me right now?" or "Which fear stories capture my attention when I'm anxious, worried, hopeless, or lonely?" awareness exposes fear as fear. Rather than merge with it, the instant we see fear clearly, we stop identifying with it. We can name it "fearing" and let it go or surround the whole fear story with love. It's a choice.

Centuries ago, Buddha warned us there'd be days like this—days when we layer untold piles of angst on top of the inherent suffering that comes with being alive. But naming which feelings and beliefs perpetuate suffering returns us to freedom.

Attention Calls Sensations and Feelings into Awareness

Anyone facing paralyzing anxiety, jealousy, loneliness, or despair knows that ditching old unconscious conditioning is easier said than done. After all, we adopted our family's unconscious conditioning as toddlers. And despite rebelling against certain behaviors in our adolescence, adulthood finds these deeply ingrained values—and the habits that support them—remain the only reality we know.

It makes sense that walking around ego's potholes—rather than falling through them again—might take some well-deserved moments of our undivided attention.

First, let's acknowledge the gifts of conscious awareness:

- Awareness notices thoughts: ego reactions, resistance, and judgments.
- Awareness notices sensations: pain, tension, numbness, and tingling.
- Awareness notices feelings: grief, hurt, despair, shame, and loneliness.
- Awareness notices ego stories: rejection, resentment, fear, and guilt.
- Awareness notices impermanence: the ever-changing truth of life.

When we align with awareness, when we notice thoughts as thoughts, sensations as sensations, and feelings as feelings, we are able to pause and remember who we really are: "I am conscious awareness witnessing my thoughts, sensations, feelings, and ego stories." But this shift—from identifying with thoughts, feelings, and sensations, as if this is all I am, to identifying with the conscious awareness noticing these—takes time. Midstream between the two, while this transition takes place, we painfully watch ourselves reenact old habits—painful, because now we are aware we are doing it but feel powerless when the old habit runs roughshod over our desire to change it.

For instance, each time Nancy felt overwhelmed at her clothing store, she threw up her arms, said, "I can't do this anymore," and stormed out, just like her mother and grandmother did before her. "Mom used to piss me off so bad! She'd never say clearly what she needed. She'd make our whole family and the whole world feel wrong, then drown her sorrow in a bottle of wine."

When Nancy interrupted this family tradition by closing her eyes and asking her heart, "Which feeling perpetuates this horrible feeling of being overwhelmed?" she let go of the family legacy. "It's my fear, and Mom and Grandma's fear, of never being good enough. Ever since I was young, I hid my imperfections to win Mom's love. Instead of receiving unconditional love, as I deserved, I coped with never feeling good enough by throwing up."

Nancy wept silently. "I never realized the pain I suffered trying to earn Mom's love. Here I am at forty-four running out of my office, still overwhelmed with never feeling good enough." When she asked her aware heart for healing guidance, it said, "You are lovable just the way you are. You never have to earn love."

As many of us learn over the years, those deep-seated childhood traumas and wounds can dampen our joy in adult life. Persistent awareness is required to meet persistent habits that repeat themselves for so many years, we forget they are there.

Instead of obliterating ego's habits, awareness wakes us up out of the stupor of past conditioning. By watching incessant thoughts and stories stream through us—triggered by long-held unconscious feelings—our heart helps us see this chain of events as thoughts and stories passing through, not who we are. Rather than waste another minute of our precious lives identifying with past traumas, awareness reminds us to choose consciously: "How would my aware heart, in this moment, like to respond to the past unconscious acts of parents, relatives, or strangers that hurt me?"

For example, Jane decided that thirty years was long enough to hate her uncle for molesting her. "I'd told many friends the story of what Uncle Al did, but I'd never acknowledged the feelings to myself. As soon as I closed my eyes and asked my heart, 'Which feelings underneath my story feed this hatred?' I first felt rage burn through my belly. Afterward my body shook with fear about ever feeling so violated. Finally I cried the tears I never could before. I can't explain why, but by focusing awareness on the feelings underneath and feeling them fully, I stopped identifying as a victim."

With awareness, Jane released herself from her rage, fear, and grief.

With conscious awareness, we can notice the instant we feel off kilter. But we still need to actively address the imbalance, rather than taking years to address the problem. We do this by taking responsibility for our inherited feelings and beliefs.

Taking Responsibility for Our Unconscious Conditioning

We cannot erase the karmic conditioning we inherited from family and culture. Nor can we reverse the traumas we suffered at the hands of our parents' and relative's unconscious and conscious acts. But through the power of responsibility, we can stop perpetu-

ating these wounds by uncovering how we perpetuate these unconscious habits. When we feel triggered, awareness gently takes our
hand and helps us peek behind ego's curtain to see which feelings
and beliefs set off our same old reactions.

The Dalai Lama, disturbed by the countless Americans riddled with
low self-esteem, encourages us to trust our innate basic goodness—
that place deep inside our heart overflowing with our other inher-
itance: unlimited joy, kindness, compassion, and inner peace.
Unfortunately many people, raised on the Christian concept of
original sin, are terrified to look inside themselves.

We grew up afraid to find in our core what we always feared:
that we are bad, boring, and unworthy of love. When my parents
drove me to the Lutheran Sunday School and Church each week,
I received a regular weekly diet of original sin. I recall sitting on
a pew between my parents, hearing the sermon, and feeling sin-
ful for wanting a new warm Easter coat—and for wishing Mom's
depression would subside. One of my good friends, raised Catholic,
spent several years in therapy healing her guilt over divorcing an
abusive husband that tried to kill her.

Such early teachings die slow. They bury our basic goodness
under piles of fear.

Most of us never want to repeat the unconscious conditioning we
suffered. Since I began seeing clients in the mideighties, I notice
the majority of my therapy clients say they never want their children
to suffer the abuse, incest, alcoholism, or depression they experienced with their parents. Yet we need healthy habits to extinguish
unhealthy ones.

These four steps replace old habits with conscious feelings and
beliefs.

STEP 1. TAKE RESPONSIBILITY

The first step to becoming more present in our choices is to take
responsibility for how we respond. This starts the moment our

aware heart watches our reactions without indulging them. When we feel judged, criticized, hurt, or rejected, ego instantly lashes out in the same old ways it has since we were little. But as we witness all of our reactions, even if ego still gets its way at first, we make progress by the simple act of witnessing alone. Awareness precedes all change.

Taking responsibility throws the possibility of blame out the window. The instant we stop blaming others, stop pointing our finger at our spouse, child, parent, or circumstance, we return home to our undefended heart. Amid anger and conflict, awareness always invites us to ask, "What is my part here?" As we stop to listen, peeling back the first unconscious layer, we see reactions as red flags calling out for attention.

Taking responsibility empowers us to greet feelings with acceptance and loving compassion.

As we walk through the dark caverns of unconscious conditioning, trusty flashlight in hand, it's crucial not to judge ourselves for past reactions. After all, we learned so young how to blame anything outside ourselves, and we have rubber-stamped the ego's need to be right for so many years, that taking responsibility for reversing these ancient but condoned ways of life takes courage.

Remember that taking responsibility does not give us license to blame ourselves for causing our cancer, pain, divorce, or suffering. Instead we take full responsibility for *how we respond*. This comes by being consciously aware and accepting of what is true.

For instance, when Tami's husband Dave revealed his affair, her first, second, and third reactions were far from "I'm to blame!" Her four-letter expletives made her fury clear. "How could I possibly have any part in your affair?' was her mantra for weeks. But as she moved past her anger in therapy, she came to admit to him, "I see now how much I withdrew into myself last year, blinded by grief after my father died. I'm sorry to hear how your loneliness pushed you to talk, then be intimate, with a coworker." Though

Dave had apologized many times, no real closeness returned until Tami owned her part.

Whenever we buy ego's shaming story of how unlovable or unworthy we are, we stop voicing our needs. We withhold affection, closeness, and joy, the whole time blaming our mate for blocking affection and closeness. We see that person we love through a hopeless "why bother?" filter. Yes, they have their part in hurting us based on their own unconscious conditioning. But we also have our part.

We take responsibility for our part by acknowledging our feelings.

STEP 2. ACKNOWLEDGE UNCONSCIOUS FEELINGS

When we take responsibility and acknowledge unconscious feelings, we dissolve any need to act out. Just as eating food satiates hunger, naming underground feelings satiates ego's need to act out anger, anxiety, fear, or despair. The instant we shift channels— from acting out to awareness—we free ourselves to ask, "Which feeling is fueling my need to react unconsciously?" Since most of us have numerous feelings moving through us at any one time, this question invites us to know the subtle layers of feelings. Once we drop below ego's story, we feel free to speak our deeper feelings.

The body can't wait for conscious awareness to arrive. Our minds may grow adept at omitting the truth and telling white lies, justifying it with "I'm keeping the peace." But our bodies cannot lie. Naked and innocent, our bodies have one gear: truth. If we fail to say, "I feel hurt, scared, disappointed, or sad," even to ourselves, our body dutifully acts out our unacknowledged feelings like a trained soldier in the front lines, obeying orders. Once we admit to ourselves "I'm afraid," our body can relax. And when we admit to loved ones, "I'm afraid you'll laugh at my feelings or ignore my needs," the body surrenders into spacious silence.

This explains why any promise, to ourselves or others, to never unleash anger again is overridden by our body's need to act out, again and again, the wrath we try so desperately to hide. Or if we stay too busy to voice our hurt or despair, our body screams louder, demanding our attention. Years later, after believing we kept our feelings secret, we usually realize our body exposed our feelings through our clenched fists, slammed doors, wild affairs, withdrawal of affection, and rolling our eyes. Our body communicates our true feelings all day long without ever speaking a word.

Most feelings, despite their intensity, only need brief acknowledgement. If we take a few seconds to tell our immature child self "I hear how sad you feel right now" or "I understand how another's remark hurt your feelings," our young self feels seen and heard, free to leap into the next moment. Occasionally, when feelings linger, our aware heart may need us to address an unmet need. We might ask, "Based on my persistent feelings, what does my heart repeatedly long for now?"

STEP 3. DESCRIBE OUR UNARGUABLE TRUTH

Acknowledging and describing feelings allows us to replace conflict with closeness. When we can see and describe feelings as visitors, rather than summations of who we are, we put breathing space around our hurt, sadness, and fear. Instead of pushing others away by acting out our underlying abandonment fears, we can identify our feeling and responsibly state our needs around it: "My fear of abandonment is up. Can you please hold me and reassure my child self that you're not going anywhere?"

Stating needs directly offers our highest chance of having needs met.

When we bring bare attention, which we learned about in chapter 1, to underlying feelings, we describe which feeling is present and what we need for it, leaving ego's elaborate stories at the curb. In addition to activating compassionate awareness for ourselves, describing the feeling engages others' compassion by teaching loved ones our *unarguable truth*: "I feel _____ in this moment, and I need _____ for it." This stops that silly habit of expecting loved ones to read our minds and blaming them for not intuiting our needs. Feel the difference between "You made me sad. You never care about my feelings" and "I feel sad right now. I need a hug." Feelings are *unarguable* because nobody can tell us what we feel (though at times they certainly try).

When we close our eyes and ask, "Where do I feel this fear, hurt, sadness, or rejection in my body?" a place of tension or pressure will stand out in our throat, chest, diaphragm, or belly. If we include *where in our body* we feel pain, fear, hurt, or sadness when we tell our loved ones, we consciously share our inner process with them. By painting the whole picture for loved ones—"I feel sadness as a pressure in the center of my chest. I need you to hold me while I cry"—such clean, clear, blameless, undefended communication instructs loved ones exactly how to respond to help us heal.

However, when describing a feeling, don't underestimate the possibility of others reacting personally. They are also strapped to their unconscious conditioning, just like us. We often need to repeat our "I feel, I need" truth four or five times to sweep out their knee-jerk, skeptical cobwebs and achieve genuine listening.

Step 4. Expose Core Beliefs

Naming vulnerable feelings—based on often-unconscious beliefs— empowers us to create fresh beliefs in seconds. Just as rabbits and moles live underground, invisible to the naked eye, core beliefs live so deep in our psyche that we have no idea they exist. Yet these invisible culprits control all our personal reactions and unconscious feelings.

In therapy, some of us may have already named our primary core beliefs, such as feeling unworthy, unwanted, unlovable, rejected, abandoned, or not good enough. But few of us know the high price we pay, in our lives and relationships, to keep believing these outdated, false gods that tell us something is wrong with us.

Just as our body acts out unacknowledged feelings, beliefs attempt to prove themselves right again and again at the expense of our happiness, health, and well-being. Luckily, we can start changing beliefs the instant we shine awareness on them.

Core beliefs joined our life when we desperately needed them to help us through a childhood trauma. When we faced overwhelming hurt, fear, abuse, judgment, guilt, or shame, a core belief rushed to the scene, ready to rescue us from confusing outer events. Since we lacked the mental capacity, as children, to understand such adult issues as depression, anxiety, addiction, or low self-worth, these limited beliefs made sense out of scary nonsense. We felt grateful. However, children developmentally see themselves as the center of the universe. So these same core beliefs that brought relief also made us blame ourselves for our parent's divorce, Mom's depression, or Dad's disappearance.

Through this less-mature filter, while Mom and Dad fought on the other side of the wall, we concluded, "Something is wrong with me. If only I had less needs, helped out more, and got better grades, maybe my family would stay together."

One example repeatedly shows up when adults try to heal childhood molestation. When the original shame of being molested is exacerbated by a parent blaming the child for the event, that child silently believes something is wrong with them. They blame themselves. The body acts out this shame, perhaps with sexual promiscuity in the teen years or by hiding its sexual body underneath abnormal weight gain. Either way, the core belief "I'm damaged goods, unworthy of love" keeps proving itself right.

As another example, when Mom's rage takes up all the space at home, we decide, "I'm unimportant. Nobody cares about my needs." We unconsciously carry this belief into our adult relationships, never bothering to voice our needs, because this belief lives below our awareness, blocking the possibility of freedom in the present.

We cannot avoid core beliefs. These false beliefs come with childhood, from our parent's acting out their own unconscious conditioning. The problem is forgetting, decades later, that these core beliefs, as much a part of us as our left hand, still mess with our choices. These unconscious beliefs lie dormant like a rattlesnake in tall grass, waiting to rear up the moment we feel loved enough and safe enough in relationship. Like a volcano asleep for years, they explode and surprise us.

We know the routine. We are having a simple argument about whose turn it is to wash dishes when suddenly we launch into a lifelong list of major hurts—anything to prove that the core belief is true, that we are unlovable. Or while driving to work on the route we always take, we find the thought of driving over a cliff more appealing than facing our current life. Or we race out of the room before hitting our young child the way we were hit.

Core beliefs can tear down our self-worth. Like we did with our feelings, we must name them to acknowledge them, so that we can stop being ruled by them. Usually our first clue that a core belief is triggered comes from watching ourselves overreact to a minor incident. Any innocent statement or quest can pour salt on those tender childhood wounds. But once we acknowledge, to ourselves and loved ones, that "I'm unwanted, unworthy, or unimportant" started somehow during a childhood trauma, we can freely ask ourselves, "How is my core belief triggering my overreaction now?" Our job is to witness underlying feelings and beliefs, then ask for what we need.

If we stay lost in acting out, our mate can help us name our core belief. For example, Nancy was putting on makeup in the bathroom, getting ready for Christmas dinner at her parents' when the phone rang. Nancy was feeling happy after opening gifts and making breakfast for her husband Don and their three teenage children that morning. But the instant Don entered the bathroom, relaying her dad's request for them to arrive an hour earlier for dinner, Nancy exploded with rage. "Dad always changes the plans, always makes it convenient for him, and to hell with us. I'm sick of it. I'm staying home and cleaning up under the tree."

Don wanted to logically talk Nancy out of her anger by offering to clean up under the tree while she got ready. But logic never worked when Nancy's ire was up. Then he remembered her core belief: "My needs always come last." He took a deep breath and asked as gently as his voice could muster, "Did Dad's call possibly trigger your core belief about your needs being unimportant?"

Nancy clenched her jaw. "NO! Don't dare talk me out of my feelings."

He dodged her anger like a left hook, repeating, "Is your old belief up?"

Nancy's inner skeptic clung tight to acting out. "Dad's needs always come first!"

Suddenly these words snapped Nancy out of the trance of her old belief. "Oh my gosh, my childhood belief is up. One more time, it told me there's no room for my needs. I'm sorry, babe, I dug my heels in. But right now, to show that my needs are important, call my parents and tell them we won't be able to come early."

While applying mascara, Nancy repeated, "My needs are important, my needs…"

As we all know, the tiniest incidents can trigger old childhood beliefs. Rather than pretend that we breezed through childhood unscathed by core beliefs, the wise choice is to cozy up to these familiar unconscious companions. When left fermenting in our unconscious, these foes raise endless havoc. Compelled to prove themselves right at any cost, they project unlovable stories onto lovers, spouses, parents, children, and friends who are doing the best they can—amid their own unconscious habits—to love us.

When we take responsibility for unconscious feelings and core beliefs, when we witness and acknowledge these rather than act out, love relationships offer a brand new playing field. Now conflict, hurt, and fear become opportunities to describe our unarguable truth, including deeply buried feelings and core beliefs.

Imagine bypassing ego's story to explain, "When you said, 'I feel unhappy,' I overreacted. I took it personally and blamed myself for causing your unhappiness. I apologize for not being a good listener and not letting you just have your feelings. But I need to explain that my fear of abandonment got triggered. I know you were innocently sharing your feelings. But my core belief, *something is wrong with me*, got triggered big time. Can you tell me that nothing is wrong with me, and that you won't leave?"

Such advanced communication takes practice and more practice. We start by identifying core beliefs to ourselves. Once named, we begin to create a new belief. If the old belief is, "I'm unwanted and unloved," we can start by telling ourselves many times a day how wanted and loved we are. If the old belief is "Nobody cares about my needs," we begin by caring about our own needs enough to voice them. Repeating our new belief eventually silences that inner skeptic who rejects the new belief in favor of the old.

Using Our New Core Belief

Once our new belief is firmly established, we should find a quiet time to teach loved ones what it is and what we need to hear concerning it. This way, during conflict, code words like "core belief" instantly signal to loved ones the root cause of an overreaction and the healing words needed.

Simple heart phrases heal best: "You are wanted and loved. You are safe. Your needs and feelings are important. You're not alone; I'm here for you." Healing words are covered more thoroughly in chapter 4.

Our unconscious overlooks any negative words such as "not" and "won't"; the unconscious hears "I won't be afraid" or "I won't smoke" as "I'll be afraid" and "I'll smoke." It's vital to heed this odd quirk about the unconscious. To see changes we desire unfold, new beliefs must be stated positively: "I am free of fear" or "I am free of smoking."

Deeper questions help us understand when core beliefs joined our life. When we close our eyes, take several deep breaths, and ask, "How is mistrust or fear of rejection familiar to me?" we might recall the first incident triggering this belief in our life. By seeing its origin, we stop projecting our story so vehemently on our mate.

Once we update our core belief, we ask our heart, "What is this repeated issue asking me to release? What do I need to do to heal this wound completely?" Conscious awareness brings choice. Conscious choice brings freedom.

A recent example from my therapy practice clearly outlines how to put these four steps into practice. Melody spoke frankly in her first session. "Frank and I had sex twice in the past six months, once on our anniversary and once on my birthday. Neither was anything to write home about. For years I've convinced myself that I'm too busy with my job, teenage son, and endless chores to be sexy. But the truth is we stopped talking and caring years ago. We live like strangers in the same bed. When I fantasize, I think about some tall, dark, exotic lover, not Frank."

I spent this session teaching Melody about taking responsibility.

Clearly Melody wanted more frequent sex. But her elaborate story blaming Frank for their lack of sex stopped her from teaching Frank what she needed. By repeating her story over and over in her head, she convinced herself years ago that she could not get her sexual needs met in this marriage. Her escape fantasy was to divorce Frank as soon as their son graduated from high school.

As long as she clung to this victim story, Melody disempowered herself from voicing her feelings and needs. When they both came for couple's work the next week, I invited Melody to ask herself two questions: "What is my part in us not having sex?" and "Which hidden feeling keeps fueling my story, blaming Frank?"

"I joke a lot about our lack of sex," she said to Frank, "but I never told you directly what I want. Every weekend we don't make love, I feel rejected and unattractive."

Frank reached out to hold her hand. "I wish I'd known, hon," he said. "After your hysterectomy, you said sex was painful. I just figured you'd lost interest."

As Melody's face contorted in anger, I interrupted, "Set down your personal reaction and say your unarguable truth, Melody. Teach Frank what you feel now and which core belief is up for you."

She took several deep breaths to calm herself. "I'm pissed! But underneath, I'm deeply hurt and sad. You know, Frank, I suffer from fear of rejection. My father was always too busy to pay attention to me. And now you're rejecting me, too."

"I'm sorry," Frank said. "I had no idea. But I'm willing to change."

"Thank you. I don't really believe you care what I like. But for the record, I love it when you stroke my hair softly and whisper dirty nothings in my ear," Melody offered. "It makes an old lady like me feel young, sexy, and loved again."

Two weeks later, Melody arrived for therapy with tears in her eyes—tears of joy. "Last Sunday we made love," she grinned. "When he invited me upstairs to the bedroom, I heard my old voice dig her heels with, 'No, don't. He'll disappoint you again. He just needs sex.' But I let the story go and said 'yes.'

"Right in the midst of lovemaking, he became my dream lover. He looked me in the eyes and said, 'I want to kiss you and love you all over. I want to pleasure you every way you want.' What happened next is too dirty to share. But who needs a fantasy man when you have a naked husband lying next to you saying that? For the first time in years, I felt his genuine love for me. I can't wait to get home and find out more secrets about this man living in my house."

Unconscious human conditioning can feel as vast and unwieldy as an iceberg with the majority of its mass invisible and under water. Our meager attempts to witness reactions, acknowledge feelings, and describe core beliefs can feel like David facing Goliath. But moment-by-moment, as we keep choosing awareness, small victories bring hope. Rather than hoping to be totally free someday, conscious awareness in this moment becomes our goal and practice. One day at a time, one moment at a time, our aware heart notices unconscious habits and chooses awareness. This becomes our new way of life.

Soon, we celebrate each moment we wake up out of fear, despair, or anxiety. Just as drops of water carved out the Grand Canyon, we too create an inner canyon of freedom for ourselves, our children, and grandchildren—one awareness at a time. And the more we do, awareness reminds us that we are all born with the grace, wisdom, and loving acceptance to handle every gift life brings.

Slowly, awareness lifts the veil of illusion hiding the truth of who we really are. We watch thoughts come and go, feelings come and go, fears and reactions come and go, even pain and body sensations come and go. But midstream, as old ways of seeing ourselves shake and crumble like earthquakes, we see possibility through awareness. Our body relaxes. Our breath deepens. And we start to rest in the conscious awareness that is always present, always here, no matter what.

Awareness is our constant, keeping a vigilant eye on invisible habits.

As our eyes open, we see ego's frequent thoughts, reactions, and feelings as passing neighbors. We welcome, tolerate, and accept old, familiar thoughts like visitors that come, amuse us with stories, and leave. But telling ourselves "I am my ego reaction" comes to feel as far-fetched as saying, "I am my neighbor." It's out of the question.

With time, we even hold our unconscious conditioning itself in loving compassion; our aware heart teaches us how to embrace even our false core beliefs. Awareness frees us to respond fresh in *this* moment. Such total acceptance returns a childlike aliveness, joy, and curiosity to ordinary daily life.

Heart Tools for Awakening

Practice each of these for one week before moving on to the next one. But if a specific tool calls you to spend more time with it, give yourself another week, month, or as long as you need in order to heal.

1. *Taking Responsibility for Our Unconscious Conditioning*

   Whenever you feel out of sorts, ask, "What story am I telling myself now?" Notice without judgment any familiar story in your head blaming a spouse, child, boss, or loved one when you feel criticized, rejected, or misunderstood. Also notice ego's impulse to lash out or withdraw. Now take responsibility for this issue by asking, "What is my part here? How am I perpetuating this unresolved conflict?" Shift the exchange by owning your part: "When you said you felt disappointed, I stopped listening and blamed myself for disappointing you. I apologize. I'll listen better now." If anger or blaming sarcasm already spilled out, ask for a do-over by saying, "Stop. Let's start over. What I meant to say consciously is _____."

2. *Acknowledging Unconscious Feelings and Sensations*

   Since feelings and pain below our awareness force our body to act out, acknowledging feelings and sensations—first to ourselves, then others—is the key. Upon waking, take ten deep breaths and scan your body head to toe, noticing any fear, sadness, hurt, pain, tingling, numbness, or tightness that is present. Allow and accept whatever you notice without judging anything

as bad. Before rising, set an intention for the day: "Today I'm willing to notice which unconscious feeling feeds my story of blaming others." During the day, at the first inkling of acting out anger,
hurt, fear, or sadness, ask yourself, "Which feeling is fueling my
ego reaction now?" Once you identify the culprit to yourself,
communicate this unconscious feeling to loved ones skillfully:
"My fear of betrayal is up. I see now that I projected my fear onto
you. Since my young self is afraid, would you give me a hug?"
Most feelings need only a few seconds of kind acknowledgment
to dissolve.

3. *Describing Your Unarguable Truth*

We limit ourselves from asking for what we need by boxing ourselves into false beliefs based on past hurts or disappointments.
We decide "If you really loved me, you'd know what I need," or
"You never care about my feelings." Shed these limitations now
and step fully into this moment, where the power always is.
Teach clearly what you feel now, where you feel it in your body,
and what you need. Start with an "I" statement: "When you said
you're attending a ten-day meditation retreat, I felt shocked. My
young kid inside feels abandoned. I feel it as a tight knot in my
chest. I totally support your retreat, but right now could you
please hold me while I cry?" When you notice you acted out earlier, ask for a do-over to begin again and speak your unarguable
truth.

4. *Revealing Core Beliefs That Trigger Overreactions*

Get familiar with one or two core beliefs that first joined your life
during childhood trauma. Whenever anger, fear, or despair flare
up in overreaction to a current incident, take a ten-minute time
out. Walk around the block or sit alone in the bedroom, close
your eyes, and ask your heart, "Which core belief is fueling my
reaction and underlying feeling?" Perhaps you already know

about your fear of abandonment, intimacy, or betrayal. Or you have noticed a propensity to feel unworthy, unlovable, not good enough, or mistrusting.

The instant you make a core belief conscious, you are free to create a new belief. If "I don't deserve love" is triggered, notice how you reacted and whisper inside, "I do deserve love." Take responsibility by saying, "When you said that, my core belief of _____ was triggered. What I need now is _____ ." If your spouse falls back into control tactics, notice your "I can't trust anyone" belief is triggered and remind yourself, "I trust our love, even if he's acting out." Whisper your new belief to yourself five times each morning for weeks to solidify your new belief. If an old core belief persists, ask yourself, "What is this repeated issue asking me to change or let go of?"

4. Your Resourceful Heart
The Power of Fearless Love

We are an ancient, ancient people who ... have been frightened, coerced, tricked, and bribed away from the source of our greatest strength: an accurate knowledge of who we are.
—ALICE WALKER

The acacia tree outside my bedroom window is in full bloom late. It's June. Every April, while the Chinese maple and aspen trees bud and bloom before the snow even melts, the acacia tree remains dormant. This spring a passing neighbor kindly suggested we cut down that poor old dead tree. But I trust the acacia's timing. More importantly, the acacia trusts its own timing, its inner wisdom, no matter what other trees do—it knows to wait till the snow passes, till the nights are warm, before starting to bloom.

We, too, can trust our inner wisdom, no matter what others do.

We, too, can accept—and trust—the innate resourcefulness of our wise heart.

Unlike the aspen and acacia trees, though, we were trained from birth to ignore our inner wisdom. Before walking and talking, we learned to look *outside* ourselves—to parents, teachers, pastors, grandparents, aunts, uncles, and older siblings—for all our guidance, approval, love, and acceptance, to well-intentioned though fallible elders.

As feisty children, any rebel who dared stand out and follow their heart was usually scolded, spanked, shamed, guilt-tripped, or disciplined back into submission. With such shaming tactics early on, we could spend the better portion of our lives doubting and mistrusting the wisdom in our resourceful hearts. Such unconscious misguidance—not life—perpetuates suffering and illusion.

Fearless love is the conscious guidance of choosing every day, throughout the day, to reconnect with our resourceful heart. As we engage with our innate wisdom, we heal ourselves of childhood hurts and false beliefs inflicted by imperfect authority figures.

The more we frantically look outside for every ounce of love and acceptance, the more we abandon our truth. The longer we postpone the love and acceptance that is always here, inside our heart, the greater the risk of turning it into a lifelong mistake.

We live our whole lives terrified to look inside. We distract ourselves, stay busy, ignore feelings, medicate pain, silence longings—all to avoid finding what we feared all along: that underneath our accomplishments and good deeds, we are really as unlovable as we think. Though we might have strong religious beliefs, few of us imagine finding anything good, let alone lovable, inside. We hang all hope on the lie that, if we never stop long enough to see ourselves clearly, loved ones too will stay blind to our true colors by focusing on our achievements instead.

From birth to death, we desperately move from parents to best friends to lovers and spouses, even strangers, to fill that gaping, empty hole inside. Secretly, we keep hoping that somebody someday out there will find us worthy of approval and love.

What we forget, time and again, is that the very person we hope will see us, hear us, value us, care for us, and love us is secretly hoping for the very same thing—from us.

Deep inside, we long to hear what we fear we won't: that we are loved and accepted for who we are. As the years roll by, as lovers and spouses come and go, we grow more frantic. Having never received the acceptance we deserve just for being who we are, we have no clue how to offer it to ourselves or our children. But by accepting the truth—that we all swim in the ocean of unconscious conditioning—we find a deeper truth: there is no greater wisdom than the wisdom in our own hearts.

Embracing the Power of Fearless Love

Conscious choice offers freedom from scary, judgmental thoughts. Simple questions engage our curiosity to name which part of us is scared, sad, or hopeless. Responsibility releases us from the victim stories that lead only to dead ends. In this chapter, the power of fearless love unveils the jewels inherent in every feeling.

Fearless love, not intimidated by any life challenges, holds our hand while we face those feelings we shoved under the rug years ago. It throws out the welcome mat to anxiety, fear, despair, grief, and shame so we can greet those feelings directly and come to know the voice of each one well. It teaches us to trust our timing, trust our changes, trust our basic goodness.

Fearless love even hears our heart-felt longings and responds with deep respect.

It stays connected daily with our body, our heart, and our young vulnerable self, addressing each need as it arises. It reminds us constantly that we are perfect, just as we are, and to celebrate every joy and delight along the way. Fearless love instills in us the courage to look inside our hearts for the loving reassurance we need. It cultivates a kind, loving relationship with us, forgiving our shortcomings, loving our unconscious habits.

Fearless loving sees mistakes, suffering, pain, and despair—the very things ego avoids—as opportunities to embrace every aspect of being human. No feeling needs to be avoided. Rather than emulating our ancestors, who spent their whole lives lost in ego's thoughts, reactions, and stories, fearless love shortcuts old habits. At our fingertips, we have all the tools needed to bypass reactions and wake up free.

Whether in our twenties, forties, or sixties, we are the ones we have been waiting for. We are the generation to help future generations greet every aspect of being human, the good and bad, with unconditional love. We have a precious opportunity each moment of this life to let our resourceful heart clue us in to how fearless love sounds, looks, and feels in our body.

Tapping into this well of friendliness toward ourselves is easier than we think.

Once we dismiss those thoughts consuming our awareness, we uncover an abundance of open space to fill as we wish. We are free to pause and ask, "What would I love to hear right now?" Maybe we feel pushed for time and would love to hear "I have plenty of time to do what I need." Maybe we are reeling from a morning conflict and need soothing words like "You are safe and loved just as you are. Stop taking others' unconscious acts personally." Maybe we have holiday jitters and need a reminder: "Take three deep breaths, see worry as worry, and let it go."

Maybe when illness strikes, instead of a harsh "I don't have time to be sick," we soften and hear our heart say, "I'm so sorry you're sick. Together let's make healthy choices today." Maybe when our lover mistakenly rubs salt on a childhood wound, we can remind ourselves, "I'm wanted and loved, despite another's unconsciousness."

Just by asking, "What do I secretly wish someone would tell me?" then saying it to ourselves, we tap into a gold mine of inner strength waiting for us inside our heart. In an instant, we shift channels from feeling lost in feelings to letting our heart love each feeling exactly as it is. This is the essence of fearless love.

For instance, Dan's mother died in an accident when he was six. He grew up placating a judgmental father. In his home, love was conditional. If he tiptoed around and gave Dad what he wanted, he felt loved. If not, Dad withheld love for days. This crazy-making formula drove him to drugs. Escaping his pain felt safer, more predictable.

"By the time high school hit, I'd get stoned daily to cope with all my anxiety. I was terrified to speak, terrified to have any needs—let alone voice them," he said. "Now with my own teenagers, I exchanged getting stoned for too many martinis at night. But alcohol makes me feel guilty, weak, indecisive, and riddled with self-doubt."

Dan agreed to close the swinging door to alcohol to allow other doors to open. When I first mentioned loving himself, he cringed and shook his head.

"I'm not ready," he said. "I feel too much shame and guilt to go there."

To help him drop below Dad's judgment into his resourceful heart, I asked Dan to close his eyes and put both hands over his heart. "Try whispering to yourself, 'I love myself for feeling guilty and ashamed.' Repeat it five times to bypass your inner skeptic."

As he spoke the words softly to his heart, tears trickled down his cheeks. "It's so hard to let in. I don't believe it. Part of me doesn't want to believe it. Love means disappearing myself and doing it Dad's way." After pausing, he shared, "I saw a shadow slipping down behind my shoulder into darkness. It feels like shame hiding."

"Even love the shame for wanting to hide. Love exactly what is."

As Dan shined fearless love on his feeling of unworthiness triggered by shame, his tears lessened. He sighed. He lay perfectly still, breathing self-love into his heart.

Our heart guides us toward this fountain of fearless love our whole life.

Telling Ourselves the Loving Words We Long to Hear

We talk to ourselves all the time. Ego especially is a Chatty Kathy. But often, without it registering consciously, we judge and blame ourselves much harsher than we would ever treat others. After hearing how we speak to ourselves, we can finally give ourselves the love and respect we've waited a lifetime to hear from others. Because we now have the ability to tell ourselves the loving words we long to hear, we feel less desperate when a loved one's words trigger hurt or disappointment in our tender hearts. The following examples illustrate the power of our choice to speak love to our pain.

At forty-two Angela had one year of sobriety under her belt. But she still believed that self-hatred, if not alcohol, was her companion for the rest of her life. In a therapy session, I asked her to say out loud the things she routinely said to herself.

"It's not pretty or nice," she giggled. "I don't want to offend you."

"It's okay," I replied. "It's important for you to say out loud what you say inside."

"Whenever I make a mistake or forget to call someone back," she said, "I whisper 'stupid' under my breath. My brother called me this for years. It stuck."

"And what do you secretly wish someone might say to you?" I asked.

She was quiet for some time. "I don't know if anyone will ever love me, but since girlhood, I longed to hear someone say, 'I love you and accept you as you are.'"

When Angela tried whispering this love phrase to herself several times a day, the negative name began to lose its power, and eventually she stopped using it.

Cheryl, twice married and twice divorced, spent her childhood wishing her mother would get off the phone to play with her or reassure her when she felt scared. She recalled one particular day in fourth grade when Cheryl's class had to hide under their desks during a bomb threat. When Cheryl, still scared, reported this to her mom and her mother just laughed, Cheryl decided that her mother never really loved her. She resigned herself to feeling unworthy of love, which made her abandon her two husbands before they abandoned her. But now at thirty-nine, she knows something has to change.

"I'm afraid if I let lovers know me," she said, "they'll find out that something really is wrong with me." When Angela agreed to stop abandoning her inner self and ask instead, "What would you love to hear?" she burst into tears. "That little fourth-grade Cheryl still longs to hear the reassuring words Mom never said, as if it happened yesterday." Now, when she notices that young Cheryl is afraid, she repeats, "I see how scared you are, hon. But I'm here with you. You're never alone. I won't abandon you."

For sixty years, John had a favorite phrase: "You stupid f—k up!" Whenever he made a mistake or had no idea how to do something, he said this under his breath. Raised by a workaholic mother, he had no clue how to respond to his wife's feelings—which is why he avoided marriage until his late forties. But it was on an airplane to his father's deathbed when he really saw how cruel he was to *himself*.

"I sat on that plane," he said, "sad for the relationship I never had with my father and sad for his miserable life. But I couldn't cry. Men don't cry. For the first time, in that plane seat, I really heard myself calling myself a f—k up, again. I felt so cracked open, it felt like a knife stabbing my poor heart at a time when I so needed comfort. That's when I asked my heart, 'What would you love to hear someone say to you?' Finally, I heard a timid voice whisper, 'That I'm loved exactly as I am.'

"I chanted my new mantra to myself all the way to Florida."

"I arrived just in time to hold my father in my arms before he died," John said. "We had never hugged, never said 'I love you.' But somehow by chanting my mantra on the plane, I found the courage to give him the embrace I had wanted my whole life."

Finding the Courage to Trust Our Heart's Truth

It takes great courage to trust our heart's truth over the reprimands of a narrow-minded culture. But, like a muscle that needs exercise to grow stronger, courage strengthens one choice, one moment at a time. As we choose to live the truth inside our own heart, we stop worrying about how it looks to others and step fully into who we are in this lifetime.

Some deem the sensitive work of self-healing and self-love strange, perhaps even an admission of weakness. But it is only strange because it is so avoided and ridiculed in our culture; it is an admission not of weakness but of strength to courageously strive for true happiness, joy, and inner peace. People talk anyway. Opinions are rampant, so in the words of singer Bonnie Raitt, "Let's give them something to talk about."

My client Julie came to my office crying. Her fiancé had just left her the day before. Fearless love was the last thing she wanted to hear about. But it did set her free.

"He left me!" she said. "He said he loved me. After his painful divorce, he finally softened and let me in. He asked me to marry him on Christmas Day after we made an offer on a new house. Finally, at forty, I'd found the man I'd spend my life with. Then while I'm fixing dinner, he packs a bag and walks out without a word."

"I hear how disappointed and confused you feel," I reflected and paused. "But I know you. I know you don't want to stay in pain very long. So would you be willing, as an experiment, to drop the story, close your eyes, and feel the grief and hurt you feel underneath? Just breathe into the sadness." As Julie breathed, she sobbed.

"As humans, one loss often triggers all of our losses," I said. "Try to identify your very first loss by asking, 'How is feeling such deep loss and grief familiar to me?'"

"My whole childhood, Mother ignored me. She was always too

busy with her profession to spend time with her daughter. I was paraded out to show off for company, then shuffled back to eat with the nanny. By twelve, with kids teasing me about my new breasts, I begged her to take me shopping for my first bra. By thirteen, since she never bothered giving me the sex talk, I hit up my best friend for a tampon in the bathroom and filled in the blanks with my imagination. Boys happily taught me about sex."

"What did you long to hear from your mother?" I asked softly.

A long silence ensued. Finally, she said, "That she loved me. That she wanted to spend time with me. That I was loved, cherished, adored, and fun to be with."

"Good. Now try saying these things to yourself."

Julie looked at me as if I had really gone off the deep end. "What? Since nobody else loves or cherishes me, the booby prize is to love myself now?"

"No, no. To your wounded child, you are no booby prize. You are her first choice. She has waited her whole life to hear loving words from you," I explained, "and hearing them from you means more to her than hearing them from anyone else. So as an experiment, close your eyes, put one hand over your heart and the other over your belly, and whisper to your young child, 'I love and cherish you, young Julie. I'm always here for you to hear your feelings, and I love spending time with you.'"

As she repeated these words to herself, a peaceful calm swept over her face.

"Wow! My whole body relaxed. I don't feel so desperate or unloved anymore. I feel like a person in the desert who got her first sip of water after thirty years."

"Each morning," I said, "say these loving words to yourself. During the day, as often as you think of it, keep telling yourself these words you long to hear."

Like Julie, we all deserve to treat ourselves with love and respect.

Telling ourselves what we need to hear acknowledges feelings. This prevents that forceful desperation down the road from ignoring our feelings too long. Once we see ourselves as fountains of fearless love, we feel less devastated when a loved one, lost in their own unconscious wound, says things that trigger our own feelings of rejection. The moment we start to plummet, we can tell our young, tender, vulnerable self what it needs to hear: "I am safe and loved. No matter how it appears in this moment, everything is okay."

The more we stand tall, trusting who we are, responding to angry words with fearless love, we invite everyone around us to step into their wise, resourceful hearts. This gives us more breathing room in all relationships to welcome and embrace the inevitable hurt, fear, and disappointment that come and go with human love.

Loving reassurance reconnects us with the unlimited kindness, compassion, and joy inside our heart. When we pause a moment to ask, "What would I love to hear?" the answer bubbles up from deep inside. Now is the time to uncover that freedom and inner peace inside our hearts. Fearless love delivers it in spades.

Cultivating a Love Affair with Ourselves

We love falling in love. When love strikes, we spend every possible moment making love. We hang on every word, every look, every sigh, and gesture. If separated from our lover by work or travel, being apart feels unbearable, and we can't wait to get back together.

Falling in love with ourselves can be just as exciting but far less time consuming. By spending ten, twenty, or thirty minutes a day watching our breath in meditation, we move underneath thoughts and reactions to know our tender, vulnerable parts:

- Our body, which speaks to us through tension, pain, illness, numbness, and other sensations.

- Our feelings, which request our attention and guide our life choices.
- Our young self, who needs reassurance when childhood wounds and old beliefs are triggered.
- Our tender heart, which speaks to us through heart-felt longings and dreams.

Stealing however many minutes we can from a busy schedule to meditate and catch our breath helps address the first signs of a cold or flu before it costs us days in bed. Likewise, meditation can throw the brakes on the unchecked tendencies of the mind. Watching our breath makes crystal clear how angry or hurt we still are over last night's rude remark by a loved one. Slowing down creates space for any sadness, hurt, fear, or rejection to rise to the surface, allowing us to consciously respond with a loving heart. Rather than medicate symptoms, watching our breath helps us hear symptoms asking for our attention.

Rather than letting thoughts drag us around by the nose, meditation helps us discern which thoughts deserve our undivided attention—and which deserve the trash. As we focus more on our breath, we drop deep into the inner silence where our heart-felt longings can be sensed and heard. Taking a few moments to understand ourselves at this intimate level begins wherever we are, at any age of our lives.

For Don, it started at age sixty-five by asking himself every day, "What am I feeling now?" and saying, "Yes" to every feeling he found.

When Don had retired from ranching the previous year, he'd felt lost and useless. He'd spent his life telling himself, "Get over it. Nobody wants to hear your sniveling." In therapy, he revamped his approach.

"My wife of thirty years wants to leave. My oldest daughter refuses to speak to me," he said. "I need to do something different. Raised in Wyoming, I was told that I'm better off shoveling horseshit than wallowing in bullshit feelings. But I see now, by taking time to name my feelings, that the young kid inside felt abandoned when nobody paid attention to him. Several times a day now, I pause in the middle of chores to ask, 'What am I feeling now?' But after ignoring myself for so many years, it still takes a few minutes to identify my anxiety, loneliness, or frustration. I told my wife I couldn't hear her feelings until I can hear my own. For now she stopped mentioning divorce."

By loving our feelings, we teach others how to value and respect them.

Cultivating fearless love is invigorating. It nourishes the heart. It warms us like hearty chicken soup on cold winter nights and refreshes us like a berry smoothie on a hot day. It is a way of making friends with ourselves, best friends, like we've never known.

Fearless love is like a dream grandmother undaunted by life's ups and downs. Nothing ruffles her calm tranquility, scares her, or erases her sense of humor. She is always here knitting in her rocking chair, ready to reassure us, stroke our hair, wrap her huge arms around our fear, and remind us of what is real—and what is not.

Fearless love is tapping into the vein of gold tucked inside our heart. It is really listening to our feelings and longings like we've never listened before and voicing our truth. It is forgiving our mistakes, respecting our heart-felt longings, and believing in our dreams. It is giving ourselves the kind caring and understanding we long for from others.

Fearless love is declaring ourselves good enough now and forever. It is replacing self-judgment and doubt with unconditional love. It is truly seeing ourselves, valuing what we see, and finally giving ourselves the understanding we long for.

It is trusting our inherent goodness one moment, one choice at a time.

Now is the time to wake up by loving ourselves unconditionally, no regrets, no apologies. Why wait for outer circumstances to change one iota when we have the capacity to be happy, free, and peaceful now?

This practice of fearless love every day changes my life, and the lives of many clients, forever.

On a recent morning, I awoke out of sorts. Besides six clients changing appointment times that week, none of my three tenants had paid their rent. The first of the month came and went with no rent checks in the mailbox and no explanations. I was too upset to write, so I took myself on a two-hour hike. After too many minutes of chewing on the blame story, I remembered to ask, "What would I love to hear now?"

I laughed out loud. Instantly I realized that nobody caused my angst. It was *my* story about how unfair it all was that kept my mind reeling. I was stealing my own joy and inner peace away by arguing with what is. Immediately I stopped.

Since I prize freedom more than anything, I could not perpetuate any imprisoning story another minute, no matter how enthralling or right it sounded. Instead, I reminded myself one more time about who I am: "I am conscious awareness in this human body. I am the space around thoughts, stories, and feelings. I choose joy and freedom now."

I repeated these truths over and over until I felt calm and peaceful inside.

Nothing changed yet on the outside. The rents remained late. Anger and lack of control kept nipping at my heels. But by accepting my feelings and breathing deeply, my resourceful heart saved my life one more time. I softened into what is.

Fearless love is not about never getting caught up. It is about noticing when we are triggered, whether this takes two minutes, two hours, or two years, and using even this opportunity to see ego's patterns. By asking, "Which feeling is ego judging here?" we free ourselves to say, "I accept myself for feeling sad and for judging my sadness."

As we grow skilled at fearless love, we have more breathing room for the human foibles that inevitably come—from ourselves and others. When we tune in to hear our feelings several times a day, we feel less desperate when a loved one lapses into hurtful remarks. As we pause each day to see, hear, accept, and value ourselves, we feel only gratitude—not resentment—when a loved one finally stops to really see and love us.

Fearless loving flows by recognizing ego strategies disguised as wisdom.

Recognizing What Doubt and Judgment Sound Like

It's important to recognize the voice of doubt as doubt. It badgers us with "what if" questions designed to confuse us: "But what if you invest all that money in your new business and can't pay the mortgage?" or "What if you leave your dead marriage and spend the rest of your life alone, loveless?" *So dramatic.* Doubt arrives before we begin any creative endeavor and leaves us curled up and paralyzed in a fetal position, unable to think, speak, or move forward.

Judgment, on the other hand, arrives after we complete something we care about. It clears its dry throat like some stuffy college professor while berating us, once again, for not working, parenting, finishing the college semester, making love, finishing that triathlon, retiring, or doing anything else good enough. Whatever we are doing, somehow judgment deems it not good enough, not right, not perfect. It leaves our self-worth in a puddle on the floor, feeling chronically dissatisfied with life and all our hard work.

Now before launching our new project, we greet doubt's arrival at the eleventh hour with our new best friend, fearless love, by saying, "Hello doubt. Have a seat in that far corner. I'm busy consciously cocreating with the universe, and I'm enjoying the process immensely."

When judgment arrives on the heels of our latest endeavor, we offer soothing reassurance: "I'm a playful, creative human loving everything I make, including mistakes. Now back to the task of being the fearless, powerful being that I am."

Locating Core Feelings in Our Body

Too often anxiety, despair, and anger flood our whole body like a tsunami. Overwhelming feelings displace all semblance of inner peace. Before we know what hit us, they sweep us off our feet with some engaging story of who is to blame.

The solution lies outside of logic's terrain, inside the heart and body. Whenever we drop below ego's compelling story and *locate a feeling in our body*, unmanageable feelings suddenly feel manageable again.

First, we must distinguish between core and secondary feelings. Core feelings—fear, hurt, sadness, joy, and shame—lead to inner peace when we focus directly on them. But secondary feelings—such as jealousy, envy, anger, frustration, irritation, rejection, disappointment, abandonment, mistrust, guilt, resentment, pride, and many more—jump immediately on the heels of core feelings before we can properly identify them.

Core feelings flash by as fast as asteroids, rarely registering on our radar. They do register on ego's radar though, which very quickly floods our mind with secondary feelings. Since ego vehemently protects us from feeling any feelings directly, as if it were a life or death matter, ego weaves tall tales of who did what to us when and how it should never have happened, all to distract us from feeling. This all happens so fast that the hurt, sadness, fear, or shame feeling remains unconscious.

Nine-tenths of the time, we collude with ego's tricks. We identify with our secondary feelings, spilling grandiose stories out to friends about which lover betrayed us, which parent or child failed to do what they should have, and how life is unfair. But as exhilarating as telling such stories can be, these watered-down versions of core feelings lead only to endless confusion and suffering. Like thoughts, judgments, and doubts, we must peek underneath secondary feelings to find the freedom inside core feelings.

By pausing to ask ourselves, "Which core feeling is fueling my jealousy, anger, despair, or anxiety now?" and by listening patiently for our heart to answer, we identify the fear, sadness, hurt, or shame we missed the instant it occurred. Furthermore, by taking fifteen minutes to locate one of these four core feelings in our body, we can uncover our heart's immense capacity to heal wounds our body has unconsciously carried as heavy baggage for years.

Long after our mind forgot, our body still feels Dad's slap across our face at nine, or the shame from someone molesting us, or the fear of additional emotional abuse.

At times, when we tune in, we feel tightness or pressure in our throat, chest, diaphragm, or belly. Other times we notice tension or pain in our neck, shoulders, hips, or back. Sometimes, if we spent years disconnected from our feelings, we may feel numb in an area of the body where a core feeling has remained stuck for a long time. But numbness is a real feeling to respect. By being fully present with the numbness, focusing directly on it, numbness soon yields to the core feeling underneath.

Allowing Our Body to Release Core Feelings

Once we turn off the phone and computer and take fifteen to thirty minutes to lie down alone in a quiet room, we prepare ourselves for locating some hurt, fear, sadness, or shame *in our body*. We close our eyes and take several deep breaths until thoughts and to-do lists yield to awareness of our body. To align our mind and heart, we set an intention, such as "I am willing to explore my fear of growing old" or "I am willing to heal my core molestation shame that holds lovers at a distance."

Now we focus directly on the place where our fear, hurt, sadness, or shame lives in our body, take a big belly breath, and send the exhale directly into that feeling.

Freedom and release comes by directly focusing attention wherever the core feeling lives inside and breathing down into the center of that pressure, pain, or sensation. Ego will try to regain our focus by obsessing about what happened that should never have happened. And we may be tempted to jump into ego's story rather than stay in this new, unknown territory. But when ego grows impatient with nothing coming right away, we simply take more deep breaths. By trusting our wise heart to guide us through the wilderness into a full-body healing, we relax into the center of the feeling until it fully releases.

Most often core feelings appear in the torso, somewhere between the neck and pelvis. But if our attention is drawn elsewhere—to our third eye for example, between and slightly above our eyes—then healing requires us to stay fully present and trust the body's calling. Telling ourselves "Usually I feel tightness in the center of my chest, so I'll focus there" or "I fear abandonment, which usually appears in my diaphragm's power center" makes logical sense to ego. But automatically obeying habit can sabotage healing by overriding the body's signal in the present moment.

This idea of trusting how the body draws our attention may sound too simple and weird to be true. Our inner skeptic sneers at such silliness, distracting us before we embarrass ourselves. It mocks the whole idea of our body possibly healing old traumas from decades ago. But the best way to silence the skeptic is to hear some real life examples, then personally give it a whirl.

For example, one year of chemotherapy for uterine cancer convinced Sue she needed therapy to avoid a relapse. By forty, her nice-girl approach had left her exhausted, handling too many responsibilities while stuffing down all negative feelings.

"I'm so pissed at my husband for ignoring the kids," she said, "I could shake him. Instead I feel like all my resentment sits like a lead ball in my belly."

After talking, I asked Sue to lie down, take several deep breaths, and bring her full attention to her belly. "Continue to breathe in your belly. With each breath, send the exhale into the center of the tightness and listen for any feelings or memories."

"It feels like someone is strangling me," she said. "I remember being thirteen, developing breasts and hips; my father called me a slut for wearing makeup."

"Right now, tell your dad whatever feeling you couldn't say then."

"How dare you shame me, Dad? You never bothered to see me or understand me."

After expressing her stuck resentment, tears erupted, allowing Sue to finally feel and release the hurt that lived as a lead ball in her belly all these years.

"I loved my dad," she said, "but I never felt important to him. He was always working or attending my brother's soccer and baseball games."

That evening Sue sat down with her husband and shared her resentments. He listened quietly, then agreed to take more responsibilities with their children. With time, Sue grew adept at voicing her feelings. But first, for two weeks, she spent five minutes alone in her car releasing all the resentments she never got to say to her father.

Dan suffered from indigestion and chronic stomach pain for thirty years. Fed up with temporary relief from doctors and pills, he tried meditative body awareness to get to the bottom of this. "When I tune in to the belly pain during meditation," Dan said, "I see images of my older brother terrorizing me while my parents looked the other way. I'm willing to heal this completely. But I don't know what to do with these memories."

"Our body stores trauma and pain," I explained. "Let's ask your body."

I asked Dan to lie down on a futon and breathe deeply in his belly to relax. "Now bring your attention to your belly. Imagine breathing directly into the belly pain."

After quietly breathing for several minutes, his legs began trembling.

"It's okay," I reassured him. "Trust your body. Allow your legs, feet, and body to tremble until the tremors reach a natural completion. Our bodies shake to release fear."

Dan kept breathing into his belly, using his breath as an anchor. Soon his hands, arms, and torso joined his legs, shaking vigorously. This continued for a minute or two. Afterward Dan sighed long and loud, implying a huge weight had been lifted.

"Who knew I needed to shake and tremble like that for decades?" he laughed.

When we locate core feelings in our body and breathe directly into them, the shaking and trembling release fear, returning us to inner peacefulness.

Gifting Ourselves with Understanding

To love ourselves fearlessly, we have one final hurdle to overcome. We need to stop clinging so tightly to that favorite role we slip into so easily, that long-suffering misunderstood one—the one who gives up communicating with loved ones because they decide "nobody understands me." This role feeds our dead-end victim stories.

The second we feel hurt, disappointed, discouraged, or hopeless, we call upon our lengthy "Nobody understands me" story. Within seconds, this unravels into all the times we felt misunderstood by ex-lovers, parents, friends, and bosses, spanning our entire life. But hidden in the background, fearless love offers a choice: to stay lost one more time in our elaborate "I'm so misunderstood" story—or drop it like a hot potato, step up, and give ourselves the understanding we've been longing for.

Anytime we don't get our way, or get what we don't want, it is such a tiny step to "Nobody sees who I really am, nobody understands me" that we barely notice making it. Soon friends and family gather round, supporting our victim stance by commiserating with us. But falling into this popular but deadly story of misunderstanding comes with a high price. It costs us our happiness, joy, freedom, and inner peace. At times, it may cost us our relationships.

An elderly friend with years of meditation practice confided to me, "After decades, Carolyn, I finally stopped playing the long-suffering housewife. I stopped hanging my happiness on what my husband says or doesn't say. Every morning I reclaim my happiness by asking, 'What sounds good to me today?' Sooner or later, we all have to wake up out of ego's lies and stories, drop our *Poor Misunderstood Me* movie, as I did, and step into the moment fresh everyday, making choices to embrace ourselves."

After all, standing in the truth of conscious awareness, loving ourselves fearlessly, we remember that we humans did not come here to be understood—or misunderstood. We did not come to grovel for approval or sell our souls for our next meal.

We came to live in integrity, aligned with the pure joy and freedom inside our hearts.

We came to carve a place in this world for who we are at the deepest level.

Understanding comes later, after we jump in and test the waters of our current life experience. Only by trusting, and letting our hearts lead us to each new moment, can we deliver the gifts that our resourceful heart brings to this world. But when fearless love yields unconventional results, when the deepest truth in our heart steps outside of the social and religious norm, following our heart leads us into the unknown.

For instance, Stephanie lived with a silent war inside that was killing her. She could not sleep. She lived with ulcers and panic attacks. She struggled to focus at work. When she finally came to therapy, she described suicide as an easier choice.

"I've been married to John for twenty-five years. Our son Jason just turned twenty. For years, our family attended the Catholic church down the street, and John and I sing in the choir. But now at fifty-two, it's too painful to keep living a lie. I've known I was gay since thirteen. But I thought if I prayed enough and lived right, God would correct me. Instead, it's destroyed my health, my sleep, and now my marriage.

"I've been a robot for years, going through the motions of life," she told me. "I had sex with my husband, not because I desired him, but to be a good wife. When I asked my pastor for help five years ago, he strongly encouraged me to cast out this evil desire for another woman and ask Christ for strength. I tried for years. But I can't keep living a lie. I'd rather kill myself than go on like this." She held her head in her hands and sobbed.

I felt deep empathy for Stephanie's dilemma. "What are you most afraid of?" I inquired. "What might happen if you tell your husband, son, and church the truth?"

"I'm afraid that I'll be called pagan and thrown out of church. That God will strike me dead for sinning, and I'll go straight to hell. That my church will blacklist me. That my husband will refuse to stay friends and my son will never speak to me again."

"I really hear how scared you feel," I said. "And since those are all fear thoughts, I want to share a secret about fear: fear doesn't know what will happen any more than we do—it just sounds like it does in our heads. Try an experiment. Try labeling each one 'fear' and letting them go." As she let each fear go, she felt newfound freedom inside.

"Now," I told her, "say your real truth in your heart."

Stephanie closed her eyes. "Between us," she said, "I'm very attracted to a female friend. We've spent time together, as friends. If I could do what I want, I'd leave my husband tomorrow and explore this new relationship. My son is open-minded. He might even accept me over time. If God loves all his creatures, maybe he loves me."

"In the safety of this office," I said, "I invite you to experiment with saying your deepest truth out loud. Stand up, look in your eyes in the mirror, and claim who you are."

As Stephanie stood up, her knees shook. With tears rolling down her cheeks, she found the courage to stand up to the fear voices in her head. "I'm listening to *my heart*. I follow the truth in *my* heart. I trust my heart as the highest authority."

When she finally sat down again, she felt uncomfortable in her body at first. "This feels so new, so foreign, so selfish. What if I'm wrong, what if God…"

"Before you let fear take you for a ride," I said, "place both hands over your heart. Now whisper five times inside, 'I understand you, Stephanie.' Drop your story of feeling misunderstood and be the source of understanding you long to feel."

"I understand you, Stephanie. I understand you need to follow your heart and stop living someone else's life. I understand you need to finally trust your heart."

"Wow!" she laughed. "I feel such peace. I want to pinch myself to make sure I'm not dreaming. I feel more alive than I've felt in years. Like all those brick-like fears are really paper thin." As I heard and understood Stephanie's truth without judgment, she replaced her poor—misunderstood—me story with feeling genuinely understood.

That evening, when she told her husband, he exploded. "How could you break up the family like this?" he repeated over and over. After overhearing Dad's rage, their son said, "But I thought we were happy together, Mom." Stephanie kept breathing and listened quietly to their reactions without abandoning the truth in her heart.

In the following weeks, she found a house five blocks away, moved out, and began dating the woman she had fallen in love with two years earlier. "I've never felt this way about anybody!" she said. "I loved my husband, but I feel *in love* for the first time in my life. And free. I can finally be honest and open about who I really am. I'm not all alone and misunderstood anymore. My pastor still gives me the cold shoulder, but several church members have called for lunch and to wish me all the happiness.

"Once my husband and son got past their initial shock, we're all happier. My ex found a woman who wants to really be with him. And my son brags about his lesbian mom. Last night, he brought his new steady girlfriend home from college to spend the night. He shrugs and says, 'I'm just happy to see you and Dad happy.'"

"When I finally opened my mouth, I feared God would never forgive me. But I feel God's love around me, holding me everyday."

Coming Home to the Buried Treasures Inside

Fearless love unlocks the buried treasure tucked inside our hearts. It is our life jacket in scary times, our magic wand in creative times. It is not some default position in between lovers or spouses to stave off loneliness. In and out of relationship, weighed down by worry, fear, or conflict, it sets us free by recalling the deepest truth: "I am loving reassurance that notices worry, fear, and despair."

Fearless love takes courage. But with time, this cutting-edge practice changes how we see ourselves and the world. When we love our hurt, fear, sadness, and shame, we stop identifying with these core feelings. When we offer loving reassurance to our wounded child each time she or he reacts in fear, we stop hiding under the bed with our scared young self. When we find ourselves lost in thought or reactions, fearless love reminds us who we are deep inside: "I am unlimited joy, loving-kindness, compassion, and inner peace dressed up in this body." Once we recall who we are, fear and despair shrivel into annoying flies to be brushed away.

Fearless love restores our self-worth to its rightful position as our birthright. It is something nobody can take away or manipulate us with. It gifts us with the approval and recognition we thought we could only receive from others, freeing us to cultivate healthy love relationships, our self-worth intact.

No matter what happens *out there* and no matter which feelings are triggered *in here*, we can turn to our resourceful heart every day for the loving reassurance, respect, acknowledgment, and understanding we need to receive in this moment.

Heart Tools for Self-Sourcing

Practice each of these for one week before moving on to the next one. But if a specific tool calls you to spend more time with it, give yourself another week, month, or as long as you need in order to heal.

1. *Begin a Lifelong Love Affair with Yourself Now*

First, spend time noticing how you speak to yourself when you feel upset, anxious, angry, or guilty. Just notice, without judging yourself for cruel put downs or past habits. Then begin your new habit. Each day, find a quiet place, close your eyes, and ask inside, "If I could hear anything, what would it be? What do I secretly wish someone would say to me?" Breathe deeply and patiently listen for your heart to respond. It may be "My life is good enough" or "I'll be okay," "I understand me" or "I am safe, wanted, and loved," "I have plenty of time" or "I'm never alone. My wise heart hears every word." Whatever phrase pops into your awareness, softly whisper these words to yourself throughout the day.

2. *Bring the Power of Fearless Love into Your Daily Life*

Pause each hour to ask quietly, "What am I feeling now?" Whether you feel worried, happy, lonely, hopeless, or scared, whisper inside, "I love myself for feeling _____." Notice how fearless love feels when you lavish it on every feeling. Whenever you wake up out of ego's stories in your head, celebrate by loving yourself: "I am happy and healthy and free. Now I remember the totally loving, totally accepting being that I really am." Spend a few moments basking in this. If you feel caught in fear or hurt, remind yourself of the deeper truth: "I am conscious loving awareness waking out of the dream of thought."

3. *Identify Core Feelings under Secondary Feelings*

Whether driving, working, exercising, reading, or washing dishes, start by asking, "Which secondary feeling is fueling my story now?" Listen patiently without judgment, allowing guilt, jealousy, anger, resentment, disappointment, frustration, rejection, mistrust, or other secondary feelings to fill your awareness. Then drop below and ask, "Which core feeling—hurt, shame, fear, joy, or sadness—lives underneath, triggering this secondary feeling?" Acknowledge it.

4. *Locating and Releasing Core Feelings in the Body*

Set aside twenty to thirty minutes. Turn off your phone, find a quiet room, and lie down comfortably. Close your eyes. Whisper an intention to yourself, such as "I'm willing to explore and/or heal this core feeling to completion." Take several deep breaths in your belly to relax and focus awareness in your torso. Then ask softly, "Where does this hurt, fear, sadness, joy, or shame live inside?" Patiently breathe and listen. When you feel a tightness, pressure, pain, or numbness calling your attention, drop any thoughts and focus directly on this area. Take a deep belly breath and imagine sending your exhale down into the center of the sensation. Repeat this several times while you trust your body. Surrender to whatever crying, shaking, trembling, or sounds occur. Allow this release until you come to a natural completion of feelings and your body returns to a calm, peaceful state. Rest a few moments in this spacious peacefulness, repeating inside, "I am happy, peaceful, and free, resting in my natural state."

5. Your Compassionate Heart
The Power of Acceptance

The opening heart is the most beautiful flower of all.
The greatest beauty in the world is compassion, love
    shining free of attachment and grasping.
—TARTHANG TULKU RINPOCHE

It is a crisp October morning. The warm sun melts last night's frost, our first this fall. Green aspen leaves, yellowing around the edges, signal the arrival of autumn. This morning, I woke up tight about time. I scheduled two couples for therapy today, shortening my writing day considerably. My breath is short, belly tight, mood irritable. Ego berates me for not being disciplined enough to get up earlier *and* for overbooking myself *and* for moving too slow most mornings. Then I remember compassion.

As my heart opens, compassion rushes in like sunrays bursting through clouds. Ego's taunting time is up. My breath deepens, mood softens, and my whole body smiles. Compassion is our superhero, rescuing us from judgment and doubt. All thoughts, fears, reactions, and feelings roll over in submission around compassion—the same way lion cubs submit to the patriarch of their pride. My mind recalls the loving phrase Buddha taught 2,500 years ago to help each of us in our own time cultivate compassion: "May I and all beings be free of suffering and the root of suffering."

As I repeat this phrase, my heart softens. I remember that I am loving awareness, holding ego's judgments and reprimands in compassion. I recall that, even now, I can let go of my attachments to life going my way and delight in the present moment.

Compassion is a gateway to freedom. We can enter at any time.

Three Simple Truths About Compassion

We usually store compassion on the top shelf of the china cabinet, along with Grandma's good silver and china, for special occasions: Thanksgiving, Christmas, and Uncle Frank's funeral ten years ago. But compassion belongs with our everyday dishes and silverware. It comes to the rescue when we forget an appointment, judge ourselves or others for making a mistake, or hear that our neighbor's back pain returned. But unlike its near relatives, sympathy and pity (which promise to bolster our self-esteem by looking down our noses at another's misfortune), compassion is an equal-opportunity lender; it offers a compassionate heart to our own and others' suffering equally, playing no favorites.

Much more than a feeling, compassion is the heart-felt warmth shared between equals, even if we don't totally understand another's suffering. Compassion becomes a lifelong companion. It blossoms into a serious commitment to free ourselves and others from suffering by leaning in to suffering and getting to know it well. Rather than perpetuate ego's lie—"If you just do it right next time, you'll never have to suffer"—the compassionate heart knows that freedom lies in accepting life as it is, free of resistance.

We learn compassion's power of acceptance by embracing three truths:

1: OUR COMPASSIONATE HEART ACCEPTS EVERY FEELING, LOSS, ILLNESS, AND CHANGE GRACEFULLY

The compassionate heart accepts Buddha's First Noble Truth: "life is suffering." And it trusts Buddha's Second and Third Noble

Truths—that we increase suffering by resisting what is *and* decrease suffering by allowing what is true exactly as it is. Compassion stops the cycle of wasting precious time struggling to avoid the unavoidable.

Like shedding a winter coat in springtime, compassion sheds ego's unnecessary habits. In doing so, it elevates our ability to be present to the highest level. With its unlimited capacity to hold all feelings and experiences tenderly (not just what ego wants or likes), compassion sees the whole scenario of events and reactions unfolding before our eyes and loves us for it: it loves the core hurt, fear, sadness, or shame that fuels our secondary resentments; it loves ego's acting out; and it even loves our childhood belief that triggers feelings and reactions. The arms of the compassionate heart embrace it all.

Compassion greets anger, resentment, disappointment, and suffering with kind gentleness. It welcomes each life experience without judging any of it, good or bad. It trusts that our caring, compassionate heart can and will embrace and love whatever arises. It rejoices each time conscious awareness greets unconscious conditioning.

2: COMPASSION CRACKS OPEN OUR HEART TO SHARED SUFFERING

Ego perpetuates another false belief: "We are all separate individuals." Ninety-nine percent of ego's daily thoughts revolve around *my* body, *my* feelings, *my* needs, *my* family history, *my* hurts and disappointments, *my* successes and failures. When anxiety, fear, depression, or shame comes knocking, we tunnel even deeper into feeling alone and separate. Buddha reminds us that we are connected to every living being. We all face illness, old age, and death.

Feelings are universal. Though they can feel quite individual and intense when happening, we all experience fear, hurt, guilt, sadness, shame, rejection, hopelessness, loss, anxiety, and depression at different times.

Since our lives all percolate in this urn of unconscious conditioning, we can save ourselves a great deal of disappointment by not resisting this truth anymore. Accepting our universal interconnectedness helps us to start each day on common ground, seeing all humans in it together, struggling with fear and doubt, judgment and guilt, anger and resentment. When scared, we can open our awareness to feel compassion for all people struggling with fear now, including ourselves. When we feel sad, we can feel compassion for all beings suffering from sadness without indulging a personal story. When another shares feelings, we can stop judging them as bad or wrong and listen. When we hold suffering in compassion, we can change the world.

Our own pain invites us to offer compassion to all humans suffering the same back pain, headache, or other symptoms we experience in this moment. For instance, if our ulcer pain returns, we might whisper softly, "May I and all beings suffering from an ulcer be free of suffering and the root of suffering." When we feel alone in our pain, our suffering increases. But including the pain of others lightens our burden and honors our ongoing connection.

3: COMPASSION NEVER TAKES ANYTHING PERSONALLY

With its broad vision that lives outside of time and space, compassion sees our own and others' thoughts as thoughts, feelings as feelings, and reactions as ego reactions. It grins at fear with that loving smile. It holds intense anger and grief in loving compassion, knowing that all feelings appear, intensify, and disappear, and that they are not who we are. Overflowing with generosity, it even holds our body's secret feelings in tenderness.

For instance, in therapy Judy moved from anger to compassion by dropping her personal reaction. She described her rage at the blatant discrimination against girls common in her Asian heritage. "Mom had me do the dinner dishes for years while my brother sat watching TV. When I asked Mom why he never did dishes, her 'he's a boy' infuriated me. Since females were never allowed to speak our feelings in the family home, I never learned to ask for what I need. Now I stand by speechless as my marriage falls apart."

"I hear your rage," I said, "and I invite you to jut your jaw out and just growl right now to express that pent-up anger for being treated less than." After Judy did this, she began to weep for all the years her mother abandoned her to live by the cultural rules.

The following week, Judy's face looked softer as she entered my office. "I realized something late one night," she shared. "After finally expressing all that rage and grief I'd bottled up for years, I stopped taking Mom's discrimination personally. I realized she received the same unfair treatment from her mother, who she still resents to this day.

"So I held my mother and grandmother, and my young child self, in my belly and surrounded all of us with deep, loving compassion. Afterward I felt deeply peaceful."

When we set aside our personal reaction, compassion fills up the empty space.

Compassion for Our Own Suffering

With ongoing practice, compassion arrives each moment as needed. It helps us see and face our naked fear, grief, hurt, loneliness, and shame directly, free of ego's story. It notices how harshly we treat ourselves when we feel anxious or overwhelmed and holds even these in compassion. It refrains from indulging our favorite escape routes—work, sex, alcohol, drugs, food, and exercise—to honor the feelings we may have avoided for years. It tenderly holds the hurt and sadness that lie invisible underneath anger without attempting to fix, shrink, or erase any feelings.

Compassion sounds so simple, we often overlook it. It is resting when we feel tired, listening when we feel sad, voicing our needs a second time when we don't feel heard the first, or pausing to acknowledge feelings. It is trusting that we are feeling exactly what we need to feel in this moment and surrendering into it.

I routinely encourage clients to imagine sitting still on a park bench with their sadness, loneliness, or rejection. We, too, can picture ourselves sitting quietly with our own pain or grief. We can close our eyes and focus a kind, loving attention on the texture and color of our pain. Instead of running away, we grow familiar with how fear or shame looks and feels. Often, if we spend two minutes acknowledging how scared or hopeless we really feel, the feeling disappears. If not, we honor our body's wisdom in these matters. We trust our grief to reach its own natural completion through full expression.

Professionally, when the time is right, I softly invite clients to hold their sorrow, pain, loss, and disappointments in loving compassion. This simple, quiet act transforms suffering into freedom like nothing else.

Personally, compassion saved my life during a tumultuous phase before menopause. In my late forties, I surfed a giant wave of hormone hell for two years. My athletic body, which had always done everything I wanted, including run six miles a day for thirty years and finish several marathons, felt possessed by demons. I slept restlessly, woke exhausted, and routinely snapped at bank tellers for no apparent reason. If I wasn't yelling or lying awake all night trying to sleep, I was crying over the tiniest things.

Finally brought to my knees, I took a week off work to address my suffering. Halfway through my daily journaling, walking, and meditating, I found the courage in a morning meditation to naively tell myself a powerful intention: "I'm willing to feel whatever I've been unwilling to feel." Nothing happened. I repeated it.

Suddenly tears filled my eyes. A lifetime of unresolved grief flashed behind my eyes. Sobbing, I relived my mother's inability to walk her last three years and her eventual death to leukemia. I recalled how my father's undiagnosed autism prevented him from saying "I love you" the first fifty years of my life and how deeply this hurt me. I pictured my young nine-year-old self sitting on Mom's bed in her dark bedroom at all hours repeatedly talking her out of killing herself.

I kept breathing and allowing this lifetime of sorrow to flow unencumbered until my heart found a calm stopping place. Shortly after, spacious peacefulness flooded my whole being. I walked more freely, spoke my truth more often, and listened to others with much less reactivity. Something changed in me forever.

When we face our unresolved sorrows with compassion, we find freedom.

RECOGNIZING OUR CENTER-OF-THE-UNIVERSE CHILDHOOD PATTERN

In early childhood, we tend to see ourselves as the center of the universe. This is normal. Our small, simple world is comprised of getting our basic needs met and getting love and attention. Developmentally, we may see ourselves in the center because we lack the mental acuity, as innocent children, to make sense out of the complex adult world.

The problem arises when we witness our parents do such adult behaviors as argue, get depressed or anxious, withdraw love, threaten divorce, or even leave. Lacking the maturity to understand what is going on, coupled with our tendency to see ourselves at the center of everything that happens, we may blame ourselves. We start believing, "If only I had better grades and didn't cost money, Mom and Dad wouldn't fight, and Dad wouldn't be leaving" or "If only I stopped having needs, Mom wouldn't drink so much and yell at me." Whatever the adult issue inside our home, we tend to blame ourselves.

When we are the target of an adult's abuse or neglect, we often stay silent; in our attempt to understand why anyone we love would do this, we again may blame ourselves. We perhaps believe, "My needs or bad behavior causes it."

Personally, my mother suffered depression and repeatedly threatened suicide when I was between age nine and sixteen. I routinely told myself, "If I get straight A's, clean the house on Saturdays, and don't leave Mom alone, she might be happy." I blamed myself until age twenty-two. Afterward, I resented her depression denting my childhood until finally, in my thirties, I felt compassion for her depression and stopped taking it personally.

Ideally a parent, grandparent, or some elder may explain to us, in childlike terms we easily understand, that Mom and Dad still love us, despite their fighting or leaving. In other words, our parent's behavior is not our fault. But without such a clear explanation, we can bury this center-of-the-universe thinking deep in our unconscious, only to have it resurface years later in a healthy love relationship, one where we feel totally safe.

This center-of-the-universe thinking from childhood, coupled with a core belief such as "I'm unlovable or unworthy," is often the root cause for us reacting so personally to loved ones. We may grow skilled at listening well to friends, bosses, coworkers, healers, strangers, and acquaintances. But when we try to practice good listening skills as our lover, spouse, parent, or child share feelings, we may still react personally—even though we may have set an intention to listen well. This is because our childhood thinking takes over.

Without seeing that possibly our center-of-the-universe thinking is running our show, ego can jump in quickly and react to another's "I feel lonely" or "I'm bored" with "Your feelings make me feel uncomfortable, blamed, or scared, and I have to discount them immediately." Or ego dominates the conversation with *why* the other is bored or lonely to eliminate any possibility of blame. Either way, our verbal dukes fly up and we are ready to fight, freeze, or flee. All these personal reactions first learned as children occur within seconds, before we have a chance to consciously choose a more healthy response.

As we have witnessed, such near-sighted loyalty to childhood patterns can block good communication and create suffering for ourselves and loved ones, allowing unresolved conflicts to fester. This "everything relates to me" perspective can become our unconscious daily practice until we make this childhood stage of development more conscious. Once we accept that possibly such childhood thinking is impacting our adult reactions and make this developmental stage conscious, we can breathe a sigh of relief. And compassionate listening to others' feelings may become much easier.

Compassion, unlike childhood reactivity, welcomes suffering and joy equally as opportunities to wake up free, no matter what is happening around us.

COMPASSION COMES FROM THE POWER OF ACCEPTANCE

We think we know acceptance. Especially in recent years, more and more people give lip service to the idea, saying, "Hey man, I accept you for who you are," or "I accept my failures and move on." But this barely scratches the surface. True acceptance accepts *everything*, no apologies or excuses.

Compassionate acceptance maturely responds to challenges. It reminds us to stop taking ourselves, our likes and dislikes, our feelings and reactions, so damn seriously. It teaches us ease in holding anxiety and despair in compassionate acceptance. It gives us permission to relax into illness, pain, and loss without resisting. It transfuses us with courage to stay with what is, stay with uncomfortable feelings, stay with the fear and grief we avoided our whole lives.

When we really get the hang of total acceptance, it changes life's playing field. It tosses victim's blame game out on its ear and locks the door behind it. It ignores ego's resistance, letting compassion fill this new open space. It expands ego's lie, "I am only my body," to fit the truth: "I am conscious awareness living in this body and responding to life from awareness." It offers understanding without any need to be understood.

Total acceptance stretches us to *accept every inch of our humanness.*

ACCEPTANCE INCLUDES LOVE'S HURTS, TOO

When we embrace acceptance one hundred percent, we can love fully. Instead of withdrawing love to protect our vulnerable heart when hurt or rejection come visiting, acceptance reminds us that our wise, compassionate heart is built to accept every aspect of love: yes, even the unexpected hurts, misunderstandings, and betrayals that come with the precious gift of loving another human.

Healing comes when we, or a loved one, finally feel loved enough and safe enough to ask, "Can you please hold me?" or "Will you listen to my feelings without any advice?" Rarely do any of us have enough self-love and awareness to voice it so skillfully. We blunder through, overreacting about some silly thing, then finally setting down our resistance out of frustration to admit, "My persistent feeling of unworthiness is triggered big time. Would you please repeat how much I deserve to voice my needs until I feel this deeper truth in my heart?" Whether our young self fell into the dungeons of a core belief or a loved one is flailing in overwhelming hurt, our response can be the same: compassionate acceptance.

ACCEPTANCE PACES OUR DEEP HEALING IN STAGES

Bringing compassionate acceptance to our deepest wounds happens in stages. It is a process. For example, Jennifer struggled with posttraumatic stress disorder for forty years. A survivor of severe childhood abuse, she still managed to practice law, raise a healthy daughter, and cope with a difficult marriage. But underneath, she suffered alone in silence with the unresolved scars of an emotionally abusive childhood.

Like many who have suffered childhood trauma, survival was Jennifer's forte. "I was married and pregnant by twenty," she said. "Who had the time back then to heal eighteen years of abuse between breast feeding, changing diapers, and seeing clients? But now, semi-retired at fifty, I find myself sobbing in my morning meditation.

"Part of me is sick of crying over the atrocious ways Mom judged, slapped, and shamed me into letting her control me like her doll. For God's sake, she's dead, but I'm also sick of walking through life like a zombie, unable to feel my needs or feelings, let alone voice them to my husband or myself. I want my life back."

"Let's help you feel your emotions first," I said. "Answers will come from that. I invite you to lie down, close your eyes, and for now, set aside the story of what Mom did. Begin taking several deep breaths in your belly. Your body and heart know what needs to unwind inside to achieve healing. More than ever before, trust your body to lead you."

"It sounds strange, but I'd love to heal the chronic pain in my left hip."

"Okay. But first, while you breathe deeply, start at your neck and slowly scan your body. Notice whatever feelings or sensations are present in your body right now."

"I feel numb. From neck to pelvis to legs, I can't feel a thing. I suck at even this."

"Oh, numbness is a real feeling," I tell her. "Your task right now is accepting, not judging, whatever you notice inside. Just allow the numbness to be here, breathe into the center of it and spend a few moments feeling how numb you really feel."

Within seconds, Jennifer's legs were shaking. "I'm going crazy. I better stop."

"Just allow the trembling to happen—let it grow even stronger if it wants to. This is your body releasing unexpressed fear that you've carried for years. Continue to breathe deeply and allow your body to shake."

After the shaking subsided, Jennifer said, "I felt terrified to feel anything growing up. The instant I blinked, farted, or laughed, Mom was on me like white on rice, correcting me, yelling, calling me 'stupid' and 'wrong.' Here I am now, a lawyer, and she called me stupid so many times I couldn't trust my own decisions for years. I had to numb my feelings. If I had felt how enraged or sad I was, I might have killed her."

"It sounds horrible beyond imagination," I confirmed. "Now refocus in your body. I notice your arms and legs trembling again, so allow that to come to its own completion."

In minutes, tears trickled down her cheek. "I'm sorry if this is too weird, but I never felt my body was my own. As long as I remember, it belonged to her. I couldn't speak, move, play soccer, or feel without her controlling my every move. I'm a brain—I live from the neck up. Frankly, I'm terrified of what I might feel in my body."

Like most of us, Jennifer needed to discover and practice compassionate acceptance. Each morning for two weeks, Jennifer spent fifteen minutes in bed breathing deeply and holding whatever feelings were present in her body in compassionate acceptance. When fear judged her pain or sadness as bad, she let it go and came back to her breath.

Compassionate acceptance opens our eyes so wide that we see and hold all things—what happened, ego's reaction to what happened, our scared child's reaction to what happened, even a parent's unconscious acts years ago—in loving compassion.

Direct Experience Transforms Scary Feelings

Nobody ever taught us to trust our body very much. But experiencing feelings directly in our body awakens compassion. With fifteen to thirty minutes and two simple tools—our breath and our attention—our body releases scary feelings, transforming them into the unlimited joy, kindness, compassion, and inner peace that we are in our core.

When we focus directly on any negative feeling in our body, something phenomenal happens. When we locate fear in our body and breathe directly into it, allowing fear to release through trembling, crying, or shaking, fear dissolves. Fear cannot withstand our full, direct attention. When we focus directly on sadness stuck in the body, we let grief take center stage and fully express itself. Afterward, we feel spacious and peaceful for no reason that will satisfy the ego.

Once we get to know how hurt and rejection feel in our body, we can witness pain as pain, not who we are, and hold it in tender compassion. When we courageously locate the shame that lives underneath fear, hurt, and sadness—shame for existing, shame for our shortcomings, shame for being molested, shame for having and voicing our human and sexual needs—and breathe directly into our shame, we can hold even this core feeling in loving compassion.

The more we bask in the unlimited joy and inner peace that compassion brings, we develop an appetite for freedom. Rather than dodge fear and sadness, we welcome the next feeling that will carry us into bliss and joy. Trembling, shaking, and grieving become minor bumps in the road when peaceful freedom waits around the next bend.

Each time we surrender ego's strategies, beliefs, and judgments that pretend to protect us from hurt, we come to trust our body's knowing to heal even more.

In Jennifer's follow-up session, she bounced into the office with a lilt in her walk. "I feel so alive after moving through my numbness and fear last week. If my body needs to tremble more today to keep me feeling so awake and alive, I'm all for it."

After she lay on the futon and closed her eyes, Jennifer began breathing into her belly. "Engaging willingness by saying an intention speeds up your healing," I said. Jennifer whispered a powerful intention: "I'm willing to heal whatever feelings are ready to be healed." Breathing, and scanning her body, she noticed her belly felt on fire. "I'm uncomfortable with rage," she spoke up. "I'm a nice girl from Kansas, but right now I'm picturing myself strangling my mother. Hurry, how do I go numb again?"

"Yes," I chuckled. "It's unnerving to feel powerful rage for the first time, especially for women. But you are safe. Use your breath as an anchor. Breathe into your belly, and ride the flames as rage ebbs and flows. Many of us carry deep rage in our core for never feeling truly seen, heard, or valued as children for who we are."

Jennifer was listening as the rage continued to burn up inside her belly. "It's never healthy to unleash raw rage on loved ones," I added. "Let's use this big pillow instead. Try alternately kicking it with one leg, then the other, and voicing your rage. This way, you can release that pressure valve."

Jennifer kicked hard down into the pillow, seething with rage, but no words came. "Damn, my voice belongs to Mom too. She stole my voice and everything else!"

"Try growling to let some sound out and clear the cobwebs out of your throat. I'll do it with you." Together, we jutted our jaws out and growled like bears until we laughed. At first, Jennifer's high-pitched soprano growl sounded like a young girl. But with this exercise her voice gained volume and depth. "Now see if any words come with your kicking."

This time Jennifer primed the pump by growling while she kicked. "Leave me alone! Don't touch me! Get away from me! I hate what you did."

With each repetition of words she would never tell her mother, she gained inner strength. As Jungian therapist Marion Woodman explained in *Coming Home to Myself:*

Deep rage is this: Nobody ever saw me. Nobody ever heard me. As long as I can remember, I've had to perform. When I tried to be myself, I was told, "That's not what you should think, that's not what you ought to do…" My life became a lie. That's deep rage.

We return to spacious inner peace in this moment by expressing this deep rage in healthy ways.

Jennifer went home vowing to play with making sounds. Since she grew up under her mom's microscope, Jennifer had stifled all the cooing and babbling that toddlers exhibit and silenced her rebellious teenager to avoid further abuse. But now these undeveloped early stages limited her adult expression. For two weeks, in the privacy of her home and car, Jennifer spent five minutes a day yelling, growling, cussing, and making silly sounds.

"I start my morning meditation seeing whatever feelings are present," Jennifer said. "Then after my husband leaves for work, I dance to my favorite reggae in the living room and babble with the music, stretching out *eeeeeh* and *aaaaah* sounds to open my vocal cords. During the day, I howl and growl in the car—which makes me giggle like a kid. At first I was scared other drivers would report me, but they're so absorbed with their own distractions, they don't notice a thing."

"The best part, though," she continued, "came after two weeks of cooing and growling. One evening I told Don I needed his uninterrupted attention. He looked shocked. After all, I'd been a silent nice girl without needs for twenty years. But he listened. I shared how depressed and lonely I'd been since 2008 when our daughter left for college. Inspired by my truth telling, he told me how he felt unloved since I rarely spoke to him or confided in him. He choked up when he talked about my agreeing to sex just to 'get it over with.' That night, we agreed to connect with each other every day."

Finding Peace by Releasing the Deep Grief for Never Feeling Seen and Heard

After we express the rage we carry inside for years over never feeling seen, heard, or valued for who we truly are, deep grief can follow.

Rage is expressed toward the loved ones who failed to see our intrinsic value. Underneath such consuming anger, we drop down into grieving all those moments we felt disconnected from our essence, from childhood through teenage and adult years, because we were so busy pleasing, rebelling, caretaking, or taking on other family roles to try to *earn* love, approval, and self-worth.

Surrendering into our deep grief from childhood or adult trauma frees us to see and hear ourselves for who we really are. By making our old unconscious family roles conscious, we empower ourselves with choice; we now can deliberately choose to keep trying to earn love by playing our old family roles in new relationships, or we can decide to hold the buried grief of our childhood in loving, compassionate acceptance.

This sadness is our core grief. Expressing it reconnects us with our pure joy of being alive. When we set aside as many uninterrupted half hours as we need, and set an intention such as "I'm willing to heal any unresolved childhood grief for not feeling seen," we return to the freedom and deep peace of our true nature—a result well worth our time and effort.

Some spiritual circles refer to this as "waking up out of the dream or illusion of unconscious suffering." It doesn't eliminate suffering, as ego believes something, *anything*, will. But it frees us to stand on the stable ground of unlimited compassion that acknowledges and sees clearly the painful consequences of unconscious conditioning.

After Jennifer discussed the new changes in her relationship, she lay on the couch, closed her eyes, and took several deep breaths.

"I notice some fear today about what feelings might arise. But my intention is to heal whatever is ready to be healed."

Within minutes, Jennifer was flooded with sadness. "I feel a heavy weight in the center of my chest that's been there for years. Scared to feel it, I've stayed busy to ignore it."

"Breathe directly into the heavy sadness. Feel how sad you really feel."

"I'm terrified I'll feel overwhelmed and never stop crying."

"I hear your fear. It's good to name fears to deflate them. But this is ego's last-ditch effort to avoid your sadness. Label it 'fearing' and focus on breathing in your belly. Then ask your heart if it's willing to touch your sadness directly."

"Yes, I'm willing." Jennifer's tears turned into loud sobs. "I feel like I'm grieving the tears of a lifetime. Images of myself at three, five, eight, and ten flash through my mind. I see sad little Jennifer looking gaunt, lonely, and undernourished." Tears overcame her. "I feel deep sadness for that little girl who endured such cruelty and terror all alone. I want to hold her and rock her and reassure her that she'll never be alone again. But I'm afraid I'll keep abandoning her like everyone else."

"Don't get lost in the story of your childhood. Keep breathing into the sadness in your chest. Stay right with the sadness and let it arrive at its own natural completion."

After her crying subsided, a soft smile came over her face. "I feel like I'm floating on my back in a warm ocean rocked by gentle waves. I feel so blissful, so peaceful that anything could happen and it wouldn't upset me. What Mom did or didn't do doesn't matter one iota in this peaceful place."

"Welcome to the abundant stillness that lives inside your heart," I whispered. "This is who you are when thoughts and feelings aren't clouding the landscape."

Jennifer devoted fifteen minutes a day to connecting with her peaceful heart.

Direct experience, like Jennifer's encounter with her unconditioned self, is the short path to freedom. When we meet unconscious conditioning directly with our compassionate heart, we can burst at the seams with more bliss and freedom than we ever dreamed possible. Direct experience transfuses us with courage to face even our shame.

MELTING UNCONSCIOUS SHAME WITH ACCEPTANCE

Underneath the tall grass of numbness, rage, fear, and grief, shame lies hidden. Most of us are clueless that shame abides deep in our unconscious, denying the joy and freedom of who we are. We recognize it by its seductive voice in our heads: "Don't speak your real truth, or they won't like you. Don't act too wild and crazy, or you'll never fit in and succeed. Don't admit how scared or sad you feel, or you leave yourself open to attack. Keep your heart closed and protected, or you'll get too hurt and disappointed by love." Yes, shame is the inner voice that insists we stay silent and invisible.

Shame joins forces with those core beliefs from childhood. It turns every doubt into proving once again, "I really am unlovable, unworthy, and not good enough." Before we are able to speak our needs, shame convinces us to silence them.

But just like fear, shame cannot withstand our full attention. As soon as we locate it in our body and breathe directly into it, that thick, black veil of shame begins to dissolve. When we find the courage to accept our humanness, our self-worth regains its rightful position: something we are born with that nobody can ever give us or take away. Self-worth is our birthright.

To dissolve this invisible culprit, we must nurture compassion every day.

Fear, rage, grief, and shame become gateways to inner peace and freedom when held in compassion. As they arise, exist, and disappear, compassion remains always present, holding each feeling in loving acceptance.

In Jennifer's next session, she reported lots of reggae and dancing. "I feel so much energy and joy, I can't wait to melt some more feelings today." After lying down and closing her eyes, she again aligned her unconscious with her conscious by setting an intention: "I'm willing to heal whatever wants to be healed."

After several deep breaths, Jennifer focused inside. "I feel a cold steel coat covering my whole torso. I don't like it. Can we just skip to the joy part?"

"Let even this be here, and breathe directly into the center of it."

"I see myself at three or four," she said after a few minutes. "Even that young, I felt ashamed for existing, as if I took up too much space and Mom was better off without me. When Mom called me stupid, shame made me not even want to exist."

Jennifer began sobbing. "I just want to be quiet. Inside, I'm holding young Jennifer in my arms, reassuring her that she's not stupid and she has every right to exist." She began rocking side-to-side and holding her arms tight to her chest as she cried.

Like Jennifer, we come to realize that we cannot change the traumas we suffered at the hands of parents and others—people who harmed us by acting out their own unconscious conditioning. But when we see this truth through compassionate eyes and reassure our innocent one inside that we never deserved these unconscious acts, a deep healing shift occurs. Rather than holding on to blame, we hold even the worst offenders in compassion.

The truth is, more than we wait for any lover, spouse, or mentor to save us, our young self will wait decades to be wholly acknowledged by our wise heart. Ego tells us we don't have hours to waste with some silly child. But a few minutes of connection with our young self when we first wake in the morning or during meditation helps us feel whole and integrated again. Rather than fearing childish outbursts, this child self overflows with joy, love, and creative spontaneity. Once we reconnect, its riches join our life.

Compassion for the Suffering of Others

We like to think of ourselves as kind, compassionate, and understanding. But when push comes to shove, when we feel cornered, blamed, or criticized in any way, we defend ourselves. No matter how much we love another, we always protect our heart. Since we are humans moving in and out of unconscious conditioning, and since we humans carry a deep-seated fear of getting hurt, we tend to quickly twist others' feelings into how they affect *me*. This entrenched ego habit requires closer attention.

If a loved one is lonely, sad, or depressed, compassion is rarely our first reaction. Our family tradition taught us well to react defensively, take others' feelings personally, and slip into rejection and blame before we even know what happened. With time, these internal hurts fester into bitterness, hopelessness, and resentment—a miserable way to live. To protect ourselves from similar hurts in the future, we withdraw, withhold love, and make do with this painful, contracted state.

Practicing the Art of Compassionate Listening

We practice this harmful routine day in and day out; our lover, mate, parent, best friend, or child says, "I'm unhappy," "I'm depressed," or "I feel resentful," and we respond not to their concerns but immediately to our own. We skip over our core hurt, fear, or sadness by jumping directly into secondary feelings of guilt, anger, irritability, frustration, or defensive blaming. We sidestep that "I did something wrong again" core belief by reverting to manipulation. "How could you still be unhappy? We have our home, our health, our kids—so much to be happy for." When this strategy falls flat, which it usually does, we hope loud anger or sarcasm will force loved ones into submission. "For once in your life," we might yell, "can you be positive and drop your chronic negativity?"

Sarcastic reactions live on the tip of our tongue, cocked to fire any moment.

Compassionate listening, including such statements as "I hear how unhappy or depressed you are," slams the brakes on all this defensive hoopla. It throws ego's false concept of perfection right out the window, never needing our loved ones to be any different than they are. It accepts loved ones through their mistakes, their guilt and shame, their hopelessness and pain, seeing each day's show as nothing more than unconscious conditioning having a field day with loved ones. Compassion is this all-loving, all-understanding, all-forgiving switch inside our heart that never shuts off.

True compassion is the direct, blameless choice. It ignores the "why" of someone's unhappiness and it knows that a simple response such as "I understand how resentful you feel" is often the most effective and comforting response. Rather than biting into the content, fueling more argument, compassion knows that strong overreactions never truly result from simple debates on who last emptied the trash or washed the dishes. Instead, compassion acknowledges the fact that some minor incident rubbed salt into a loved one's childhood wound.

By skipping over the content and reflecting only feeling words—"I hear how sad or scared you feel"—compassion invites loved ones to share deeper feelings. By leaving personal reactions and clever solutions out of the equation, compassionate listening helps others feel seen and heard for who they are.

For compassion to flow through us, we first acknowledge—to ourselves and loved ones—our ego habit of avoiding discomfort and clinging to the familiar. But listening with compassion can be far more challenging than it sounds. On good days, we hear another's feelings without reacting. On bad days, we take another's feelings personally and react unconsciously before we even realize what happened.

Even those of us skilled in healthy communication can fall back into reactivity easily. For example, my therapist friend Randy, who teaches couples communication workshops in California, shared this story about the sticky wicket he stumbled into with his wife. Despite years of meditation, he still fell into personal reactivity.

Last year, during a midlife transition, his wife Sally shared, "I feel unhappy." Through his skillful communication training, most times Randy responds with "I hear you feel unhappy." But this time, he instantly blamed himself for Sally's unhappiness, making her feelings all about him. "What have I done wrong this time?" he asked.

"You always make my feelings about you. I'm sick of it," Sally rebutted.

Challenged to defend, he said, "I'm sick of your chronic unhappiness. We have so much to be grateful for; how about you practice gratitude today?"

Luckily, Randy felt this escalating, about to ruin their Sunday. So he quickly changed directions: "My unarguable truth is that I feel hurt and criticized by your statement. So let me take a few minutes to teach you why criticism is such a trigger for me.

"My dad criticized me endlessly. I could never do anything right. And Dad would never take the time to teach me how to do things right. Since I was the oldest, he'd just immediately start yelling at me. Later in my first marriage, my wife complained that I either worked too much or wasn't working enough. I couldn't win with her."

Hearing the origins of his rawness around criticism, Sally dropped her defenses. Instead she immediately went to him to hold him as he wept.

After Randy expressed his deep grief for never feeling seen or valued, he was able to turn to Sally and say, "I'm sorry I made your feelings about me too often. But now that I told you the source of my reactivity, I feel clear to hear about your unhappiness."

"Your overreactions make more sense now that I know the source," she said in a compassionate tone. "It'll be refreshing to share my feelings with you now fully present and listening."

When serious conflicts erupt in relationships over minor incidents, it's important to pause and ask ourselves, "Which childhood wound is triggering my·reaction?"

Even if we bless loved ones in our morning meditation or prayer, we can be so filled up with opinions, judgments, and self-righteousness during the day that the art of compassionate listening can take years to perfect. The trick is to dance a jig and toast the air each and every time we are able to set aside reactivity and, instead, simply listen.

Compassionate listening is the advanced course in compassion for others. It unveils the freedom found in remembering that this person trying to love us, with all their foibles and confusion, struggles with the same unconscious fear, doubt, judgment, and delusion that we do. By greeting our own ego habits with loving acceptance, compassion helps us see others move in and out of their own unconscious conditioning.

Compassionate speech follows good listening. As we drop ego's need to blame, blameless speech is clean and simple, spoken with a kind tone. It invites us to *describe* our visiting feelings rather than merge with them. It sounds like "I notice my old feeling of being unlovable flared up after you said you needed alone time this weekend. Would you spend a few minutes telling me that I am lovable?"

COMPASSION FOR LOVED ONES, FRIENDS, ENEMIES, AND ALL BEINGS

Buddha taught that compassion opens our hearts to the suffering of all beings. But consciously opening to pain, our own or another's, defies logic. It grates against ego's common sense mantra: "avoid pain at all costs." So we begin to practice compassion on the easiest subjects first—our loved ones and ourselves.

As many times as we want to repeat it, we say, "May I and my lover, child, and/or loved one" (naming each one) "be free of suffering and the root of suffering." If someone is ill or in pain, we specifically state, "May Uncle Fred heal from colon cancer." After weeks of practicing this, if we feel ready to include our circle of friends, we repeat, "May my friend Marie who suffers from back pain and my elder friend Linda with arthritis be free of suffering and the root of suffering."

As we continue, we can begin to include "neutral" acquaintances by saying, "May the UPS driver who cut me off be free of suffering and the root of suffering." We widen the compassion circle by including the most challenging, our enemies: "May Lydia, who hurt me, and John, who I dislike, be free of suffering and the root of suffering." Each time we express compassion for those our ego never thought deserved compassion, our heart stretches further. Finally we include all people and all beings by saying, "May I and all beings be free of suffering and the root of suffering."

Cultivating compassion in our morning meditation and prayers opens our heart to our shared human suffering with all beings. But being prepared on the spot to meet another's unconscious anger, fear, and judgment with compassion remains a challenge.

COMPASSION HEALS OUR DEEP-SEATED FEAR OF LOVE

As a marriage and family therapist, I see couples create suffering for themselves by defending their hard-won personal reactions— and blaming their mate for the existence of such reactions. In my therapy sessions with these couples, I first acknowledge how frustrating it can feel for us humans to set down our personal reactions and skillfully respond to others with compassion. Then I ask them to do just that.

Despite our grand efforts to love one another day in and day out, we rarely put ourselves in a loved one's shoes. We rarely choose "May you be free of suffering" as our trusty bedfellow to get us through the night. Over the years, as resentments pile up, partners become roommates residing in opposite corners.

But when we peek underneath those scoundrels hiding in our unconscious, perpetuating conflicts and destroying intimacy, we come face to face with something we least expect: a deep-seated fear of love.

This little-known truth, that humans fear love, is rarely acknowledged or discussed.

We talk a good game. Yes, we all insist we want love, crave love, and can't relax until we find love. We spent youthful hours on the phone telling friends what our next lover needs to look and act like. And after we find love, we spend an equal number of hours telling friends what horrible things our partner did—or failed to do. We devote years trying out lovers, hoping to find that special one who makes our heart sing. And do it all over when the fairytale ends in divorce.

After the honeymoon ends, when things get hard in any of our human relationships, we need to ask, "What is my real practice?"

At the first whiff of hurt or rejection, we withdraw and escape to our cars or computers, afraid to leave ourselves open. When a partner or family member yells rudely and blames us for their depression, we rarely respond with compassion. We don't tell ourselves, "Her unskillful words come from unconscious conditioning. Her words are not about me. I'll be the bigger person and speak from my heart." In the heat of the moment, it can feel like it takes a saint to respond with compassion.

But as we get the hang of it, as we meet fear and anger with compassion again and again, we find freedom in the life-changing results. The truth is, the wider our hearts crack open, the more terrified we really are, deep inside, to give and receive love. The deeper we let love in, the more terrified we are of losing it, caring too much, or trusting and getting burned. Love scares us because, as fun and juicy as it is at times, love makes us vulnerable to hurt. And if someone we've invested all our heart and trust in abandons us, this is far more devastating than an acquaintance blowing us off. Thus, ego exhausts itself hoping to avoid hurt, pain, rejection, and suffering altogether.

Lucky for us, our compassionate heart is built to handle all suffering.

Besides being misguided by romance novels and Hollywood movies, we swallowed yet another false lie from ego: "If someone really loves me, they will never hurt or disappoint me. Someone who loves me knows what I need without asking." By never questioning this lie, we kick and scream long past childhood. And when these fail, we wonder if maybe we chose the *wrong* Mr. or Ms. Right. By not questioning ego's lie, we never stop long enough to see that the hurt and disappointment we so tried to avoid is the very suffering that matures us through compassion.

HOLDING LOVED ONES' DEEPEST WOUNDS IN COMPASSION

About two years into a good love relationship, once things fall into a smooth rhythm, is often when all hell breaks loose—or so it feels. What really happens is that, once our spouse feels safe and loved by us, their past traumas and wounds surface to be healed. Past wounds and hurts want in on the love action.

Such a surprise can hurl us into questioning the entire relationship. Luckily we have already been cultivating compassion for ourselves. We know how to hold our unexpressed rage, grief, and hurt in compassion. We know firsthand the empty hole or tightness in our chest from never feeling seen and heard for who we really are. We may be scared. But we are prepared to step up and hold these same scary feelings in understanding and loving compassion for our lover as we did for ourselves. Their pain may look like an angry ogre, but we can love even their ogre side.

Compassion rises up from a deep understanding of our human predicament. In *Stillness Speaks*, Eckhart Tolle describes the precious lens through which compassion sees life: "If her past were your past, her pain your pain, her level of consciousness your level of consciousness, you would think and act exactly as she does. With that realization comes forgiveness, compassion, and peace."

To help heal another's suffering with compassion, we must know the basic rule of healthy intimacy: only one person's wounds can be healed at a time. In other words if, while addressing our partner's wound, our own unconscious fear of rejection or abandonment is triggered, we need to recognize our personal reaction and set it down quickly, before it snags center stage. This becomes an opportunity for us to practice setting ego's reactivity aside and choosing the higher ground. This frees us to respond from our compassionate heart: "I'm here for you, and I love you. Go ahead and feel how sad or scared you feel." Compassionate listening heals, bringing closeness and freedom.

Kate spent several months healing her rage and grief from growing up with an alcoholic father. She loved the idea of similarly freeing her husband Jeff from never feeling seen or heard or valued. But Jeff, a gifted engineer pushing forty, was still licking his wounds from his first wife, who had cheated on him with his best friend. To keep a safe distance from Kate, Jeff avoided sharing his tender feelings by throwing himself into reading newspapers, magazines, anything he could get his hands on.

"Hon," Kate said, "we vowed at our wedding to be open with each other."

"Mmmhmmm," he said, never lifting his nose from the paper.

To move past his usual defensive reaction, Kate repeated her words like a broken record. "No really, what's up? You seem withdrawn and distant after sex."

Again, Jeff held her at arm's length. "Nothing. I just want to read."

Determined not to give up like before, Kate's third try broke down his defenses. "I have my compassionate listening hat on. Is your fear of letting love in up again?"

Jeff looked up from his paper. "I don't know what's wrong or how to address it. But the closer I feel in lovemaking, the tighter my chest gets. I'm terrified that, when you get to know me, you'll find me inadequate, just like my ex did."

Rather than talk him out of his fears, as her ego wanted to do, Kate held his hands. "I'm here for you, babe. I love you madly, and I hear how scared you are."

"It sounds stupid," he said, "but I love you so much that I feel scared in every direction: scared you'll leave, scared I'll feel trapped, scared there's no room for my needs, scared I'm not relationship material, scared I'll open my heart and you'll die."

Jeff teared up as Kate held him in her arms and made comforting sounds.

Afterward Jeff smiled, "Wow, my chest feels lighter than it has felt in years." They both agreed to share their feelings and needs for a half hour every Monday night.

The more we recognize that the person we love struggles with the same fears we do, the more the words of the Dalai Lama ring true. "Everyone wants to be happy and be free of suffering," he says. Far from settling for imperfect love, compassion opens our eyes to see and celebrate the inherent perfection of life, and love, just as it is.

DO-OVERS TOSS US OUR LIFE JACKET

As we quickly notice in love relationships, personal reactions die slowly. Long after we set a daily intention to respond with compassion, we still watch our personal judgment, blame, and reactions take front row, center stage. This can be frustrating. Sometimes the process of awareness feels worse than being oblivious to all that acting out. At least before we were unaware of our unconscious reactions. Now, suddenly, we are conscious of our reactions—and conscious of how our reactions create more suffering for ourselves and loved ones. In other words, we see clearly how our anger toward our spouse's unhappiness escalated into one more unresolved argument. But this doesn't stop us from blurting out our two cents.

This is where a do-over throws us a life jacket. Moments or days after we put our foot in our mouth with some sarcastic, defensive, personal reaction, and after we've cooled off, we can go to our loved one and gingerly ask, "Could I please have a do-over?" It's a way of saying, "Please erase those unskillful words that flew out of my mouth, and let me carefully speak the loving, conscious words I choose to say." If both parties spoke words they later regret, do-overs offer opportunities to practice choosing acceptance, understanding, compassion, and forgiveness.

Do-overs can save the day—and maybe even save the relationship.

After reacting unconsciously, do-overs allow us to practice speaking our truth with kindness. Rather than "You never listen to my feelings," a do-over might sound like "Would you be willing to spend five minutes after breakfast listening to my feelings?" Rather than "You always trash my car when you use it," a do-over request might be "Could you please empty your trash after using my car?" Do-overs help us turn defensive blurts into clean, direct, conscious "I feel, I need, I request" statements.

It takes time and practice (and plenty of do-overs) to be able to treat loved ones with the loving compassion and respect we all deserve. But after seeing and hearing our own intrinsic value, and holding our hurt and grief in compassion, we feel inspired to bring this same freedom to loved ones. Just like us, their tender hearts have also waited their whole lives to be seen, heard, loved, and valued unconditionally.

Compassion blossoms out of a willingness to be present, curious, aware, and resourceful. It offers understanding without being understood, forgiveness without being forgiven, and unconditional love without love in return.

CROSSING THE LINE INTO FREEDOM

When that moment arrives, when we wake up and see through the eyes of loving compassion, we cross a line into freedom. It feels like reaching shore after weeks or years of being lost in a sea of emotions and thoughts. Compassion forgives every mistake, comforts us after judgment shames us, and reassures us when fear instills doubt.

By seeing and hearing our own intrinsic value for who we are, compassion gives us courage to face our core feelings directly and hold them in loving compassion. By dropping ego's lie that we are separate, our compassionate heart steps up, again and again, to wish that us and all beings be free of suffering and the root of suffering.

As our own compassion overflows into compassion for others, we stop twisting others' feelings into how they affect us. Instead, we meet others' unconscious acts with conscious acceptance. Instead of arguing over the content of another's feelings, we acknowledge their feeling words with no personal input. When needed, we help loved ones identify which core feelings and beliefs are triggering their overreaction. In other words, we commit to practice compassionate listening and blameless speech daily.

Our lifelong challenge is to meet all suffering with compassionate acceptance.

Though anything can instigate ego's fear of trusting, fear of caring, fear of believing in ourselves, we always have the option to choose compassion, even now. Amid utter chaos when overwhelming fear, grief, rejection, or despair trigger our fight/flight anxiety, we can still breathe deeply and let our compassionate heart reassure us that we are safe and we are loved, always.

Choosing to Live in Compassion

Compassion changes us forever. Once we open our heart to see all humans through the eyes of compassion, and see them struggling with the same fear and shame, aging and illness, sorrow and loss that we struggle with, we strengthen our heart connection to all living beings. Once we touch the freedom found in forgiving others' unconscious conditioning, even that of the bad driver who cut us off or a self-absorbed mother, ego's resistance seems pointless.

We are free to join compassion, which trusts the wisdom of life.

As compassion cracks our heart wide open, we see nothing but wise beings walking this earth as carpenters, doctors, plumbers, store clerks, teachers, parents, and countless other roles, all learning compassion through the trials of being human. Against this backdrop, ego's fearing and wanting seems nothing more than illusion, a thought that only exists in our head. Compassion teaches us to value everything and everyone, even the life experiences and people we don't like.

Like a mountain that welcomes rain, snow, wind, cold, and heat without flinching, our compassionate heart stands tall and still as a mountain inside us, welcoming each season, each challenge, each new moment with "Hello. I'm excited to see you."

Freedom emerges from our deepest level of self-love and self-acceptance.

Heart Tools for Compassion

Practice each of these tools for one week before moving on to the next one. But if a specific tool calls you to spend more time with it, give yourself another week, month, or as long as you need in order to heal.

1. *Cultivating Compassion for Yourself and the World*

Toward the end of your morning meditation or prayer time, practice compassion for yourself. Place one hand over your heart and say, "May I be free of suffering and the root of suffering" or, to address specific needs, "May I be free of back pain, headache, despair, or illness and the root of this suffering." Repeat this phrase several times until it feels like your heart and body receive it. When your heart is ready to include loved ones, repeat the phrase, "May my spouse, child, parent, or best friend be free of suffering and the root of suffering." As you feel ready to expand, bless the grocery clerk, mail person, and other neutral acquaintances you encounter in your day: "May the UPS man be free of suffering and the root of suffering." Once you're comfortable, find the courage to include people you consider enemies: "May my sister-in-law that I avoid or dislike be free of suffering and the root of suffering." Finally, bless everyone by saying, "May I and all beings be free of suffering and the root of suffering."

2. *Sitting on a Park Bench Accepting Visiting Feelings*

When anxiety, loneliness, despair, or rejection visit you, pause a few minutes, close your eyes, and imagine sitting on a park bench getting to know these feelings better. Without needing to fix or change the feeling in any way, accept each feeling as it is. Notice how each feeling manifests in your body. Notice which stories the feeling triggers in your head. Let these "visitors" share the same space with your joyful, compassionate heart.

3. *Compassion for Self through Direct Experience*

Find four weeks during a quiet time of year when you can consistently take time to heal each core feeling. At least once each week, set aside twenty to thirty minutes to shut off your phone, ask your family not to disturb you, and lie down in a quiet room where you can be alone. Close your eyes and set an intention, such as "I'm willing to explore or heal any core feelings in my body" or "I'm willing to feel whatever I've been unwilling to feel." Pace your healing process by addressing only one core feeling at a time. Take ten deep belly breaths and scan your body for whatever feelings pop up. When hurt, rage, grief, or shame appears for all those times you never felt heard and seen for who you are, in your core, travel backward in your memory to the first time you felt unseen and unheard and reassure your young self.

If hurt appears, locate where you feel it in your body and let a sound out to match the degree of hurt. When rage appears, give yourself permission to alternately kick one leg, then the other, into a large pillow. See if you can voice the words and sounds stuck in your throat. Deep grief for not feeling seen and heard often comes on the heels of rage. When waves of grief appear, let yourself cry each wave until your body reaches natural completion. Shame hides deep inside, so after you release the hurt, rage, and grief, set an intention, "I'm willing to see and heal any shame I carry for existing or having needs." Often shame feels like a thick, black, tar-like shell covering your torso, specifically around your chest or genitals. Keep breathing into the center of it until it lightens and dissolves into a spacious peaceful feeling inside. With each healing, energetic aliveness returns.

4. *Compassionate Listening and Speech*

Practice setting down your personal reactions and listening attentively to a loved one share their truth. Then say, "I hear you, and I love you" or "I hear you feel _____ and you need _____ around it."

Since you will often notice that a spouse's core belief is triggered before they do, gently ask, "Is your core belief up? Would you love to hear how lovable and worthy you are right now?"

When speaking, practice clean, blameless communication, such as "I feel _____" (without blaming yourself or others) "and what I need to hear around this is _____." As you grow skilled at naming your childhood wounding, you might add which core feeling and belief is triggered for you.

Whenever any dialogue escalates into confusion, yelling, or unresolved conflict, become the first in your family to say, "Pause! I'd like a do-over. Let's take five minutes to calm down, then come back together to speak our truth in a blameless, kind way." Remember, do-overs are your life jacket during conflict.

PART II
Bringing Freedom and Inner Peace into the World

The past five months, we have looked inward, coming to see, hear, value, and accept ourselves, brand new through the loving eyes of our wise heart. We catch ego's countless thoughts, stories, and feelings quicker now, allowing us to fill the empty space more often with healthy habits: presence, curiosity, awareness, resourcefulness, and compassionate acceptance. Our newfound abilities to accept what is, love all feelings, set down personal reactions, take full responsibility for conscious choices, and offer loving acceptance have prepared us for the next step: becoming the change in the world.

By leading with our wise heart, we can model freedom and inner peace in all our relationships. As we practice kindness, gratitude, forgiveness, and integrity in our daily interactions with loved ones, friends, coworkers, and strangers, we invite these next five heart powers to become our conscious choices. True freedom is found by remembering our connection with all beings and showing respect for the sovereignty of all beings each moment, each day in contact with others.

6. Your Kind Heart

The Power of Generosity

In life we cannot avoid change, we cannot avoid loss.
Freedom and happiness are found in the flexibility and ease
     with which we move through change.
—JACK KORNFIELD

It is a rare, bitter cold January morning. A Canadian cold front dipped into Colorado last night, causing record low temperatures. It dipped down to minus twenty degrees in Denver last night at midnight. Outside the kitchen window at eleven o'clock, my thermometer said four degrees. This morning's sparrows struggled to flap their frozen wings.

The emotional climate inside is bitter cold, too, this morning. After waking up an hour late and just now sitting down to write at noon, I've heard plenty of booing from ego's section of the bleachers. My morning meditation sounded like nine Supreme Court justices, all scolding me for being downright lazy and lacking in commitment. Kindness was nowhere in sight as my ego chanted, "You're late! How can you ever call yourself a *real* writer?"

Lucky for me curiosity and awareness came to my rescue, reminding me that I don't have to listen to ego's rants. I shrugged, labeled them "judging," and tossed them in the recycling bin while asking my heart for compassionate advice. Her soft, tender voice whispered, "Relax. You're in perfect timing, always. Whatever is happening now is perfect because it is what's happening. Just enjoy writing."

This ring of truth, real truth, signaled my body to relax and take several deep breaths. "Ah, yes, this moment is the only moment there really is. Whatever happened or didn't happen is history now. In this moment, I choose kindness."

Kindness is choosing to respond, to ourselves and others, with warm words and acts and a loving tone. It is responding to whatever comes toward us with an open, generous heart.

Meeting Life's Imperfect Moments with Kindness

Most of the time, just like my cold, cold morning, things don't go as expected. Life rarely matches ego's perfect picture in our head (especially in love relationships). Ego derails us with pictures of what life and love should look like, what understanding and forgiveness should look like, and even what enlightenment should look like.

This conflict between what is and should be often holds us hostage for years, wasting precious time and destroying perfectly good relationships until, finally, we stumble upon our kind heart. Rather than trying to change life all the time to fit ego's ideal picture, we might respond differently; we might consciously choose these gifts of kindness:

- Kindness is dropping ego's judgments and trusting this moment as it is.
- Kindness is greeting another's anger and fear with "I'm here for you."
- Kindness is feeling our angry rebuttal explode inside and setting it aside.

- Kindness is responding with respect to our body's symptoms and feelings.
- Kindness is dropping the plan when flexibility includes everyone's needs.
- Kindness is stopping the inner war between what is and how it should be.
- Kindness is never taking ourselves or our current reality so seriously.
- Kindness is pausing amid a busy day to ask, "What am I feeling now?"
- Kindness is embracing our warm, generous heart that is always available.
- The spirit of generosity welcomes who we are, and what we feel and need, exactly as we are. Free of indulging any personal reactions, generosity never pulls back to think "but how does that affect me?" Like a loving grandmother, a generous spirit accepts everyone just as we are.

RECLAIMING THE LOST ART OF KINDNESS

Kindness feels like a thing of the past, a lost art. In this speed-driven, high-tech, "me" culture, kindness has no place. It is for sissies, weaklings, brownnosers, wimps, cowards, old ladies, and the faint at heart. Nobody has time to be kind these days. We have bigger, more important things to do. Listening to someone's feelings or heart-felt longings, even our own, can feel like a waste of time. We are too busy chasing our potential—which too often translates into filling our bank accounts—and redefining what it is to be human and healthy at thirty, forty, fifty, or sixty. In this rat-race world, women and elders are more likely to get the finger than be given that choice parking spot nearest the store.

Random acts of kindness live more on bumper stickers than daily reality. But kindness may be the missing puzzle piece we are looking for.

We think of ourselves as kind. We love to believe, "I'm a kind person. If my spouse, children, boss, and community only knew how much I sacrifice daily." But our ego loves to flatter itself with what we want to hear. The truth is, we move in and out of kind thoughts and deeds depending on our mood, our stress, our fear levels, and whether or not we are getting our way. It can be hard to stay kind if we feel hurt, down, or ill. For that reason, a daily commitment to kindness helps exercise our conscious awareness and kind heart. If we pick one day a week to tally up how often we actually respond with kindness versus irritability, frustration, or negativity, we might be surprised by the final count.

Just yesterday a client in her late forties started therapy. In the middle of a messy divorce, she is living with the painful reality of her husband running off with a young woman while he begs her and their two sons to stop being angry with him.

"When my oldest son asked his dad why he left after twenty-seven years for a younger woman," Sheila said, "Mr. Self-Righteous answered, 'I gave this family everything I could for years. Now it's *my* turn!' But his turn starts with a $500,000 income while I worked nights for years to help him get his medical degree."

After expressing her rage and grief in therapy, Sheila eventually found kindness easier on herself and her boys than closing off her heart with resentment.

We are rarely kind to ourselves. Inside, where nobody can hear, we harshly judge ourselves for never measuring up. We are quick to snap at our mistakes, to deem ourselves "shameful and unworthy." Years after a critical parent, teacher, or priest has left our lives, we internalize these voices and repeat theses cruelties in our head.

Too often, kindness is short-lived. We may express kind words and actions when we wake up rested and refreshed in the morning— but then something unexpected happens, and we feel disappointed or jealous from another's actions. Or we feel overwhelmed, criticized, or ignored in a vulnerable moment. Watch out; kindness flies out the window, quickly replaced by hot anger, harsh judgment, seething resentment, or mean words we soon regret.

When did "kind" become a dirty word?

Kindness Is One Breath, One Choice Away

Kind thoughts, words, and acts are always just one breath away. No matter what is happening, we can whisper, "I choose kindness now."

Kindness is a talisman, a lucky charm in our purse or back pocket, handy at a moment's notice. To watch our breath and label thoughts "thinking" for ten, twenty, or thirty minutes a day is more than just a meditative practice. It is one of the kindest gifts we can give ourselves. Even if someone is yelling angrily at us, we can take a deep breath and respond with kindness. Even if our spouse is scared about money, and they are blaming us for our financial situation, we can choose kindness—for both ourselves and for them. During the worst conflicts, we can sink into our wise heart and respond with kindness.

Loving-kindness is our true nature. Along with joy, compassion, and inner peace, it is one of the four unlimited qualities forming who we are in our core. It is respecting our bodies, our feelings, and our hearts *enough* to listen to their needs. It is enjoying the daily process of reaching our goals with ease, joy, and inner peace. A dash of kindness, placed carefully amid all of our striving, can upgrade our quality of life.

Kindness comes in countless shapes and sizes. For Karen, who rides the disappointment roller coaster each month when she finds out she's *not* pregnant yet at forty, kind patience allays countless doubts and fears. For Tina, who struggles with her weight and back pain, kindness morphs into self-care by getting up a half hour early each morning to run on the treadmill and strengthen her core muscles.

For Dave, kindness is turning guilt into forgiveness for ignoring his wife's needs the past thirty years. "When I remember," he said,

"I stop beating myself up for never seeing my sexist arrogance all those years and forgive myself." For Bonnie, kind words bolster her self-worth with "I'm free to speak my truth to protect my seven-year-old daughter" when she faces her ex-husband's bullying ways in family therapy. For Bob, kindness is loving the anxiety in his chest rather than unleashing it on his wife. For myself, after being sick two weeks, it is resting on the couch every other day rather than launching myself back into daily hiking.

The Power of Generosity Begins with Ourselves

Kindness practice begins at home. Through the power of generosity, kindness is pausing five times amid a busy day to ask, "What am I feeling now?" and welcoming the answer. It is setting a morning intention: "I'm willing to treat myself and others with kindness today." It is taking three deep breaths before responding to anything ego hears as judgment, criticism, fear, or doubt.

As we mature, kindness is slowing down enough to be aware of who we are *now*, and what we feel and need *now*. It is voicing our needs like a broken record, speaking up as many times as it takes to feel heard without giving up—on our needs or another's capacity to hear us. Flexibility and acceptance pave the way for all this to go smoothly.

When we stay present and connected with the feelings and needs in our body, or when we experience our feelings free of story, we see our human predicament through clear, kind eyes. Such honest seeing allows us to soften those "You stupid idiot" judgments that come with a mistake into "It's okay. You're human and humans make mistakes. Just learn from it and let it go." If we wake up sick, we can flip ego's "You'll never get this project done" into "I have plenty of time to nurture myself back to health and finish the project." Exchanging judgments for reassuring words polishes the rough edges of any diamond, even our own.

Cultivating Kindness with Simple Morning Phrases

In Buddhism, loving-kindness is practiced with specific phrases. Many of us can begin our day by spending a few minutes, after a morning meditation or prayer time, repeating to ourselves, "May I be filled with loving-kindness. May I be safe from inner and outer danger. May I be happy and healthy in body and mind. May I live with ease and joy and well-being in this world." These simple but powerful phrases plant seeds of kindness. As we water them with daily repetition, they remind us of our basic goodness amid challenges. When starting out it's best to focus kindness on ourselves.

When we feel ready, we expand our kindness circle by cultivating loving-kindness toward a mentor or teacher who greatly benefited our life: "May you be filled with loving-kindness. May you be safe from inner and outer danger. May you be happy and healthy in body and mind. May you live with ease and joy and well-being in this world." If an elder is facing illness or death, we can say phrases specific to their needs.

After a few weeks, we include loved ones in our practice by saying their name—"May John be filled with loving-kindness. May he be free of inner and outer danger"—and so forth as we stated for ourselves. We expand the circle further by including friends, neighbors, and acquaintances in our kindness circle.

The hardest step is practicing loving-kindness for someone we dislike or who hurt or wronged us somehow. But as we include even these individuals in our practice, our heart softens, and we begin to see even their basic goodness that ego, for its own sake, has blinded us to, resisted, or denied. Finally, as with compassion, we include all beings. "May I and all beings be filled with loving-kindness. May I and all beings be free of inner and outer danger. May I and all beings be happy and healthy in body and mind. May I and all beings live with ease and joy and well-being in the world."

Midway through my morning hike, I say, "May I, my loved ones, friends, and all beings, including the elk, deer, and coyote I share the trail with, be happy, healthy, and free."

Kindness Toward Ourselves Takes Courage

Whether we admit it or not, we are all tender, sensitive, vulnerable human beings. Our feelings get hurt so easily. Our good intentions become misconstrued so often, we slip inside an invisible cocoon of hopeless discouragement without noticing it. After all, if we're truly honest, we are like turtles without shells in the big world, with one added drawback—we know our life could be snuffed out any moment. Equally as bad, we know our beloved mate or dear parents could devastate us by suddenly disappointing us, abandoning us, or dying. No wonder we cling so tight to anything ego promises that looks remotely secure.

Underneath working, parenting, exercising, and earning accolades to cover up this tender vulnerability, we are afraid—afraid to trust ourselves or love or life; afraid to believe that there is room in this world for us to be who we really are; afraid to care too much for fear of being called a sissy, or worse; afraid to dive into love and wind up in the middle of the lake alone, another fool who took the bait. Bottom line, no matter how rarely we admit it, we are afraid of being hurt. We hide behind cell phones and other devices, work, exercise, and TV—anything to avoid feeling our feelings and speaking our truth. This is why we jumped in bed with ego in the first place—to uncover strategies to avoid pain.

Kindness toward ourselves is accepting our vulnerability and acting accordingly. As we age, kindness is slowing down to reach today's finish line healthy, not exhausted. It is pausing amid a busy day to listen to our body, our feelings, and our heart-felt needs. It is practicing kind speech by flipping "I'll never find love" on its head, like a pancake, into "I love myself, wrinkles and all, and I trust the universe's timing on finding love."

After we devote ten minutes each morning to cultivating loving-kindness, we need to see throughout the day what our *real practice* is. Do we practice kindness, or do we respond in the same fearful, judgmental ways we always have?

Personally, I spent the last two weeks rebuilding my stamina from a sinus infection. Now I'm ready to cross-country ski at 11,000 feet and get my daily hike with the elk and coyote. After all, it's a balmy forty degrees in early March. Warm sun calls me outside to play. But I can't. I tweaked my left knee falling through soft snow while skiing last Sunday. Not the way I pictured this morning going. As someone committed to health, I hate being sick or injured. Personally, I feel angry, sad, and discouraged—anything but kind in this moment. I feel royally picked on by the powers that be.

Aging is the crash course in kindness, forcing us to listen to our bodies before the symptom gets louder. My ego rants non-stop, blaming me for this predicament: "If you took better care of yourself and ate everything organic, you'd be strong by now. You shouldn't be this exhausted from just writing a book and seeing clients—you must have cancer. If only you'd worn your knee support skiing, you'd be hiking today." Ego really knows how to kick us when we are down.

To choose kindness over discouragement takes great courage.

Kindness is the advanced course in presence. When we call on kindness, the first thing it does is submerge our pain in a spacious pond of loving-kindness, a pond that is always available to us. This allows us to spend a few moments softening, opening, and accepting our predicament just as it is. No, we never expected this particular struggle and may not wish this on our worst enemy. But right now, in this present moment where all the power always is, we can lighten our load by saying "yes" to what is.

My knee still requires ice. My strength is taking longer to recover from illness than ego tells me it should. But holding my situation in acceptance makes it tolerable. Today, like most days, will look different than my ego thinks it ought to.

Kindness is sticking with our morning intention to be kind today, even when life's ups and downs escalate into hurricanes. Most importantly, kindness is asking ourselves, "Does my heart really need all this protecting? Or is my heart built to handle hurt, loss, discouragement, and even the truth?"

For instance, when Joan's husband died unexpectedly during heart surgery, she jumped into staying busy. After all, tending the family hogs and cows and endless chores is how she survived—and avoided—her abusive alcoholic mother as a child. But after two years of colds and pneumonia, Joan chose the kind action: facing her grief.

"Mom was so angry all the time, to cover up her drinking, that she never taught any of us four girls about sex, periods, or how women care for their bodies. Now at forty-eight, I'm learning to slow down, trust my feelings, and take a damn bath." For Joan, kindness came in the form of self-care. "The more I get to know my feminine qualities," she said, "the healthier I feel."

Kindness is a conscious choice as fresh as today's just-plucked oranges. A wake-up call may arrive on our doorstep at any moment, any season, any age, inviting us to stop hiding and running away from feelings or life.

At thirty-four, when her father died in a head-on collision, Tiffany woke up to her own mortality. She left her stale marriage, dropped fifty pounds, and moved across country to start a new life away from a controlling extended family. Sara had a pattern of ditching lovers before they ever reached a two-year anniversary. She finally saw the truth that she was habitually running away before her partners could see how "messed up" she was. For her, kindness included getting sober and loving all aspects of herself.

Whether it is through a painful life event or years of meditation or therapy, somewhere along the way, our hiding and covering up becomes crystal clear; finally, we feel ready to let our vulnerable self be seen and heard.

Crossing the Line into Basic Goodness

Somewhere, somehow, when we least expect it, we cross an invisible line. We wake up, as if from a dream, and the fog of reacting those same old ways lifts. Our values and priorities shift. We see the preciousness of life clearly.

On the other side of this line, we still argue with our spouse, children, and coworkers. We still eat, sleep, exercise, and play in our free time. We still experience disappointment, fear, grief, shame, doubt, and judgment—all the perks of being human.

Once we cross this line, though, we discover what Buddha called our basic goodness. This bottomless well abounding with patience, understanding, generosity, and wisdom is our true nature. As pure and untouched as a high mountain stream, it remains undaunted by the hurts, losses, and wounds we suffer in life. This basic goodness burns away the fog and shines a kind heart on all we encounter. In coming to know fear, anxiety, and despair clearly, we stop allowing those monsters hiding under our bed or in our basement from overstaying their welcome and running our lives.

No longer needing to avoid any feeling, freedom expands into the open space.

Once we stop pressuring ourselves constantly to improve (implying we're never good enough), basic goodness warms us like sunshine with kind thoughts, words, and actions.

Cheryl ditched her basic goodness years ago in favor of her driving ambition and her many accomplishments. She felt proud for holding a PhD in a male-dominated field, architecture, and for being the youngest senior partner and only female in her architectural firm. She eats healthily, jogs daily, and last year, she designed and built her dream home.

But at forty-five, home alone every night, she drinks a bottle of cabernet to cope with depression. When I suggested she try to feel kindness toward her feelings, she sneered.

"I never got where I am in this man's world by wallowing in feelings," Cheryl said. "Feelings are just a waste of time—time I don't have if I want to make senior partner."

But since antidepressants failed her, she agreed to spend thirty seconds five times a day asking herself, "What am I feeling?" Kindness practice can begin small.

Two weeks later, she said, "It is probably sheer coincidence. But ever since I acknowledged my depression in the daytime, it stopped waking me at night."

"Let's name what the depression asks you to give yourself," I suggested.

"Stop work. Lie down. Stop being productive—all the things I hate," she shouted angrily. "I can't do a damn thing when it strikes but drink or lie down with my eyes closed and hope the hell it leaves soon. I just wish it would go away."

"While you are lying down," I said, "are you willing to practice kindness?"

"I guess it can't hurt, but I'm not a touchy-feely type. Don't push me."

The following week, whenever depression forced her to lie down, Cheryl practiced her own customized version of loving-kindness. "May I and my dog Putts be happy, healthy, free of danger, and filled with loving-kindness."

Cheryl's curiosity was sparked. "It's odd, but I feel a childlike innocence that got buried years ago. I'm slowing down, smiling, and playing more often with Putts. I don't want you turning me into mush, but I actually felt less depressed this week."

"Yes, underneath all the pressure you put on yourself to achieve," I said, "your basic goodness inside is waiting to reconnect you with your kind heart. Once you let your kind heart and high achiever coexist, the depression can leave."

"I have no time for foolishness. But if it ends depression, I'm game."

Two weeks later, Cheryl looked so refreshed, I barely recognized her.

"How is your loving-kindness practice coming?" I asked.

"Too bad you can't bottle and market this stuff. You'd make millions. I'm not a Buddhist and never will be, but every time my depression appears, I pause and tell myself, 'May I be happy, healthy, and filled with loving-kindness, free of danger.' Hell, don't tell my boss, but I even include him and his heart condition in my practice. I'm sleeping and feeling so great that wine stopped tasting as good. My associates tease me that I must be getting some great sex to be this happy and productive.

"Last weekend," she continued, "I got on my mountain bike for the first time since college. If this is basic goodness, I'll order thirty every month, one for each day please."

Our basic goodness is that open, trusting, wise innocence we entered this world with. It remains undaunted by any pain or rejection we have suffered. It melts the clouds of judgment, fear, anxiety, and despair we adopted years ago to earn full membership into the inner sanctuary of our family and culture. We can trust it, lean into it, and respond to life from its perspective. Our basic goodness meets all difficulties with a kind, generous, loving heart. It helps open our eyes to see the perfection of each moment just as it is.

When we meet our own human dilemmas with basic goodness, it becomes easier to respond to loved ones with this same kind presence and respect.

Holding a Loving Space for Loved Ones

Listening attentively is one of the kindest gifts we can give anyone.

Kindness is giving someone our full, uninterrupted attention with no agenda or personal reaction of our own. It is dropping our anger, jealousy, and resentment—everything unlike love. From the open space of our basic goodness, we can understand how another person might feel so unhappy without making their feelings about me. This selfless attention takes practice.

First of all, kindness requires a warm, generous spirit. Each morning we start with an intention: "I'm willing to choose kindness toward myself and loved ones today." Kindness asks us to be an open loving space to hold others' feelings in acceptance and understanding.

Like water running down a hill, defensive and sarcastic reactions take no thought or effort. But giving our ego free license to react, in the end, destroys relationships. Responding with kindness when a loved one is contracted in anger or fear truly takes courage.

As we set down ego's reactions, we freely witness a loved one's fears and reactions unfolding before our eyes as ego's drama—not a representation of who they are. Able to see our own ego stories as just stories, our kind heart understands that the unkind words and acts of loved ones as they struggle to voice their feelings are nothing personal.

In my work with couples, I call this "holding a loving space." When our mate is contracted due to old wounds and core beliefs, overreacting, our job is to drop all personal responses and feed back only the words they expressed, such as "I hear how depressed and sad you feel." Or we might just say, "I hear you. Tell me more."

The instant we drop ego's need to aggressively push and shove to get our way, we surrender into what wants to happen. We begin holding a loving space for others to feel whatever they feel deeply by simply being open and present. Our silent attention invites a loved one's truth to unfold, however clumsily or defensively they began. Kindness requires far more acceptance, understanding, and patience than we ever thought we could muster.

At forty-one, five years into her second marriage, Marie thinks about leaving daily. She even has divorce papers in her desk drawer. "Living alone is looking better and better," Marie chuckled. "We live like roommates, barely tolerating each other. At first, his great listening skills were one big reason I married him. But now, on his way from the front door to the TV at night, he sucks on a beer rather than kiss me. I have two choices: I can resign myself to a boring, lonely life with Jon, or I can pick up my toys and start over."

"You both have your parts in letting the marriage fall apart," I said. "Would you be willing to bring Jon in for couple's therapy to learn good listening skills?"

"It's no use," she rebutted. "He always hears my feelings as criticism."

"Sometimes," I said, "with a threat of divorce, men suddenly listen better."

Reluctantly, Marie brought Jon the following week for couple's therapy. After explaining the importance of kindness and listening attentively without interruption or personal input, Jon agreed to listen first.

Marie figured she had nothing to lose, so in this safe setting she shared the feelings she had never risked sharing before. "A few months after we married, Jon, when my mother died suddenly, you expressed great understanding during the funeral. But a few weeks after the funeral, when the reality of Mom's death was really hitting me hard, you yelled, 'How long do I have to keep dealing with your mother's death?' I felt so shocked and devastated; I've been scared to openly share my feelings with you ever since. Inside, I wondered why I married such a selfish, moody man.

"I think about divorce every day," she said. "I don't know if my heart can open again."

As Jon listened silently, he began to weep. "I am so, so sorry that

I was so rude five years ago. My parents fought constantly and never apologized or forgave anyone. But I ask you to please forgive me and let me show you how I love you."

Jon rushed to hold Marie in his arms and they held each other tight. "I know I've been a lousy listener, hiding behind my beer and TV. But I do hear how hurt, scared, and hopeless you feel. I knew something was wrong. I was scared to address it."

Both left that day committing to be honest, open, and kind with each other. Over the next few months, they took baby steps. Jon stopped drinking, which meant a great deal to Marie. They set aside thirty minutes each evening to share and hear each other's feelings, which slowly rebuilt the trust they had lost. Jon practiced loving-kindness toward himself and Marie every morning before work, which helped him hold a loving space for Marie without taking it as criticism when she shared her tender feelings. Hope replaced hopelessness. Kindness replaced judgment.

Marie changed her core belief from childhood, "Nobody cares about my feelings," into "I love and care about my own feelings, *and* I teach Jon how to open to and hear them." As they held a loving space for each other to share the fears, hurts, and resentments built up over five years, trust slowly returned. Marie finally arrived in that place in her heart where she could forgive Jon around her mother's death.

In our last session, Jon said, "The more I shut up and listen, the more Marie shares secrets I've never heard. We've grown so adept at talking about the old fear stories we used to tell in our heads; now we laugh out loud at fears that used to paralyze us. When we ride horses together, we laugh at our fears all the way back to the stable."

Kindness includes our willingness to step, brand new, into the present with understanding and forgiveness, despite past hurts. It includes a willingness to start over, letting go of resentments again and again. It includes dropping ego's "he'll never" and "she won't" stories in our head to see fresh possibilities each moment, whether we are five, ten, twenty, or forty years into a relationship.

Kindness is resisting ego's compulsion to ask, "*Why* are you so sad?" Instead, our kind, loving heart mirrors back to our loved one "I hear how sad you feel," because it knows that, no matter how it looks or sounds or why it's there, another's grief is always about the other person—not us.

Kindness Includes Exposing Our Unconscious Habits

Daily meditation and prayer, along with spiritual readings and a daily intention to choose kindness, reveal the illusions and core beliefs driving our unconscious actions. But confessing these unconscious culprits to others takes sheer guts. It can feel scary and embarrassing to be this honest with our spouse, parent, or loved one, but sharing vulnerability rekindles closeness. When we finally see how past fears and hurts drive our actions, forcing us to withdraw love, kindness nudges us toward right speech and right action; what we express and how we express it reflects our willingness and capacity for healing.

Rather than withholding our truth, we can create a safe container for it by asking for our mate's undivided attention. Once they are listening, we might say, "I have something hard to share, so I need you to listen attentively without interrupting. I can see now that my fear of rejection sabotaged our lovemaking the past six months. The rejection story in my head makes up various versions of, 'If I open my heart to you while we're making love and really expose how tender and vulnerable I am, you'll find me unmanly and reject me.' To avoid feeling devastated, I hide my feelings. But then you never get to see who I really am."

Ego fears that such confessions will destroy the love. In fact, they only deepen our closeness. When we describe our actions from a kind heart, miracles happen. Our deeper truth invites others to share their deep truth from this tender, vulnerable place.

Kim arrived home feeling joyful after a ten-day meditation retreat. Instantly hit with the brick wall of her stale marriage, she decided to open up and share the revelations about herself that came during her loving-kindness practice.

"Hey Tom! Do you have a sec? I have something to tell you," she called to her husband, who was out working in their garden. He came inside and sat down, frowning. Because he was used to Kim acting distant toward him, Tom was skeptical about what his wife was up to this time.

"I fear you won't like what I have to say," she said. "But it feels so tender and fragile to me, since I saw it myself at retreat, that I just need you to listen.

"After the first three days of loving-kindness practice in sitting meditation, I continued wishing me and you and everyone health, happiness, and freedom from danger. It's hard to admit, but practicing loving-kindness toward you felt like swallowing a bitter pill. I am so resentful for having to make all the major decisions for both of us all these years, I could barely include you in my meditation.

"Then one morning on my walking meditation, an epiphany came over me. As if I was watching a movie, I saw how my trying to control you must have given you the message that I didn't trust you. No wonder you avoided me. I had to sit down and weep. Movie frames of my dad controlling my every move growing up streamed before me. I felt how his control made me lack confidence in my decision-making."

Through deep breaths and tears, Kim said, "I deeply, deeply apologize. I was so busy these past twenty years struggling to come up with the 'right' answer, so mistrusting of you and myself, that

I missed all the ways you love me. I hope someday you'll forgive me." Tom patiently listened as Kim went on bravely exposing her unconscious habits.

"The first forty years of my life, I never trusted anyone. I never knew what trust looked like or realized it was missing. I don't know how to trust. But maybe if I practice my loving-kindness practice each morning and set my new intention, 'I'm willing to trust myself and Tom and the present moment,' my fear of making a mistake will lessen."

After sincerely thanking Kim for admitting her part in their dissatisfying marriage, Tom told his wife that he too had realized some things while Kim was on retreat.

"I never took your needs seriously," he said. "My father taught me to *show* love to women by working hard, remodeling the kitchen, or building a garden. He said feelings were a waste of time, something to avoid at all costs. But while you were gone, I saw that listening to your needs and feelings is how I make you *feel* loved. All these years, while I ignored your feelings and needs, you felt unloved and unimportant." Understanding that her own sharing had opened up a softer, more tender dialogue than she'd ever known, Kim listened intently and felt deep gratitude for her husband's generous display of kindness.

"While you attempted a zillion times to teach me your needs, I ran out of the house to show my love through chores. But while you were gone on retreat, I missed you horribly. I feel deeply ashamed for cheating you, and me, out of the love we could have had these past twenty years. I'm committed to honoring your feelings and needs with kindness."

Tenderly, Tom and Kim held each other and agreed to begin fresh.

When we find the courage to share our inner secrets, closeness prevails.

After tapping into the basic goodness and unlimited kindness we are born with, it grows easier to see all of our mistakes and short-comings as part of the shared human struggle to wake up free, in harmony with our unconditioned self.

Kindness flows naturally, deeply respecting what it means to be human.

Respecting the Wisdom of Our Kind Heart

As we practice listening attentively to loved ones, it behooves us to also listen to—and trust—the visionary wisdom pouring forth from our own hearts every day. Curiosity jostles awake the gems of wisdom buried inside back pain, illness, and migraines. Depression demands our attention and forces us to switch directions away from avoidance tactics and toward kind attention. But when a lovely dream pulls us out of the doldrums, or a longing to live by the ocean repeatedly fills our thoughts, these bits of heart wisdom can guide us in new directions.

At seventy-nine, following heart surgery, Ralph found himself depressed for the first time in his life. A busy man cramming each waking moment with grandchildren, daily walks, weekly choir practice, and world travels, he said, "I'm shocked that anyone as active and positive as me could ever get depressed." But in therapy he learned that "busy" left no time to listen to his heart. "Once I started spending thirty minutes a day breathing deeply and asking my heart what it had to tell me, the depression gradually packed its bags and left. I can't explain it, but I love my quiet time now." Like an internal rudder, our kind heart gently nudges us at each junction toward health, happiness, and freedom.

Our kind heart showers timeless wisdom like an endless fountain of possibility day after day, week after week, year after year until one day we do embrace the unlimited joy, kindness, compassion, and inner peace that we are in our core. One day, we step beyond the fog of doubt and fear, judgment and delusion into the lush green field of our birthright, basic goodness. Finally we chuckle to ourselves, "*Oh*, that's what I need to learn from these lovers that keep leaving me or the promotion I can't get." What relief. What joy and freedom.

Our timeless heart can wait forever for us to learn lessons.

Our heart is far more than an organ pumping blood through our veins and arteries. Whether we are seven, seventeen, thirty-seven, or sixty-seven, our heart is conscious awareness noticing everything all the time: what is true, what feelings and core beliefs are reacting to what is true, how those around us are reacting, and the deeper lesson this experience is bringing us. When we listen, our kind heart reminds us that we are safe to bask in the sacred miracles present in ordinary life.

Our kind heart calls out to us every day, several times a day, whispering its infinite wisdom. If we are smart, we will listen attentively and respond with respect.

Now is the time for our ego to take its rightful place, serving our heart.

Kindness toward our heart begins with honoring and respecting its wisdom. It begins with sitting quietly with our feelings and heartfelt longings, with naming and accepting them.

Teaming up with our kind heart gives us the courage to make a deep commitment to well-being, a commitment to drop hurt and create anew the loving self-relationship we want now. Possibly for the first time we trust life enough to stand up for what we believe in and voice our truth. Despite fear's voice of caution, kindness teaches us that there is room in this universe for us to live our dreams.

John started listening to his heart in his late fifties. A gifted naturopath, he relieves symptoms and teaches patients how to keep their heart, lungs, digestion, and immune systems healthy. A strong, gentle man by nature, he has done this tirelessly for over thirty years. And with alimony payments to his ex-wife, two children in private colleges, and a baby on the way with his second wife, he needs to work. His countless responsibilities leave no room for self-care.

But last winter, when John contracted pneumonia, he realized the high price he paid for never listening to his own heart. John's full recovery involved healing his childhood abuse and changing a core belief that perpetuated unhealthy choices.

"Whenever I didn't do *exactly* what Dad wanted, he hit me with a belt," John said in therapy. "But watching him hit my oldest sister when I was too young and weak to do anything hurt much worse. That belt taught me that never, under any circumstances, are my needs important. From five years old on, my needs didn't exist. I spent my childhood either pleasing or avoiding my father. Now, pushing sixty, I'm super responsible but have no skill at asking for or even knowing what I want."

Hearing his hopelessness, I spoke directly to the wisdom of his heart. "If you could give yourself whatever you want or long for, and if you knew your wife, children, and patients would support it, what would you give yourself?"

Slowly, John's truth found a voice. "When I was lying in bed with pneumonia, I noticed a longing that I've had off and on for years, a longing to take a whole month off work for myself—not to go on a family vacation but to wake up each morning and ask myself what *I* felt like doing that day. I never even did that as a kid. Years ago I convinced myself I could never do that until I retire. My patients, our baby on the way, my financial obligations…"

"Stop right there," I said. "This is exactly how you talk yourself out of taking care of yourself and your own needs. This is how you perpetuate your core belief from childhood that there's no room for your needs. But before you dismiss your wise, heart-felt longing that's been trying to get your attention for years, would you at least be willing to look in the mirror and say it out loud to yourself?"

Looking into his own eyes in the mirror, John began to cry and said his longing out loud. That night, after dinner, he told his wife Janet that he wanted to take a month off work for his own health. She freaked out at first, mumbling about money. But as he explained how, for his entire life, he had felt unable to address his own needs, her fear turned to compassion. She calculated their savings and, together, they picked the month of March. His patients, ex-wife, and grown children not only supported his need but respected him for vocalizing it.

When I saw John after his time off, he looked peaceful, like a different man.

"Instead of believing there's never room for my needs," he said, "I let myself out of prison by telling myself daily, 'There is *always* room for my needs, no matter what is going on around me.' I'm planning to take March off every year."

As we trust the longings, symptoms, and clues from our kind heart, we stay on course and create the whole life we deserve.

Our heart constantly calls us awake to *this* precious, sacred moment.

Our kind heart is open, allowing, surrendering. It receives life on life's terms. It lives in the here and now, basking in the abundant freedom and joy of each ordinary moment. It finds happiness with the most mundane aspects of life because it knows happiness is always present, no matter what external turmoil goes on around us. There is nothing the kind heart needs to get or have or keep from this world in order to be happy. In its infinite wisdom, it knows that joy, love, compassion, and inner peace are always right here at our fingertips. It trusts the innate perfection of each moment.

In a million ways, our heart invites us to choose kindness again and again.

When we surrender—when we step fully into *this* moment, *this* love relationship, *this* opportunity to be fully awake and alive—our heart takes the wheel. Finally, we pause long enough to see the miracles of this present moment, free of thoughts, plans, and busyness. Finally, we really see the rain falling outside the window, see the kind, loving compassion in our beloved's eyes and really feel the magic and beauty that is present, always.

Our kind heart whispers to us constantly, calling us back into this body, this heart, this breath, this precious love affair with life just as it is, right here and now. It reminds us that we have nowhere else to be and nothing more important to do.

There is no greater wisdom than our own wise, kind heart.

Kindness as a Way of Being

The more we choose kindness day to day, it becomes our way of being.

By telling ourselves, each morning, "I'm willing to be kind to myself and others today," we set the wheels of kindness in motion. Throughout the day, kindness appears just when we need it. With practice, we discover that kindness really is our true nature. As the clouds of fear, judgment, resentment, and illusion part, kindness shines forth as our natural way of being. With time and commitment, we grow to respond to ourselves, loved ones, strangers, and to life with the kind heart we were all born with.

Cultivating kindness is like planting a flower garden. We mulch ego's incessant thoughts down into rich fertilizer for planting petunias, delphiniums, and geraniums. We water the fresh seeds and young shoots daily by gifting ourselves, our loved ones, and all beings with loving-kindness. We routinely weed out the countless fears and judgments that masquerade as wisdom, including those deeply ingrained either/or thoughts: "*Either* do what everyone else is doing to fit in, *or* foolishly follow your irrational heart."

Just as we trust the tiny flower seeds to grow and blossom, we begin to trust kindness to blossom in our thoughts, our words, our actions, and our lives. The key is holding an intention in our heart to choose kindness everyday.

As kindness flows, life takes on a playful tone. We experience joy and bliss more often. As angst and frustration come and go, we smile inside at the happiness, joy, and inner peace standing in the background, quietly reminding us who we really are.

We grow up. We wake up. With kindness, we become that person in the room we were all hoping for—the one exuding kindness, patience, understanding, and love.

Heart Tools for Kindness

Practice each of these tools for one week before moving on to the next one. But if a specific tool calls you to spend more time with it, give yourself another week, month, or as long as you need in order to heal.

1. *Cultivating Loving-Kindness as a Morning Practice*

No matter how you start your day, spend five minutes generating seeds of loving-kindness. Begin with yourself; repeat the phrases "May I be filled with loving-kindness. May I be free of inner and outer danger. May I be happy and healthy. May I live with ease and joy in this world." Even if you feel silly or self-conscious, do it for two weeks and notice how you feel. If you suffer from back pain, headaches, or anxiety, customize the practice to fit your immediate need: "May I be free of back pain and enjoy a healthy, happy, pain-free body." After two weeks, include a mentor: "May_____, who taught me so much in life, and I be filled with loving-kindness. May _____ and I be happy and healthy and live with ease and joy in this world." Every week, include a new loved one, friend, acquaintance, stranger, and enemy until you arrive at

"May I and all beings be filled with loving-kindness." If you have only a few seconds, simply say, "May I and all beings be happy, healthy, and free."

2. *Expanding Kindness Toward Yourself*
Before getting out of bed, place both hands over your heart and continue kindness with a daily intention: "I'm willing to notice ego's habitual reactions today and choose kindness instead." Repeat this five times to dismiss your inner skeptic and go about your day. When fear, anger, disappointment, or pain arises, see even this as an opportunity to practice kindness. Evenings, as you crawl in bed, take a few moments to acknowledge your kind acts that day. Be as kind as you can to yourself with such loving, reassuring phrases as "I see you. I love you. I understand you." Take baby steps across that line and reconnect with your basic goodness.

3. *Broadening Kindness Toward Loved Ones*
Broaden your morning intention to say, "I'm willing to choose kindness toward myself and loved ones today." As conflicts arise, practice listening attentively and feeding back the main points and feeling words you heard. Whenever you see clearly how your own unconscious habits have sabotaged closeness with your lover, spouse, or child, invite them to listen without interruption while you share your tender, vulnerable truth. It might sound like, "I see now that my need to control, hide, stay busy, avoid sex, or withdraw love has created distance between us. I apologize. I hope someday you find it in your heart to forgive me."

4. *Practicing Kindness Toward Your Heart*
Begin by paying attention to heart-felt longings and intuitive hunches as they flit through your awareness. Journal about longings and dreams to make them more real. Breathe life and motion

into special dreams and goals by acting them out in your living room. Even when dreams and longings make no logical sense, pay attention. Try it on. See if your body feels more peaceful, joyful, and spacious with it joining your life. Before fear kills your dream (as it has countless ones) by asking snidely, "But how will you ever pull that off?" bring kindness to the table. Inquire softly, "How might this longing or dream relate to my current life?" Ask during your morning meditation or walk how this repeated longing might fit into your current life. It doesn't matter how or when you ask, but ask. Honor and respect your heart's direct line to universal wisdom. Watch kindness become your new way of being.

7. Your Grateful Heart
The Power of Appreciation

To be grateful is in itself a blessing and an open door to joy ...
You might even, as Albert Einstein suggests, begin to see
that everything around you is a miracle.
—JAMES BARAZ AND SHOSHANA ALEXANDER, *Awakening Joy*

I feel steeped in deep gratitude and grace this July Monday. The peacefulness bursting in every cell of my body feels untouchable, as if I could never again be ruffled by anything. Yesterday my love of nature entered a heavenly realm. A herd of two hundred elk—mamas, babies, and young males with fuzzy antlers—stampeded past me so close that I felt the ground shake under my feet from the weight and strength of their powerful bodies. This precious moment will live inside my grateful heart forever.

We'd woken up at six on Sunday morning to hike in the San Juan Mountains above tree line, above 11,000 feet, before afternoon thunderstorms and dangerous lightning arrived. For four hours my heart felt drenched in the peak summer blossoms of lavender and white columbine (Colorado's state flower), neon pink Perry's primrose, and purple fringe—three wildflowers that only grow near creeks. Later, meadows of magenta Indian paintbrush and mountainsides of tiny bluebells stretched as far as the eye could see.

When my friend and I sat atop a rocky ridge to eat our turkey sandwiches, we spotted twenty-five female elk grazing in the meadow below with their frisky babies. As a nature lover who adores the quiet feminine strength of elk, I felt truly blessed.

But this elk sighting is not all of why I feel steeped in gratitude.

After lunch, as we stood to leave, we heard hooves running in the distance. I looked over my right shoulder to spot a huge brown female elk running full speed toward me. I looked into her eyes, and she into mine, as if we looked directly into each other's souls. She leapt to her right, midair, steering her entire herd of two hundred males and females away from us by eight or ten feet.

My friend and I squatted behind a short ponderosa pine, our mouths agape. Two hundred huge elk breezed past us as one dark brown blurry body with the grace of a flock of geese. They looked straight ahead, dutifully running toward the ancient yet familiar call of their elder grandmother. Baby elk, barely three feet tall, baring the round spots of youth on their backs, panted hard as they strained their gangly legs in order to stay by Mother's side. Though it lasted only ten minutes, this sacred gift from nature exploded into a timeless eternity that altered us both for several hours after.

Even as I write this the day after, tears of gratitude fill my eyes.

Gratitude for What Is—Not Just What We Want

I love glimpsing wildlife in its habitat. It helps me touch my own animal nature—that place of pure joy inside all of us bursting from what we see, hear, and touch in the now.

In such moments, gratitude arises spontaneously. It is easy to feel grateful for things we love. Gratitude overflows when we fall in love (every single time), hold our newborn baby, make a new friend, visit old friends, celebrate graduation, or earn a raise. When recovering from serious illness or surgery, we feel grateful just to be alive. Gratitude flows naturally when things unfold in our favor.

But what about those other 364 days of the year? Can we stretch our notion of gratitude to include moments ego doesn't like? Are we willing to align with our heart that feels grateful even when we feel sick, hurt, lonely, rejected, or out of sorts? Can we allow our grateful heart to point to the joyful wisdom inside *all* of life's gifts?

Too often we use up our words in complaining, wishing our spouse, work, or child were somehow different and better. Too often we withhold every morsel of gratitude for a good spouse until it's too late—after they've ditched us. Or, likewise, we forget to be grateful for our health until we've lost it.

At work, petty grudges and competition can rob from us decades of gratitude for the opportunity work affords us in serving others. Even with our children, we can get so caught up in the daily hassles and pressures of parenting that real gratitude for blessed moments comes after they leave home.

To our ego, it makes no logical sense to be grateful for illness, pain, loss, or change. But tucked inside each life experience is a kernel of truth and wisdom that can help us mature into kind, compassionate, forgiving human beings. Gratitude comes with time.

Just before biking the Ride the Rockies tour for his tenth year in a row, Jake injured his knee. As he lay in bed icing his knee, realizing the seven-day ride he loved was not going to happen this year, several choice four-letter words spewed out through gritted teeth. But weeks later, after healing enough to do short rides, he admitted, "Slowing down helped me see how I'd been neglecting my lover for months." Inside the injury he first despised, Jake found opportunities for healing his knee and his relationship.

When Pat's fiancé tired of her complaining and called off the engagement, she realized that, in the stress of wedding planning, she had forgotten to appreciate how understanding, patient, and attentive her partner Todd was. Quickly, she stepped into deep gratitude, both for Todd and for the opportunity to see how she had lost focus on what truly mattered. When they married last June, she was able to enjoy some of the hidden fruits of gratitude in a renewed closeness with her husband.

My friend Anna stormed into her first appointment with her new cardiologist declaring, "I refuse to take drugs. I'll lower my cholesterol naturally or not at all." But once the doctor told Anna that, at fifty-seven, she was not far from a massive stroke, she leapt into gratitude. "I thanked her for finding the problem and knowing a solution."

When Erin heard her husband say, "I want a divorce," gratitude was the last thing on her mind. "I always dreaded the idea of parenting alone," she said. "But one year later, I like living alone, not having to share my bed or closet, not fighting with someone who no longer loves me. I never pictured myself as a single parent, but I'm grateful to be out of an unhealthy marriage that affords me more quality time with my girls."

Whenever disappointment, illness, pain, or conflict enters our world, gratitude is seldom our first reaction. As we know, ego instantly judges anything we might not like. For example, Erin's fear of parenting alone appeared first, calling up many fears, negative beliefs, and feelings. But most of these melted into gratitude as Erin stayed present in her new life. When presence and curiosity help us watch for ego's latest version of "You won't like being alone or rejected, and you should avoid change at all cost," we can drop ego's distracting stories and choose gratitude, even for the changes we never wanted.

The Power of Appreciation Holds Secret Powers

Seeing the moment of today exactly as it is, appreciation transforms a bad day into a good one without changing our outer circumstances one bit. The power of appreciation wakes us up out of our favorite victim stupor and shows us how to create the relationship we dream about.

Gratitude trusts that the same wisdom that keeps our heart beating and lungs breathing is bringing us a gift right now, if only we open ourselves to receive it.

On her sixtieth birthday, Alice started therapy. "My body tortures me," she began. "I have arthritis in my left hip, and the doctor says I'll need knee replacement surgery within the next year." But once Alice shifted into gratitude, she began listening to the loving message coming through her hip and knee. "My whole life I've put lovers, children, and family first. The only time I stopped to rest was when my hip or knee hurt. Now that I listen to my body, I stop pushing at the first sign of pain and ask my family to help cook dinner. I'm happier. My body is happier. Even my family is happier."

No matter what feelings are "up" for us, we can whisper to ourselves, "I feel grateful for all the good health, love, joy, and abundance in my life," and bring a peaceful, relaxed feeling to the whole body. Smile softly and surround outer turmoil with a light heart. Instead of jumping past this moment into possible pain, panic, or anxiety about what might happen in the future, gratitude wraps us in a blanket of compassion, reminding us that even this current predicament will all work out okay.

For example, Vickie complained that her husband Bill never shared feelings or bothered to listen to hers after sixteen years of marriage. While cleaning house, exercising, and driving to and from work, she chewed on this story all day for years. She bombarded her friends with the same story so many times they stopped listening.

But when she explored gratitude in therapy, her marriage got a fresh transfusion. "Each morning, I agreed to notice any ways Bill showed his love during the day," she said. "I expected disappointment, like usual, but instead I felt ashamed of the rumors I'd spread about him. He kissed me every morning on his way to work. He hugged me at night when he came home. He called to bring dinner home when I was tired. And the real shocker came when I asked him nonchalantly to hold me while I cried. He did!

"I called all my friends and apologized for lying to them about Bill's love. I now have the loving relationship I always longed for—and it's with my same old husband."

When we only feel grateful for things we like, we feel a little happy, but only when we have those likeable things in our grasp. When we feel grateful for everything, happiness can become our constant daily companion.

Feeling Gratitude When Sadness Visits

Sadness is a basic human feeling. Yet when it appears, we struggle to hold it at bay. We need to learn to trust its timing, to welcome both sadness and joy with open arms. Sadness knows that, like an old friend, tears arrive just in time to carry us downstream through pain to whatever is next—acceptance and compassion, if we choose. When we finally surrender into sadness, giving our bodies permission to feel how sad we really feel, every cell in our body sighs in relief. Our loving heart holds us tenderly, strokes our hair, and whispers, "Don't be afraid. You're safe to let the tears flow. Breathe into the sadness and be with it."

For example, Josh felt elated to find buyers who loved the home he and his late wife built on forty acres twenty years ago. But as the reality sank in of losing this land he loved and the home where he raised his family, tears overcame him.

"I look at the basketball hoop where the boys and I played HORSE countless times and start to weep," he said. "When I see the shed where I repaired broken faucets, door knobs, shovels, and rakes, I'm flooded with nostalgia. The boys are grown now, and I need the money from the house sale to fund my retirement. But that doesn't change all the ways this home held my family for years."

Josh let himself grieve every day for a week. Then he signed the escrow papers, blew a kiss goodbye to his beloved home, and stepped into a new chapter of his life.

Gratitude for what we had helps us step forward into whatever is next.

Finding Gratitude When Loneliness Strikes

Loneliness can strike at any time, night or day. It can strike when a loved one leaves, even if we want them to leave. It can strike in the middle of our marriage, even when the living room is filled with children. It transports us back in time to fourth grade when we stood knock-kneed and shy as classmates picked us last for the softball team. When loneliness strikes, we feel paralyzed. We desperately want the phone to ring but dread anybody finding us in such disarray. Loneliness's victim story impedes our ability to reach out for comfort, convincing us to clean or pour a second glass of wine instead.

But gratitude sheds new light on loneliness. "Out in the world, I'm a successful businesswoman with a beautiful home," Sally said in therapy. "But last Saturday, I did something I haven't done in forty years. I lay frozen in bed in my remodeled master bedroom watching reruns of *The Waltons*. I desperately longed to attend my son's college basketball game like we have for three years. But if I did, somebody might ask me where Phil was. And I'd have to explain why my husband of thirty-two years left me for his twenty-six-year-old employee. I burst into tears at just the thought of it."

Sally stayed home in bed watching the game on TV. But between commercials, she stayed present with the loneliness she had never expected to feel at fifty-five. "The more I focused on the loneliness in my heart and really felt it, the more grateful I felt for the woman I am, with a loving son and beautiful home. By feeling grateful, even for the loneliness, I stopped feeling alone and, instead, felt how strong, blessed, and healthy I am. This turnaround surprised me."

Now when loneliness visits, Sally shifts into gratitude for her life as is.

Surrounding Shame with Gratitude

When shame envelops us, we find ourselves swirling in the eye of a nasty tornado. Shame can sound as firm and right as the Pope himself. It berates us for all the ways we have been or ever will be bad, worthless, and unacceptable. Shame silences our voice and hides our creative expression, demanding that we never stand out but always fit in with that nonexistent norm. It is that familiar "never good enough" voice in our head that insists we never be seen, heard, or valued in this lifetime.

Gratitude swoops in to save us from shame's dank, gloomy life in the cellar. It applauds our uniqueness with, "There's nothing shameful or silly about you. You are perfect just the way you are. Let loved ones really see who you are." We open and soften into our grateful heart. We trust who we are, trust our decisions and choices. We trust our basic goodness. We step back into the real reason we are here: to enjoy life.

As an experiment, try voicing gratitude for any shame you carry secretly inside. Say "yes!" to any shyness around your body or shame you carry for being molested. Say "yes" to any shame you still carry in your heart for getting divorced or for coming from a divorced family. Try saying "yes" about the money you lost in the recession and any ways you still blame yourself for it. Even say "yes!" to the promotion that passed you over last year or the shame you feel over your son getting caught for smoking pot.

Saying "yes" to unwanted feelings often expands into gratitude for other aspects of our life. For example, you might find yourself adding, "And I'm grateful for my loving friends and for the divorce that forced me to look at myself." Or "I feel gratitude for my health, even the neck tension that reminds me to relax and worry less." Try expressing gratitude for five good and bad situations and notice how this feels in your body. If fear tries to block gratitude, ask, "What is this unwanted situation trying to teach me?"

Gratitude reminds us to trust whatever experience we are having, like it or not.

If we remember to whisper, "I feel gratitude for my pain reminding me to slow down," even if we don't yet fully grasp its goodness in our life, gratitude will slowly seep into our awareness. Rather than "I have to drive the kids to soccer practice," gratitude helps us say, "I *get to* take the kids to soccer and be part of their daily life." Patience and gratitude bring deep trust in the life wisdom that sees and knows things we don't know yet.

In our back pockets, we all carry stories of pain, sorrow, suffering, and fear. We humans share a backlog of tribulations we never expected, wanted, or easily digested. But when we look back, some of those dreaded experiences held invisible jewels in their seams whose subtle power carried us forward into the wise, mature beings we are today.

The more we practice gratitude, the more we soften, open, and surrender.

Joining Our Heart's Unlimited Capacity for Gratitude

Gratitude's vast capacity extends far beyond the limits of sheer positive thinking. Ego fears that if we feel grateful for being sick, we'll never get well. Or if we act grateful for a cancer diagnosis, we are signing our death certificate. We live under ego's mistaken belief that gratitude will bring more of what we don't want.

Instead, it replaces negative thoughts with joy by regularly switching over to our mind's gratitude channel. Trust replaces mistrust. Acceptance replaces resistance. Humility replaces pride.

I could not write this if my heart had not experienced the exponential power of gratitude in my own heart and life. Several years ago, during a time of deep resentment, I walked and walked on elk trails behind my home in nature. I'd hike, ski, or snowshoe one or two hours each morning, looking up rarely from my ruminations to peruse for wildlife. Slowly, when I would spot a coyote loping uphill, a mother and baby elk grazing nearby, or a hawk circling above a grassy meadow for lunch, my mood changed. Exit resentment. The unpredictable novelty of seeing wildlife in nature called me out of my story and into the beautiful present. Sighting elk, owls, coyote, and hawks made that same resentment story boring. Then one spring when I least expected it, gratitude woke me up.

We had a drought winter, which meant our high desert plateau received too little snow. Instead of rushing creeks and muddy trails, spring's snowmelt evaporated early, leaving creek beds dry, pine trees limp, and trails dusty. Without lush streams, my friendly elk, deer, bears, and hawks migrated elsewhere. I hiked and hiked, hoping to see more than a horny toad or grasshopper. But weeks passed without sighting a deer or elk, and negative resentment returned.

One day while meditating under a tall ponderosa pine that I had hiked by for years, I turned and said to the tree, "Thank you for being here and for providing shade." Suddenly my vision of the landscape burst at the seams, revealing a new world my mind had never seen in this new way. I looked from the towering ponderosa pine to the spindly juniper trees I had passed so many times, and, for the first time, I said, "Thank you, ancient beings, who receive strong winds, pouring rain, and cold snow without ever complaining. Thank you for mirroring the possibility of stillness back to my being."

I felt my heart crack open to finally see all this grace in my everyday life.

I stood on a knoll above Elk Corridor, a place I fondly named after seeing the winter herd of fifty elk warming themselves in the sun after a cold January storm. I expressed gratitude out loud for all the simple things I'd ignored for too many years: "Thank you, precious life, for the warm sun on my body, the cooling breeze on my arms, the baby blue sky, the wispy clouds across it, and the musky smell of elk."

"Thank you," I went on, "for the tiny green oak leaves bursting with chlorophyll in perfect timing every spring. Thank you for the snow-covered 14,000-foot La Plata Mountains in the distance. Thank you for the dove's morning song and for the occasional elk bugle interrupting this vast silence we share. Thank you for the yellow daisies, purple larkspur, wild irises, and white baby's breath sprinkled throughout this high, dry desert plateau. Thank you for the monarch butterflies migrating here from Mexico."

As I continued tearfully, gratitude overflowed into all arenas of life: "Thank you for my spouse's kind, generous, loving presence in my daily life, despite past hurts. Thank you for my lifelong friends on Maui and in California holding me in precious love. Thank you for all the good health, joy, and abundance in our life and all lives. Thank you for thirty years of clients who have trusted me with their pain and struggles. Thank you for my injured knee helping my aging body transition from running to hiking."

Back home, I tearfully shared the resentment story I had secretly harbored too long and apologized for the ways I had withheld affection. Luckily my spouse of twenty-six years, a long-time practitioner of meditation, understands the unconscious potholes we humans slip into. Once I expressed gratitude for Jo's consistent daily love, we both laughed at how bamboozled even I had become in resentment.

Since then, I commit to gratitude on a daily basis. Each day on my morning hike, I stand on that grassy knoll and express gratitude for everything I am seeing, hearing, smelling, touching, and feeling in life, the good and the bad. At the end, kindness practice joins in with, "May I and all beings be happy, healthy, and free."

Gratitude radiates inside all our relationships through appreciation.

We Feel Seen and Valued with Daily Appreciation

Year after year, as routine dulls our senses, we forget to appreciate loved ones. Appreciation slips through the cracks, unspoken, as we race through our busy lives. In a few years, all that undying love and devotion in our romantic phase dissolves into complaints and blame. After a decade or two of living together, resentments are honed into an art form. Soon we compete for the role of "biggest victim" in a relationship.

But if we consciously invite a daily dose of appreciation into our love relationships, we can turn a corner we never knew existed. Active appreciation creates an attitude shift—from complaining about to valuing this person we share life with. In short, appreciation matures us, stretching our hearts and minds to feel love in all its surprising forms and embrace what we have.

One single daily appreciation can change how we view ourselves and loved ones. It calls the gifts of each moment into awareness. When a loved one stops to say, "Thank you for cooking, mowing, working, losing six pounds, or taxiing children to gymnastics," we feel seen and valued, often for the first time.

Because ego thrives on judgment, doubt, and complaining, it wants nothing to do with our attempts to appreciate. Suffering from a case of chronic restlessness and dissatisfaction, ego can't waste time appreciating anything. Rather than appreciating all our efforts—to run a 10K or marathon, graduate from high school or college, score a good job, or complete chemo—ego is always on to the next thing, chattering nonstop about what we need to get, do, have, or keep next to be happy and good enough.

Fortunately the power of appreciation, gratitude's sidekick, neutralizes ego's runaway train. Appreciation brings value to those small, unspoken daily acts, done by loved ones and strangers, by verbally acknowledging things that help life go smoother. For instance, with ourselves, we might look in the mirror and whisper, "I appreciate my valiant efforts to swim twice a week and eat organically for my health." With loved ones, we might say, "Thanks for bringing groceries home after a tiring day at work" or "Thank you for working, tending the baby, driving the kids to school, or cooking today." With a stranger, we might acknowledge, "Thanks for giving me that primo parking spot."

Appreciation pats those around us on the back for putting energy, effort, time, and attention into each day without being asked. It replaces ego's chronic habit of lumping experiences into "good" or "bad" with "this moment is good enough, perfect as it is." It reminds us to pause long enough to appreciate the things our spouse did do today to keep the family functioning rather than the one thing they forgot. And it reminds us to thank our child for doing their homework, even if they need help with it.

Years ago, psychologists studied appreciation in marriage. In the experimental group, couples agreed to only appreciate each other for four weeks. The control group appreciated good behavior and addressed bad behavior. After one month those couples that complained and praised each other reported little change. But the daily diet of appreciation created such a safe, loving environment that, to their surprise, couples reported "all bad or negative behavior" fell away without saying a word.

When I work with couples, the first two things I teach them our first session is to listen well and appreciate each other daily. "Start appreciating each other every day for small and not-so-small things," I say. "Appreciate your mate for eating healthily, starting an exercise program, playing catch or shooting hoops with the children, listening to your feelings, staining the deck, waking up a half hour early for yoga, being a good mother or father or lover—whatever you see or feel or think of."

For instance Ralph and Linda had perfected their complaining skills over the past nineteen years. Their marriage had deteriorated into yelling matches and loud silences.

"We love each other," Linda said. "We just forgot how to get along."

"Your best choice is a crash course in the art of appreciation," I said. "I need you to appreciate each other daily for all the small things you take for granted.

"Ralph, would you be willing to thank Linda for cooking your low-cholesterol meals, so you don't have a second heart attack, and all the ways she shows you love?

"Linda," I said, "would you appreciate Ralph for working hard to support you and your teenage boys for nineteen years? Thank him for playing with the boys after a long day's work, for holding you when you cry, for saving gas money by bicycling to work, for keeping his temper in check—whatever comes to mind. See how it feels to appreciate and be appreciated for the little daily things you both do each day.

"For this to work," I said, "you have to refrain from angry quibbling for a month."

They stared at each other in disbelief. Reluctantly, they agreed.

One month later, after saying goodbye to a client, I heard soft whispers and giggles coming from the waiting room. I peeked around the privacy screen to see Ralph and Linda snuggling and laughing like teenagers on the couch. Both looked twenty years younger, happier, and light years less inhibited to be their unabashed selves.

"When Linda lay on the bed with me, looking into my eyes, and told me all the things she appreciates about me, I melted like a school kid," he grinned. "I fell in love with her all over again." Linda shrugged shyly and snuggled deeper under his arm.

We still had work to do. Both carried a pile of resentments from years of unresolved conflicts. But appreciation paved the path toward forgiveness.

Appreciation is love in action, offering support amid tough changes.

Appreciating Changes Rekindles Love Feelings

Changing ourselves, changing those unconscious habits we've practiced for decades, can feel like pushing boulders uphill. It requires focus, attention, effort, and a strong intention to respond differently. It's just as hard for our loved ones. When we ask our spouse to stop yelling, judging, manipulating, ignoring, or discounting our feelings, we need to acknowledge how hard change is—and show appreciation each time we see even the tiniest incremental changes.

For example, Sam's temper appeared two years after he and Trish got married—when he felt safe and loved enough to show his true colors. But Trish, a child of raging parents, had no tolerance for anger. Yelling back, she only escalated matters. And when she saw him wilt at the tiniest threat of divorce, she soon realized such a paramount change in him would require kid gloves.

In therapy, Trish discovered the power of appreciation. One night, she asked Sam to sit on the couch beside her as she held his hand. "I watch you struggle with anger. I know you feel guilty after you yell mean things at me. But I need to feel safe with you again. I need you to drop below your angry temper and tell me how hurt, sad, or scared you feel underneath. I need you to soften and tell me which vulnerable feelings are triggered for you. In return, I'll appreciate every effort you make to change."

Sam nodded hesitantly, mumbling, "I'll try, but I don't know how."

Over the next weeks and months, Sam struggled to speak his feelings, slipping back into anger at times, but Trish praised each effort. "Thank you for leaving the room last night when you couldn't stop your anger. And thank you for telling me how my words hurt you. I appreciate you naming 'I feel angry' rather than acting it out."

One Saturday night during a conflict, deep grief welled up inside Sam—too big to hide from Trish, he struggled to describe his inner experience: "I feel stuck in a vise with a ton of grief pressing down on my chest. I feel too terrified to move."

Trish held Sam tight while his body trembled with fear. Tears poured out of him for nearly an hour. After a long silence, he said, "I'm crying for that terrified little Sam who watched his parents break up over and over again, and I'm crying for the adult Sam who's scared to let your love in fully." They fell asleep in each other's arms.

After releasing his lifetime of grief, Sam's temper rarely flared up anymore.

Appreciating others' changes opens our heart to kind compassion and forgiveness.

Around the time Tom and Kathy entered therapy, Tom had been sleeping in the spare bedroom. After throwing themselves into exciting careers and triathlons years earlier, they suddenly felt like strangers on weekends. When Kathy pursued her desires for more nonsexual affection, Tom felt rejected sexually. Whenever Tom initiated lovemaking, Kathy brought up all her disappointment and rage that he never addressed. Fifteen years later, their son Josh was the only glue holding them together.

"We're friends," Kathy said, "but the marriage is boring and dead."

"I haven't given up," Tom said, "but at least once a day, I consider leaving."

We spent weeks practicing listening, kindness, and forgiveness. But with years of unresolved conflict, they kept retreating in hopelessness to their own bedrooms.

As a last resort, I suggested appreciating the small changes they saw in each other. They both smirked in disbelief. But with coaxing, they were desperate enough to try.

"I appreciate how much more kind and patient and less judgmental you've become," Tom said. "Instead of getting stoned and going mute, I feel safer to tell you what I really feel and think. I feel like you're really listening for a change."

"I appreciate you for letting me cry when I'm sharing my vulnerable feelings and for not making it about you," Kathy said. "And I really like you sharing your feelings with me. It's something I've begged of you for years."

As they appreciated each other daily, trust slowly grew. Tom refrained from anger, and Kathy decided to share a secret she had never told anyone, not even her parents or brother.

"I was molested," she whispered between tears. "When I was seven, the neighbor boy who babysat me touched me sexually. I knew it was wrong, but I was afraid Mom would blame me, so I never told anyone."

Tom held Kathy as she wept. "I appreciate your courage to tell me this," he said. "I feel so much compassion for you. Now all your requests for nonsexual affection make sense. I apologize. Please forgive me. I'm sorry I wasn't there for you."

Appreciation helped them respond to each other with kindness and love.

Gratitude for This Precious Human Life

When I look at the photo on my fireplace mantel of my dad and stepmom riding up the Telluride ski gondola, I think, "They're gone now. I'll be gone too someday." In that moment, I pause amid my to-do list, and I feel the preciousness and joy of being alive.

Gratitude calls attention, again and again, to life's basic goodness. When we rest in our grateful heart, we melt into the unlimited joy of being alive. We stop giving orders, stop ranting about our latest upset, and admire the lilacs outside the window or soak in every detail of our child's beautiful eyes. We even feel grateful that the ten-year-old Toyota still drives us to doctor's appointments, dinner out, and the grocery store—and to a new precious national park come vacation time.

Suddenly, for no good reason on a Wednesday morning, we acknowledge all the grace that brought us to this precious moment. Or we drop our grudges and feel grateful for all the ways Mom and Dad did love us. Or we pause amid a busy schedule to email an old friend and tell them how grateful we are to share life with them. Since all things arise, exist, and disappear, including ourselves someday, the time for gratitude is now.

When we live in gratitude, we enter the unbounded reality of a grateful heart. We start flowing downstream into each precious moment with lighthearted abandon, less attached to notions of how life should be and utterly delighted in how it is.

Heart Tools for Gratitude and Appreciation

Practice each of these tools for one week before moving on to the next one. But if a specific tool calls you to spend more time with it, give yourself another week, month, or as long as you need in order to heal.

1. *Discover Joy in Gratitude For What Is—the Good and Bad*
Upon waking in the morning, name five good things you are grateful for in your life. You might start with, "I'm grateful for all the love, good health, joy, and abundance in my life." Notice how it feels in your body to express gratitude for one tiny portion of all the grace in your life. Next, take a deep breath and name five things you are willing to feel grateful for, even if you don't like them, such as "I'm willing to be grateful for my recent loss, my back pain, or my current conflict." Invite into awareness the gifts

these less desirable experiences might bring into your life. Now notice how gratitude feels in your body for things that ego judges as "bad." Whenever you think of it in the day, say anything you feel grateful for.

2. *Daily Appreciation of Yourself, Loved Ones, and Strangers*
First, bring the gift of appreciation into your love relationships by appreciating lovers, spouses, children, parents, and friends for the small and not-so-small things they do routinely. Appreciate loved ones for working, exercising, cooking, mowing, meditating, eating healthy, saving money, prepping dinner, and being a good mother, father, lover, or child—anything that takes time, effort, attention, and a generous heart. Notice how it feels inside to appreciate loved ones. Extend appreciation to friends by taking time to appreciate the countless ways they have been and are there for you, year in and year out. Once appreciation is your new habit, pause a few moments each day to appreciate yourself for five things you do. Watch appreciation become your lifelong daily habit while dissolving those habits of complaining, judging, and blaming.

3. *Appreciate Changes in Yourself and Loved Ones*
Since changing bad habits requires near-heroic effort, acknowledge any incremental changes you witness along the way. If your spouse, child, parent, or friend is working on being less judgmental, applaud them whenever they succeed in big and small ways. If you yourself are working on naming your hurt and sadness before they escalate into anger or resentment, appreciate yourself each time you accomplish this feat. As we appreciate ourselves and others more often, the changes swiftly become our new habits in a way that is friendly and healthy for ourselves and loved ones.

4. *Gratitude for This Precious Life as It Is*

Starting today, pause to appreciate this precious, grace-filled life you are living. Despite current challenges, name ten things your eyes are seeing or ears are hearing that you appreciate. Especially include things about your life you have habitually taken for granted. While commuting to work, pause the CD player for a few seconds and name ten life experiences, good and bad, that brought you to the precious being that you are in this moment. Let gratitude be your new mantra.

8. Your Forgiving Heart
The Power of Letting Go

We are terrified of trust,
terrified of making ourselves vulnerable.
The leap into forgiveness is immense...
It's the body that's terrified.
—Marion Woodman

It's an ordinary Monday in April. After riding our bikes in mid-sixty-degree temperatures last week, two inches of snow cover the lawn, driveway, aspen tree branches, and blooming crocuses. Anyone who has ever lived through spring in the Rockies knows how unpredictable it is, which feeds the common saying: "If you don't like the mountain weather, wait five minutes. It'll change."

Indoors, behind closed doors and closed lips, it's also an ordinary Monday. Diane still resents her husband for never giving her an engagement ring twenty years ago. John feels rejected that his wife refused sex again last night. Marsha regrets that her seventy-year-old husband refuses sex every night. Lynn's fear of abandonment is triggered as her partner flies out tonight to teach midwifery in Nicaragua. Lisa feels betrayed by her son's pot smoking. Dave silently resents that his wife's midlife pregnancy postpones his retirement another twenty years.

Let's face it. Our daily lives dangle precariously between unconscious habits and the reality that any little thing could cause old wounds to flare up. It feels impossible to avoid rejection, hurt, and disappointment in such a slippery inner climate. Toss in ego's habit of avoiding all pain, discomfort, and dislikes, and the walls of resentment build.

We have all been caught in the human storms of hurt, resentment, and anger. Despite years of meditation practice, I still find myself in the eye of the storm occasionally.

Today I feel kind, peaceful, joyful, compassionate—our unlimited natural states. But quite recently, I found myself in yet another painful predicament, a disappointment that had me seething with anger.

I am one of those Leos who really celebrates her birthday; I spend the entire month on Maui each August. As my sixtieth approached, I called my six closest friends, whom I call my "heart family," ten months early and asked them to clear their calendars for my Maui beach ritual next August. Since I had flown to Hawaii and San Francisco for their decade birthdays, my celebration felt like a shoe-in.

But when all of them declined, except the two who already live on Maui, I sat in disbelief. In my shock and disappointment, I forgot to account for our aging. One retired couple lost too much in the 2008 recession to splurge on anything more than food and utilities. Another's precarious health keeps her out of intense summer heat. With time, I gradually accepted all these deeper truths. But months later, while visiting on the phone with one of these six friends, she casually mentioned that the four living in the Bay Area were planning a last-minute Christmas trip to Maui—after I had other Christmas plans. I vacillated between feeling angry, hurt, sad, and feeling betrayed by these dear friends of twenty-five years. My stomach contorted in knots when I focused on it. The first offense had inflamed my childhood wounds, and this second one rubbed salt in them.

My wise heart that has practiced insight meditation and for-giveness for thirty years, knowing better than to react personally, received their legitimate reasons with spacious understanding. After all, our special needs have only grown bigger as we age. But my young child self—the one excited to share my August swims with dolphins, sea turtles, and manta and eagle rays with my closest friends—felt wrongly dismissed.

Simply labeling my feelings and letting them go failed to quell the raging fire in my belly. But my strong overreaction signaled to me that raw childhood pain from countless childhood disappoint-ments with a depressed mother had been triggered. With the help of a trusted therapist and friend, I breathed through my own lay-ers of anger, hurt, disappointment, and fear—into spacious, loving presence.

Such release brought compassion and forgiveness. I couldn't imagine holding this against my beloved friends—and causing us all more suffering—another second. After expressing my feelings, I could remember all the ways my friends did celebrate me with birthday calls, cards, a visit to my home two months earlier, and buying me an expensive hotel room on Lanai.

Now I could forgive and let go and wish them a great holiday on Maui.

Each moment along the way, conscious awareness clarified my options: feed my disappointment story and create more suffering, separation, and distance—or choose forgiveness, which felt like the light, smart choice for freedom. It was a no-brainer.

As long as we keep bathing ourselves in ego's narrow, prickly lies and telling ourselves, "My identity is limited to ego's reactions, judgments, and opinions," we suffer. We remain one among mil-lions swimming in the ocean of unconscious conditioning. But the second we stick our nose above water for air, the instant we choose awareness and forgiveness, we take the next step in our own evolution.

Out of loving acceptance, freedom blossoms, allowing us the space to choose forgiveness. As tender, vulnerable beings with our emotional toes stepped on daily, it's smart to learn the art of forgiveness. Fortunately curiosity, awareness, compassion, and kindness have all prepared us for this moment, this leap into forgiveness.

Curiosity is now our new habit. Each time we ask, "What story am I telling myself now?" and "Which part of me is feeling rejected, angry, jealous, or guilty—my young child self or reactive ego?" awareness hands us our core feelings and beliefs. Soon enough, we hold all personal reactions in loving compassion, leading to forgiveness. A dash of kindness reminds us to soften, open, allow, and accept.

As Jack Kornfield explains, "To let go does not mean to get rid of. To let go means to let be. When we let be with compassion, things come and go on their own." With practice, forgiveness frees us to let go and start fresh. Each moment we choose to set down our burdens, we wipe the ledgers of our life clean.

Facing a Lifetime of Grudges and Resentments

We all have skeletons in the closet. We have all felt burned, used, hurt, and violated, most painfully by the people who love us, or say they do.

Forty years ago, after our favorite Uncle Fred, the family drunk, abused us at age six, we stopped speaking to him for good. When our best friend slept with our lover or spouse, we stopped speaking to either one. When our daughter brought her girlfriend home or our son brought his boyfriend home to meet us, grief replaced years of fantasies about weddings and grandchildren, at least until surrogate mothering and artificial insemination became viable parenting options. When our father abandoned us for his brand-new wife and her children, we never really forgave him.

Grudges die hard. A client recently told me that her father called her mother to wish her a happy Thanksgiving, twenty years after their divorce. "The instant Mom heard his voice," she said, "she berated him all over again for causing the painful separation. Even after ten years in AA, Mom stubbornly clings to self-righteous blame."

We secretly hope that maybe the worst suffering will happen to someone else—until we happen to see in his email or cell phone that our husband of twenty years is cheating on us. Or we walk to the other side of the street to avoid our ex-business partner who embezzled a million from our company fifteen years ago and got away with it. I too resented Mother's depression for forty years—until I finally realized her depression was about her, not me. Then I felt flooded with compassion for her suffering.

How do we forgive atrocities committed by people who say they love us? Even with kindness and compassion as trusty allies, forgiveness is hard. It doesn't sound fair that any adult who abuses a child, or who lies and cheats others, deserves forgiveness. Yet grudges carry such a high price tag for us. Resentments shut down our aliveness and kill our joy. Together, they numb our heart from feeling happy or sad or anything.

Perhaps the man exiled from leading his beloved Tibet, the honorable Dalai Lama, serves as a great living example of forgiveness. Despite the reality that the Chinese military ruthlessly killed and raped millions of Tibetans and destroyed Buddhist monasteries, he continues to forgive the Chinese their horrendous unconscious acts. In fact, the Dalai Lama teaches forgiveness as an act of kindness toward ourselves. If we can forgive every action of others and ourselves, we can set our heart free.

But before we leap into the forgiveness lane with the Dalai Lama, we should take a close look and clarify what it is we need to forgive.

Resentment is our first clue. After the first six months of a relationship, during which we share everything and feel so heard, seen, and understood by our new lover or mate, something happens. They say or do something and crush our feelings, and we feel devastated. "How could you betray me so?" we cry out. "I thought you loved me." With time, or right after a heated embrace, we may mouth the words "I forgive you" between gritted teeth. But inside, our ego has joined forces with the fear of getting hurt, chanting another lie: "If they *really* loved you, they'd never have hurt you to begin with. "

We withdraw, we stop trusting, and we silently question the wisdom of staying totally open and vulnerable with this person—or staying at all. Rather than feeling love, we feel hurt, resentful, and misunderstood.

Soon a debate between our demanding ego and forgiving heart ensues:

Ego's Voice of Fear:	Don't be a fool. Last time you opened up and trusted someone, you felt rejected. Just close your heart and still enjoy the good sex without being too vulnerable. Say only what they need to hear to give you what you want. If you want to avoid feeling hurt and rejected, stop being an idiot and sharing tender feelings.
Your Forgiving Heart:	Remember: hurt, disappointment, fear, and rejection are part of the unconscious conditioning we all struggle with. Hold your hurt in compassion and forgive your partner's unskillful actions. For the future, teach them how to describe rather than act out their hurt feelings and ask directly for what they need.
Ego Fear:	If they don't understand you by now, they never will. Once they get away with hurting you, you'll never be safe to trust them again.

Never let them forget what they did to you. If you give them another chance, be sure to stay busy and hold a grudge so they feel righteously punished. Make them earn your love back.

Forgiving Heart: Help heal the situation with "I see by your overreaction that your childhood wound—feeling misunderstood and mistrusting—is triggered. I forgive you for lashing out at me when your core sadness blinded your clarity. I let it go. Next time you're triggered, try telling me what you need to hear in order to heal."

Ego Fear: Resentment protects your heart from future hurt. Since those who love you hurt you the worst, feel righteously resentful whenever you feel hurt, disappointed, betrayed, or rejected. Whip up a story about what loved ones did to you and milk it as long as you can. To avoid being caught off guard again, read their mood and tone of voice and prepare your next attack. Always keep them on the defensive, too preoccupied with how they hurt you to even notice how you might respond differently.

Forgiving Heart: Offer healing by saying, "I forgive your resentment and I let go of mine. I stopped expecting perfect years ago. I love you as you are and know you are doing the best you can. So let's set aside our mean words and have a do-over. You say what you feel and need while I listen intently, then we'll switch. Let's set our burdens down and create a close, loving connection fresh with what we want now."

Both voices—that of the ego and that of the heart—have their logic, but their dialogue by itself goes nowhere. It's up to us to choose which voice will be our guiding authority. Despite different circumstances and challenges over the years, ego offers the same old tools for the same old outcomes again and again. It promises to keep us safe through pride, judgment, guilt, blame, shame, fear, instilling doubt in others, and a dire need to be right. Ego corners us between bookends, resisting what is at the outset and attaching to its desired outcome at the end.

Though ego promises a secure outcome, for days, weeks, and years at a time, if we just do what ego says, that promised outcome seems to be ever-retreating. Such resistance and attachment pits us against others and life itself, forcing amnesia about our lifelong connection with all humans struggling, just like us, with the same unconscious habits. When all else fails, ego resorts to urging us to hurry up and forgive so we can get to more important tasks.

Our forgiving heart smiles, amused by ego's tricks. Then it gently reminds us to experiment with kindness, compassion, and forgiveness, and see how these feel inside. Our heart is always up for teaching us to name our unconscious childhood wounding, so we can voice our adult feelings and needs skillfully.

Forgiveness brings a critical choice point: to perpetuate ego's lies, aligning with its false sense of security, or choose the freedom found in forgiveness.

The Power of Letting Go Helps Us Forgive

If suffering is a self-made prison of grudges and resentments against parents, lovers, children, friends, and strangers who have hurt us, consciously or unconsciously, then forgiveness is our get-out-of-jail-free card. Genuine forgiveness happens through the power of letting go. Finally we let go of our attachment to needing life in this moment to be any different. We stop wishing our childhood or past had been different. Eventually, with practice, we let go of taking others' unconscious words and acts personally. We let go of our secret hope that someday our spouse will miraculously become the lover, provider, or listener we dream about. Finally we let go of all hopes and fears of a different reality, relaxing into what is. What a relief.

When Doris's coworkers attended a lunchtime Pilates class without inviting her, she felt devastated—for a couple hours. Then she recalled forgiveness. She woke up out of her childhood pain of being teased about her weight and used this current hurt as an opportunity to heal her rejection. Once she spent a few moments loving herself for feeling rejected, she let go of her current "nobody likes me" story.

When Jane's mother left her and her sister with their father after the divorce, she spent years blaming herself and feeling unlovable. But finally, in her late thirties, after pushing two husbands out the door, she forgave her mother for abandoning her. This one act gave her the courage to soften and be vulnerable with her new lover.

When Sue found out her boss had withheld overtime pay from her for months, she felt so betrayed she wound up sick in bed. But rather than sidestep confrontation as Sue had done for years, she called her boss and addressed the oversight that night, then let it go. Her boss apologized and corrected it in her next paycheck.

When Ann was diagnosed with breast cancer, her daughter said, "Don't worry. I'll quit my job and care for you." Instead of gratitude, Ann blurted out, "Why? You were never here when your father was dying." Once Ann cooled off, she apologized. Ann let go of her grudge in order to receive her daughter's caring.

True forgiveness lifts our burdens. It returns us to joy, inner peace, and freedom.

Forgiveness sounds good. But how do I not react personally to my wife's depression and weight problem? How do I *not* take my husband's affair personally? How does my teenager's school suspension not reflect badly on me as a parent? How does Grandpa's womanizing around town *not* shame our family?

Letting go into forgiveness takes commitment and practice. It is not about glossing over hurt, dismissing it, or making excuses. It comes after we stop taking others' unconscious acts personally, even when they impact us very personally. It comes after we locate our core feelings and core beliefs that are triggering our wound, even when our resentment feels totally justified. It comes after we truly acknowledge how hurt, sad, scared, and ashamed we feel, even if it is years later. It comes after we see that loved ones struggle with the same judgment, doubt, and fear that we do.

Forgiveness is a process. It takes the time it takes.

For example, at thirty-two Diane includes spirituality in her daily life. Each morning she wakes early to practice meditation before jogging. Twice a year for the past twenty years she attends a ten-day meditation retreat. Despite her daily devotion to waking up, she still resents her husband Ted for shaming her two years ago.

"I'd never boated this section of the Grand Canyon; I had no idea where the takeout point was," she explained. "Suddenly our friends in the boat behind us yelled 'Get out! You're headed for a thirty-foot falls.' Ted panicked. He jumped out of the boat to drag us upstream to shore. He saved our lives, but the whole time, he screamed at me about how I spaced out and nearly killed us. When I repeatedly tried to explain my innocence, he shut me down. He never apologized, never allowed me to bring it up again."

Diane tried to forgive Ted in her meditation. But fear and resentment remained. In therapy, when she closed her eyes, took several deep breaths, and located the fear in her body, she was able to be present with the fear itself, free of the canoe story. For the first time, Diane felt how scared she is of Ted. Tears rolled down her cheek.

She agreed to tenderly acknowledge the truth to her young child self: "I'm here for you. I feel how his anger terrified you and still scares you. But he was scared too. In his fear he lashed out at you. I'm sorry he blamed you, and I'm sorry he was unwilling to hear your truth. Despite his angry reaction, you didn't do anything wrong."

By finally speaking and hearing the truth, her whole body relaxed.

That night, Diane explained to Ted that she was scared to fully open and trust him since that incident. He apologized and vowed to speak his feelings in a softer, kinder tone. Once Diane forgave him, she let go of her resentment.

Forgiving those who lose themselves in a moment of panic is one thing. But forgiving loved ones and strangers who chronically ignored, betrayed, or abused us, causing untold suffering, takes time, patience, and great courage.

Forgiving the Unforgivable Is a Four-Phase Process

True forgiveness takes time: Time to be honest with ourselves. Time to heal the layers of outrage, resentment, grief, and hurt still pulsating in our young self. Time to realize that—although this hurt, rejection, or betrayal feels very personal—it's more about the unconscious habits of the offender than it is about us. It takes time to recognize that, in an ignorant or impassioned moment, others acted out their conditioning on the closest target nearby, which happened to be us.

Time to reach understanding, compassion, acceptance, and forgiveness.

When I first heard that nothing we take personally is personal, I felt personally offended. After all, my husband divorcing me at the tender age of twenty-three, throwing me into a dark depression, felt very personal. My mother's depression resulting from her unhappy marriage vastly impacted my childhood—that felt personal. In two seconds or less, my ego can conjure up all the lovers, parents, bosses, therapists, and friends who caused me hurt, rejection, disillusionment, and betrayal over the years.

However justified our hurt, we still have to choose between the righteous indignation that perpetuates suffering or the freedom of forgiveness. When we keep focusing on how hurt and betrayed we feel, we find others' painful actions hard to swallow or stomach. But once we turn the compassion corner and stop taking others' unkind atrocities personally, forgiveness flows in and out of our hearts—for ourselves and for the life struggles of others.

Forgiveness does not mean we forget or condone another's cruel acts.

Forgiveness does not mean we agree to stay in an abusive relationship.

Forgiveness flourishes when we stop withholding love, stop closing off our heart, and let go of resentment. It unfolds naturally along a four-phase process:

1. Facing Our Betrayals and Resentments Honestly
2. Allowing Core Beliefs and Feelings to Carry Us to the Shore of Forgiveness
3. Acknowledging the Truth to Our Young Self
4. Settling into Forgiveness and Letting Go

1. Facing Our Resentments Honestly

After wasting years lost in bitterness and resentment, we finally realize that we hurt ourselves the most by hanging on tight to old grudges. Now, we must be ruthlessly honest with ourselves by setting an intention. We pause, take a few deep breaths, and sincerely ask, "Which resentment prevents my heart from being fully open with loved ones?" We quickly see the same resentment story we listened to for years as just an embellished ego story.

Ego aggressively gears up to defend when threatened—especially when our heart sees it clearly for what it is: a collection of elaborate, embellished stories. But our forgiving heart watches ego rise, vie for our attention, and dissolve. Honestly seeing betrayal as betrayal and resentment as resentment opens a tiny crack in the door of forgiveness. It warms us up to the slim chance that another's horrendous acts were possibly not all about us.

For instance, Jane moved past the pain of her father's addiction years ago. After all, she and her husband moved two thousand miles away and had their own teenagers to focus on now. But one evening, while her husband played poker with the guys, she watched a movie in which a young girl waited and waited at the curb for her father to pick her up for the weekend. As the girl waited longer and longer, Jane began to rock back and forth, comforting herself. Soon she ran into her bedroom where she wept for over an hour. The young girl on TV triggered her own raw wound.

"I lost track of the countless times I waited excitedly for Daddy to pick me up every other weekend," she said, "only to be disappointed. I cried so hard I looked like hell the next morning and called in sick at work. I thought I'd forgiven his selfish addictive ways when, as a teen, I refused to see him anymore. But the other night I felt flooded with pain and resentment for the hundreds of times he promised he'd come for my birthday or Christmas, only to hear the next lame excuse."

Despite being forty-five and a mother herself, Jane wept profusely for the deep pain still lodged in her heart that she never felt safe to express as a child.

After releasing her grief, Jane found a place of peace in her heart. She forgave her dad. By facing our resentment stories directly, and experiencing the core feelings triggered by our original wound, the process of genuine forgiveness begins.

2. ALLOWING CORE FEELINGS AND BELIEFS TO TRANSPORT US TO THE SHORE OF FORGIVENESS

Achieving the leap into forgiveness is like crossing a stream. The shore we stand on is familiar, riddled with defensiveness, personal reactions, and elaborate stories of blame. It thrives on frustration, irritation, anger, loneliness, and guilt—all the surface feelings that distract us from true healing.

The journey across this stream, from reactivity to forgiveness, is rarely clear. But we do know that endlessly chewing on ego's stories only holds our guilt, resentment, and anxiety intact. And it holds forgiveness and freedom at arm's length.

By asking ourselves, "Which core feeling—hurt, fear, sadness, or shame—is triggered?" we bypass ego stories and surface feelings and deepen the healing process leading to forgiveness. Each time we feel upset, angry, or resentful about another's actions, we owe it to ourselves, and loved ones, to name our core feelings and beliefs triggered. This is our responsibility.

For example, Jenny found out about her husband's second affair with the same coworker through his emails. She felt shocked, enraged, and devastated.

"Damn you!" she told Frank in therapy. "I told you in the beginning, forty-five years ago, that if you ever cheated on me, I'd divorce you. Five years ago, when you cheated on me with this lonely hussy at work, I forgave you against my better judgment. Now I'm sixty-five, my five children have children of their own, and I have to grow old alone because you're a stupid fool. Pack your bags and stay in a hotel for now. You're not welcome in my bed anymore."

Jenny filled out the divorce papers and kept them in her top desk drawer. But guilt thoughts shamed her for not being attractive enough to keep her man and for not seeing the affair earlier. Her friends begged her to file and leave him a pauper. But Jenny spent fitful nights crying herself to sleep, torn between leaving and forgiveness.

In session, I asked her to name which core feelings and beliefs were triggered.

As Jenny closed her eyes and peeked underneath her rage and guilt, she was overcome with grief. "I never feel good enough. Mom ran off with her boyfriend when I was twelve, leaving Dad to raise me. Now my own husband goes elsewhere for sexual favors. What's wrong with me?" she said.

Slowly, Frank and Jenny continued to work on their marriage. Frank apologized repeatedly, swearing he wanted to grow old and someday die in Jenny's arms. Jenny took the time she needed to move through her rage, loss, grief, and betrayal.

"I wouldn't let myself think about getting caught or how deeply it would hurt you," Frank said. "I felt sorry for her being a widow. If I could, I'd erase it all in a heartbeat. All I can do now is keep telling you that *you* are the love of my life."

Although Jenny had come a long way in processing her grief, it was Frank's genuine tears of remorse at the fear of losing her that ultimately softened Jenny into forgiving him. He made a point to come home and share lunch with her daily, so she could stop worrying about where he was at lunchtime, and they began traveling together again. But even after she forgave Frank, and after he shored up his integrity in therapy, it still took several more months to heal her broken trust.

"When I finally forgave myself for not seeing the affair," she said, "I could forgive him. And when I worked through the grief and despair I'd sat on since I was a girl, I didn't have to keep telling myself that I'm good enough. Now I feel it in my bones."

In April, on their thirtieth anniversary, Frank and Jenny renewed their vows.

Our forgiving heart always shares the same moment with ego. It welcomes all emotions with the compassion of a loving grandmother. It gently reminds us, "You are safe and loved. Nothing is wrong.

You are simply a human being releasing pent-up fear or sadness or shame. Let go and allow it to pass through you."

Facing core feelings, coupled with acknowledging the truth of what really happened, is a true source of freedom, joy, and inner peace.

3. Acknowledging the Truth to Our Young Self

We are built to handle hurt. We are built to hear the truth, no matter how much that truth stings in the moment. What can disturb us the most are lies and omissions of important details, the times we agonize over the secrets and hidden truths of a situation. Left in the dark, we swirl downward into the abyss of ego's reactions, stories, and fears, desperately searching for something to hang our hat on. We hunger for truth.

I'll never forget ten-year-old Orion sitting in my office begging his father, "I wish you'd told me how bad you were hurting. When Mom died of cancer, I hurt too. We could have cried together. Instead you hid behind working overtime."

Countless clients, after the initial shock of a spouse's affair, all said, "It's not the affair that hurts the worst. It's the number of years you lied about it."

Whether child or elder, female or male, we all deserve to hear and speak the truth. If offenders are too scared to speak up, we can at least acknowledge what really happened to our young self. Without truth and forgiveness, we suffer.

For instance, John turned forty-eight when his daughter Sara called him on his birthday. Sara had been a challenging child growing up, requiring therapy as a teen for addiction and weight issues. Following her divorce at twenty-three, John helped her financially until she got back on her feet and found a job. This relationship had its ups and downs, but nothing prepared him for what he was about to hear.

"I've been doing hypnosis therapy, and I know you abused me at six and seven, Dad," Sara accused him. "I remember a man slapping me repeatedly, and I presume it had to be you. I can't believe you'd do such a thing."

Shocked, John took a few deep breaths. "I'm so sorry that anyone struck you at such a tender age, hon," he said, "but I guarantee it wasn't me. I know I never touched you inappropriately. How can I help you heal from this?"

Sara hung up. That was their last conversation for twelve long years.

But at sixty, in his meditations, images of Sara kept appearing. He knew forgiveness was the next step, but he didn't know how. In therapy he insisted, "She's the offender! She wrongfully accused me of a crime I didn't commit."

Rather than argue with him, I taught John how to distinguish between his young self and his forgiving heart. I helped him acknowledge the truth to his young boy inside who felt hurt. Anxious to get started, John closed his eyes and soon described a young six-year-old boy in blue jeans and a blue sweater swinging in the schoolyard.

"First, I love you, and I know what good morals you have. You didn't do anything wrong. I hear how confused and hurt you feel. But you can stop taking this lie personally. I hold your hurt in compassion, and I'm holding my daughter Sara in compassion, too. I want to help you see that she lashed out at me because I'm the man closest to her, the man who has always been there for her." John's body sighed with relief.

"Your old belief, 'I don't deserve love,' was triggered," he told his young self, "so let's replace it with 'You are lovable.' I imagine holding you right now while you cry."

John covered his eyes with both hands and wept quietly. Tears streamed down his cheeks until he went for a walk later to make sense of all these raw feelings.

Two weeks later, John returned. "I called my daughter," he beamed. "I said what a shame it is to let precious years go by without sharing the highlights of our lives. Tomorrow I'm flying to visit her and meet my new grandson.

"During our goodbyes, she said, 'Daddy, I'm sorry. I was in a lot of pain.' I told her I knew she was hurting and that I forgave her. I even told her I would be happy to help her talk about it when she is ready."

Whenever another's hurtful words trigger strong reactions in us, we can rest assured that a core belief is raw and bleeding inside. Through a simple intention, such as "I'm willing to name which core belief is triggered by my reaction" and "I'm willing to use this opportunity to repeat my new core belief, such as I'm lovable and worthy," we release resentment, hurt, and fear—everything unlike love. Speaking the truth to our young hurting self, soothing its tender wound, allows forgiveness to flow.

4. SETTLING INTO FORGIVENESS AND LETTING GO

Even with these first three phases, forgiveness can be hard to pull off. Deep inside the secret caverns of our heart, devastating loss and pain can feel like a Himalayan-sized crevasse between "us and them." Painful unconscious acts can make us question everything: the way people feel about us, whether something is wrong with us, whether true love exists at all. When someone who says they love us hurts, betrays, or rejects us, we need a little time to hide in a corner and lick our wounds. But the step we take next either creates freedom or deepens suffering.

This leap across the abyss—from ego reactivity to being vulnerable, open, compassionate, and forgiving—happens slowly over time as we are ready. Ego sees only how we leave ourselves open to more possible hurt. But our forgiving heart knows that moving through our rage, grief, and hurt is the short path to freedom.

As Jack Kornfield says in *The Art of Forgiveness, Lovingkindness, and Peace:*

> True forgiveness does not paper over what has happened in a superficial way. It is not a misguided effort to suppress or ignore our pain. It cannot be hurried. It is a deep process repeated over and over in our heart which honors the grief and betrayal, and in its own time ripens into the freedom to truly forgive.

As we take time to be honest with ourselves, time to grieve fully and feel how hurt we really feel, time to feel compassion for our tender self, forgiveness sprouts a few buds. At first, we may practice secretly under the covers at night by whispering, "I'm willing to forgive my stepdad for molesting me" or "I'm willing to forgive my ex-wife for betraying me." We try it on safely and see how it feels.

When our heart feels ready to take the leap into forgiveness, we know it. If not, we give our heart more time to heal. And eventually, as we reach a place of peace with it in ourselves, we may say, "I forgive you" to the violator themselves. Or we may choose to say this in the comfort of our home or in a meditation practice, rather than having to tell them directly. The key is stepping into compassion for ourselves and for the unconscious conditioning driving any human cruelty.

By the same token, when we have hurt, disappointed, or betrayed others, intentionally or unintentionally, we should allow them to move through the four phases of forgiveness in their own timing. We may apologize and say, "Please forgive me," but healing occurs in each of us at our own individual pace. In the interim, we must bring patience, kindness, and compassion until they are ready.

Forgiveness changes our rules of engagement. It shatters our naive, Hollywood version of romantic love. It stretches our hearts to see that true love includes, even embraces, those imperfect acts delivered by our mates and loved ones. Love holds all our ordinary human feelings in a warm, loving, forgiving embrace, knowing these very ordinary feelings help us mature.

Though traumatic at the time, each loss, each disappointment and hurt, puts one more puzzle piece in place. The deep truth is that each anguish exists for a noble purpose: pain burns through ego's lies quicker than anything to wake us up to who we really are—conscious loving awareness. Though scary and disconcerting, each trauma brings us to this moment of understanding, compassion, wisdom, and forgiveness.

After forgiveness, our rules of engagement change. We let the pain of a lifetime go. We stop chewing on old resentment stories. We surrender our license to throw pain back into a loved one's face in a fit of anger. We meet another's scared, angry words with a forgiving heart. This takes committed practice.

Sean entered therapy five years into his marriage. "I can't forgive Sue," he whispered. "After the first year, she judged me for the way I shared feelings, the way I snored, the way I kissed and made decisions... Even though she apologized, I'm afraid to open up and risk being judged again.

"Part of me wants to make it work," he went on, "and part of me wants a divorce."

Sean spent time working with the phases of forgiveness. He owned his story of resentment. He acknowledged how deeply his trust was broken by such harsh judgments to his young, wounded self, who had felt judged incessantly as a child. He addressed his core belief, fear of being unlovable, by expressing and loving his grief fully. And he mustered up some compassion toward Sue's unconscious wounding.

But genuine forgiveness stayed just out of arm's reach.

Finally, one night as he was falling asleep, a light bulb went off inside Sean's head. "Somehow I switched channels, from my same old resentment story to compassion and forgiveness—for me, for Sue, for my critical father, and for our relationship. I lay in bed holding young Sean in compassion when suddenly I thought about holding Sue also in compassion. I wept for the past four years while she patiently waited for me to open up to her again. I grieved all the loneliness she quietly suffered for years while I was lost in my resentment story. And I wept for the closeness I missed out on by keeping those judgments alive. I fell asleep chanting, 'I forgive you, Sue.'

"The next morning, I spilled my guts to Sue, withholding nothing. We cried together and made slow passionate love. It was like waking up out of a long, dark dream, one I made up and kept alive daily. Now when it revisits," he said, "I chuckle."

Sean sees Sue freshly now, as the same loving, kind woman he fell in love with.

Forgiving Ourselves Our Human Imperfection

Let's face it. We are each a work in progress. We resist, rebel, procrastinate, deny, avoid, tell white lies, demand our own way, and repeat the same mistakes over and over. We explode into righteous anger moments after promising to never get angry again. We set an intention to be kind and forgiving in our morning meditation or prayer, only to be unkind and unforgiving minutes or hours later. We set New Year's resolutions, only to abandon them weeks later. We rage against inevitable sickness, old age, and death, squealing like pigs. We do all this simply because we are human.

As humans, we struggle with strong opposing forces.

When we begin to see our unconscious patterns, we can get discouraged fast. Once the veil of self-righteous blame lifts and we first see our own part in losing our marriage or job, it hurts. We are filled with guilt, remorse, or judgment.

"How could I be so stupid and not see this coming?" we implore.

"Why was I so loyal to the company that laid me off six months before retirement?" we ask. "How could I not see that affair right under my nose?"

All day long, year after year, we berate ourselves for being human. Mostly this happens unconsciously, below our awareness. While we drive, work, eat, exercise, even make love, ego taunts us for not getting it right again. When illness or loss brings us to our knees, ego beats us up for not being savvy enough to avoid it. But our forgiving heart reminds us that, rather than try to avoid being human, we need only be awake and compassionate. As Buddha taught, the three main pitfalls we humans fall into are ignorance, craving, and aversion. If we fall into these while truly awake, we can simply forgive ourselves.

We are not permitting ourselves to be cavalier, irresponsible, reckless, or uncaring in our relationships—just awake and aware of how our acts affect others. Forgiveness begins by asking, "What have I been unwilling to forgive of myself?"

When Dana heard her two-year-old daughter say, "I'm sorry. I'm sorry, I won't do it again," Dana felt shame-stricken. "Great! I taught my daughter to apologize for existing the same way my cowardly mother taught me. I swore I'd never do this to my kid." It took some weeks, but Dana finally forgave herself.

Five years ago, Leanne's father died while she was at the pharmacy getting his medications. "I grieved then. But I still feel guilty for not stroking his face when he took his last breath, like I promised I would. I loved my father. I quit my job to care for him his last two years of life." She held her face in her hands and wept. But when she put both hands over her own heart and repeated, "I forgive you, Leanne. I forgive you," she felt a huge weight lift from her chest.

Forgiving our human imperfections can feel the hardest of all. It's easy to see how others need to change. It's easy to see when others are lost in fear, hurt, rejection, or abandonment. But seeing ourselves clearly is a whole different animal. When we do finally "wake up" out of our current story and see that we spent the last two minutes, hours, or years chewing on a judgment or resentment, ego judges us for being lost in a story. It starts to feel like we can't win for losing.

But before giving up, let's look at why self-forgiveness is so hard. We were born into a vicious cycle. School taught us our three R's and how to socialize in public. But nobody taught us how to love, parent, cope with aging and death, or invest wisely. We learned what not to do by watching our parents.

For years, we humble and fumble our way through, hiding our shameful mistakes as best we can, gathering hints on how to get by, more or less, by overhearing bathroom or dinner conversations. The instant a parent, peer, or authority figure witnesses one of our poor judgments, we are judged, berated, ostracized, or fired for "not knowing better." If we are naive enough to share a dream or heart-felt longing, we are teased and ridiculed. Such a formula begets self-conscious judgment and doubt. Meanwhile shame festers underground, destroying confidence.

Forgiveness comes by loosening our tight grip on fear.

Forgiveness comes by seeing our mistakes with compassion.

Forgiveness comes by letting go of everything unlike love.

As a therapist and workshop leader, I hear the pain our hidden life of shame causes. I witness how we hold ourselves imprisoned with painful guilt and regret for years. Forgiveness releases us from this life sentence. It allows our heart the freedom to speak our truth and our life the freedom to change. Even if our sorrow and resentment from horrible wrongs are justified, the time to choose compassion, forgiveness, and freedom is now.

Steve convinced himself that his wife would never understand his need for a new vehicle. So when patients paid him cash, he stashed it in a secret envelope. One day, with $6,000 saved, he drove home with a refurbished Dodge pickup. But when he faced his wife and explained this splurge, his guilt and shame multiplied tenfold.

When Dan retired at sixty, he felt remorse rather than freedom. Ten years earlier he had advised an elderly couple to invest poorly to increase his own profits. Unable to forgive himself, he drove to their house and handed them a check for $20,000.

Sharon woke at 3 a.m. nightly, riddled with guilt and blame. "If only I'd said no when my daughter asked if she could attend that graduation party, she'd never have been assaulted. If only I'd hired the best attorney in town, her rapist would be in prison now instead of Harvard. If only I'd been a better mother, she'd have called me for a ride home." When Sharon finally said, "I forgive you, Sharon," she slept better at night.

After last year's audit, Dave regrets cheating on his taxes. Aaron regrets riding his snowmobile in soft spring snow and separating his shoulder. Susan regrets having an affair with her husband's best friend and breaking up the family. Linda beats herself up for not somehow saving her marriage, winding up hopeless and alone.

We all carry some regrets in our back pocket. Lucky for us, forgiveness is always available the moment we wake up out of our guilt, confusion, and shame. Rather than waste more precious time ruminating on past events we cannot change, we can forgive ourselves now. We can pause, put both hands over our heart, and whisper to ourselves, "I forgive you. I forgive you now." Make sure to say your name out loud. We can repeat this simple phrase whenever regret or remorse robs our attention.

Applying the Four Phases to Forgiving Ourselves

Long-term love relationships give us time. Time to exit the honeymoon phase and act out unconscious habits. Time to explode in anger and see if, afterward, we are still loved. Time to feel betrayed, withdraw love, and return again. Time to make up stories like "I can't trust her to tell me the truth" or "I can't trust him not to judge me." And time to see our story as story, forgiving loved ones and ourselves for the closeness we missed.

We are silly creatures. We spend years looking for Mr. or Ms. Right, who gets us, loves us, and understands us. But after two years with this individual, we begin an unconscious attempt to prove our core beliefs right—we truly are unworthy, unlovable, unwanted, or undeserving of love. Baffled and confused by our angry outbursts and sullen withdrawals, our mate begins to question if we are worthy of their love.

To exit this maze, we practice the phases of forgiveness.

"I'm stupid," Jim said. "I spent Christmas Day on the roof out of sheer ignorance while my family ate dinner inside. I know how to listen and not react defensively. But Christmas morning, when my lover Toby jokingly said, 'Move over and give me space' in our tiny, crowded kitchen where he was cooking dinner for twelve, I disappeared. Feeling offended, I held a meditation retreat of one on the roof, repairing shingles and licking my wounds. Since our parents accepted our gay marriage, I'm stupid not to enjoy family."

"Not stupid, just human," I smiled. "You have practiced self-judgment for decades, so be patient and kind with yourself. Face whatever resentment story you made up about Toby honestly, and let it go. Then acknowledge the truth to young Jim inside. Forgive yourself for falling back into your old survival habit of running."

He placed both hands over his heart. "All that happened, young Jim, is Toby asked for space. You reacted from your childhood belief, that there's no room for your needs, and bolted. I forgive you, Jim, for being impatient and for judging Toby."

Within seconds, Jim's breath relaxed. He chuckled, shaking his head.

"I was unrealistic, expecting myself to change overnight without any setbacks," he said. "I need to lighten up and be way more forgiving of Toby and myself."

The sooner we forgive ourselves and others, the more time we have for cultivating kindness, compassion, inner peace, and forgiveness. By lying still and allowing these qualities to expand in our body, such natural states become familiar.

As much as another's unconscious words and actions hurt—and they do—we always have choice. We can react on autopilot the way people have for centuries—or we can choose kindness, compassion, and forgiveness. It is our moment-to-moment choice. When we want freedom more than anything else—more than being right or clutching our resentment story tight to our chest, performing a victim's righteous indignation—forgiveness unburdens us.

On this lifelong path to waking up, forgiveness trumps being right every time. The power of letting go returns us to the pure joy of being alive. Time and time again, we slip up and act unconsciously, even if we swear we are present. But remembering we are all born into the same soup of conditioning—and all get lost in resistance, doubt, judgment, fear, and illusion—cracks our heart wide open to forgive everyone's flaws.

Experiencing how deep grief and pain transform into unlimited joy by moving through the forgiveness process ultimately makes life more enjoyable. Forgiveness is taking one long, huge exhale and finally letting go. Discerning between ego's voice and that of our wise, forgiving heart is vital.

By placing both hands over our heart and whispering, "I'm willing to feel the hurt and also feel all the ways this person loves me," our heart opens. If tears of letting go arrive, we release them. As we breathe the love that surrounds us into our heart, we gradually awaken to the truth that, on the deepest level, there is no separation. The love we feel for ourselves inside our heart and the love entering our heart from another human being are one and the same.

Whether we know it consciously or not, we live our entire lives in an unlimited field of love. We are love; the bones, muscles, cells, and skin forming our body are all permeable, allowing love to hold and support us at all times, under all circumstances. This universal love holds all living things, including ourselves.

From this expanded place, love is never dented by hurt, disappointment, betrayal, or rejection. Such things come and go. Since love is the invisible fabric holding all living beings together, nobody can really take love away. We will miss the face and voice of a loved one if they leave or die, but we remain held in love. At the deepest level, in the core of our forgiving heart, we are love.

This love evens the playing field. We are imperfect human beings loving imperfect human beings as best we can. Just like us, our partners and loved ones also struggle for freedom from unconscious habits. Just like us, they also long to be happy, healthy, and free of suffering. Just like us, they also move in and out of consciousness, spilling anger, fear, frustration, and suffering over onto us.

On waking up, the truth that we have been and will be betrayed, rejected, and hurt by other people acting out their unconscious conditioning is somehow easier to swallow. And the fact that we will continue to disappoint, frighten, and scare others with our unconscious acts grows easier to admit. It opens the door to freedom.

By practicing the four-phase process of forgiveness, we touch the inherent warmth and openness that live in our great compassionate heart, where our unlimited capacity to be kind, generous, and forgiving lives. With time forgiveness softens and opens our heart. Like fruit, we ripen toward the light of true forgiveness.

Forgiveness unfolds through the transformative powers of letting go.

Heart Tools for Forgiveness

Practice each of these tools for one week before moving on to the next one. But if a specific tool calls you to spend more time with it, give yourself another week, month, or as long as you need in order to heal.

1. *Find the Courage to Face Resentments Honestly*
   Grudges and resentments gain power and kill our joy by festering below our awareness. Before rising out of bed or during a meditation, spend ten minutes asking, "What am I unwilling to forgive?" Ask, breathe deeply, and listen patiently for an image or feeling-sense to bubble up. Keep asking four or five times without judging the answers. As awareness of resentments joins your day, ask repeatedly, "How have I and my partner suffered by clinging tight to my resentment story?" Awareness brings choice. Next time this resentment story visits, ask, "How do I choose to respond now? Will I buy in to the story or label it and let it go?" In time, as forgiveness grows more comfortable, ponder, "What am I willing to forgive?"

2. *Forgiving Others with the Four-Phase Process*
   Dive in and face the most painful hurt in your life. (After forgiving this one, minor hurts become easier.) Say or write down the entire resentment story you have carried for years to yourself so you face the story consciously. Sitting upright on a meditation pillow or chair, close your eyes, take some deep breaths, and picture your young self in your belly at four, nine, or fifteen—whenever

the violation occurred. Notice what they are wearing and their facial expression. Acknowledge the truth of what really happened to your young self. You might say, "Yes, your relative bullied you and used your humiliation for his own amusement. I'm so sorry nobody believed you, and I'm sorry he never admitted it. I'm sorry for how painful that must have been for you." Take some days or weeks to allow the core feelings of rage, fear, hurt, and sadness their full expression until each feeling arrives at natural completion. Acknowledge any core beliefs that joined your life at this traumatic time, such as "I can't trust anybody" or "No one cares about my feelings." Reassure your young self, "Nothing is wrong with you. Though it felt personal, their hurtful acts were about their unconscious conditioning, not about you." After these three steps, gently ask your heart if it is ready to forgive. If it says "no," honor it with patience. When your heart does say "yes," whisper out loud to the person who wronged you, "I forgive you, I forgive you." Make sure to say the person's name aloud. Notice how this feels in your body. You may or may not choose to voice these words to the violator.

3. *Asking Forgiveness from those We Have Hurt*

Using the same four-phase process, start by honestly asking yourself, "Who have I hurt with my unconscious anger, resentment, or fear?" First acknowledge the truth of the situation to your wounded young self and forgive him or her for letting this fester so long. Acknowledge whatever core feelings and beliefs were triggered. Forgive yourself by saying, "I forgive you, I forgive you" out loud to whoever you wronged, making sure to say their name. Genuinely apologize to your victim and say, "When you come to a soft place in your heart, please forgive me." Be patient in respecting their personal timing to reach that opposite shore of forgiveness.

4. *Forgiving Ourselves Our Human Conditioning*

It is exhausting to hold grudges against anyone, especially ourselves. Set quiet time aside this week to close your eyes, breathe deeply, and honestly face those resentments you've held against yourself for years. Speak or write the resentment story so you can hear ego's story as a story, not truth. Hold your young self in your belly and genuinely acknowledge the core hurt, fear, sadness, and shame kept alive by repeatedly blaming yourself for being human and making mistakes. Feel fully the deep grief, fear, and shame, allowing each layer to release and heal in its own timing. Witness any core beliefs triggered. When your heart feels ready, say "I forgive you, I forgive you" out loud, making sure to say your name. Repeat this exercise as often as you need to.

9. Your Truthful Heart
The Power of Integrity

Virtue and integrity are necessary for genuine happiness.
Guard your integrity with care.
—JACK KORNFIELD

Our truthful heart is born with the innate ability to discern right from wrong, lies from truth. But sometimes ego tries to convince us that telling a white lie, or omitting the whole truth, will avoid conflict, save the marriage, or keep the paychecks flowing. Once we make an unwavering commitment to live in honesty and integrity, we stand grounded in the intrinsic dignity and sovereignty of our being, no apologies or compromises. Integrity helps us freely speak and act our truth, no matter what, based on our personal values and principles.

However, these days integrity is rare. Discerning good from bad, healthy from unhealthy, and wise from unwise requires a savvy moral compass inside. Between TV, computers, iPads, and cell phones, we are constantly bombarded with a smorgasbord of ads and commercials, all saying, "Pick me! Pick me! Buy me! I'm the best!" until our head spins. But with get-rich-quick scammers stealing people's lifesavings and hacking our identity while we sleep, we have to discern between right and wrong. More than ever, we need to make the highest choices, based on our own integrity.

Even with things we want, like health, countless choices leave us overwhelmed. Exercise is a good idea, but what kind of workout is better for my age, weight, and body type? Organic foods and nuts may help prevent cancer and heart disease, but if I'm not wealthy, is it really necessary to eat only grass-fed beef? Bodies need vitamins, but which supplements do I need? Which brands can I trust? When investing in stocks, which are environmentally conscious? Do I go with stocks showing the best returns or those helping save wildlife?

I recall a simpler time when today's greed-driven worlds of medicine, politics, and business thrived on integrity. I grew up in the fifties in a small Minnesota town. With barely a thousand people, downtown Main Street stretched one block, lined by Sally's Café, Red Owl Grocers, Woolworth's five and dime, Bill's Pharmacy, Gambles Hardware (my dad's store), the bank, one movie theater, and a corner post office. Men only gathered at the Billiard's Hotel across from the train station to drink beer, smoke cigars, and play pool. We kids joked that if a stranger blinked while driving on the highway, they missed our town.

I loved the homemade banana cream and chocolate cream pie at Sally's Café, where Mom took me after school on cold winter days. Each morning Dad rolled dice here with his friends, the butcher and grocer, to see who paid for coffee. The town was originally a settlement of Swedes and Norwegians; everyone knew everyone on a first-name basis. And everybody attended the Lutheran church on Sunday morning to gossip after the sermon.

Integrity spelled survival in such a tight-knit community. Accountability and neighborly goodwill were not just nice ideas—they were the dire means for any smart businessperson to stay afloat. In fourth grade, when my best friend's father (literally, the milk man) flirted with someone's wife while delivering milk door-to-door, gossip turned into blacklisting him. One year later, they sold their house and moved to Minneapolis.

Today, our interconnection with all living things is still here but harder to see. Strangers in large cities ignore each other on the sidewalk to rush to their next meeting; people relocate every few years for work, love, health needs, or an itch to move. Integrity is no longer held in check by church gossip and dwindling business.

In this modern "do-whatever-you-can-get-away-with" world, quick money (and lots of it) trumps the power of a weak moral compass. For many today, success means millions in the bank, vacation cruises, the best private schools for our children, million-dollar bonuses for swindling those less savvy out of their savings, and a vacation home or two around the world. With the bar of success rising nonstop, anything we achieve is never good enough—at least not for very long.

Like kindness and patience, integrity is a lost art. We are so busy chasing fame, money, and success that integrity lies discarded like a bone by the roadside, left for the weak and foolish to gnaw on. Aggression and competition replace kindness. "Me first" replaces patience. In the lying-and-cheating scuffle to the top, integrity becomes a moot point.

In this climate of rampant greed, integrity is fool's play of the past, a good idea gone sour. When greed and fear of never enough consume us, integrity slips through the cracks, along with honesty, kindness, and inner peace.

Yet greed comes with a hefty price tag. Greed blinds us the same way alcohol blinds an alcoholic. No matter how much money, success, sex, drugs, property, or stocks we have, greed always wants more.

Greed makes us forget that we are all interconnected.

The Power of Integrity Restores Our Moral Compass

Our truthful heart holds our winning ticket out of greed's messes. It points out how integrity offers plenty of room for success, money, and following our dreams. It guides us through treacherous waters to achieve our goals without harming innocent children, trusting employees, and faithful spouses. It is the medicine this aching planet needs.

If we feel lost in doubt and confusion, integrity is our inner moral compass that always knows the difference between right and wrong. We need only pause and tune in. When we stand on our own two feet and live our lives with a strong daily commitment to integrity in all our relations, we land on the side of astute judgment to recognize clearly the right choice.

Our wise heart helps us routinely unravel moral dilemmas:

- Should I take this high paying job, even if it damages the environment?
- Do I reveal my lesbian longings to my husband and seven-year-old son?
- Do I fudge on my taxes this year when money is so tight?
- Do I buy ivory earrings since poachers kill elephants for their ivory?
- Do I expose the engine fire to a new buyer of my beat-up 1979 Volvo?
- Do I tell my daughter about my teenage abortion during our sex talk?
- Do I let pneumonia take my mother at ninety or use heroic measures?
- Do I quit my job when my coworkers have lost their integrity?
- Do I tell my spouse about my affair, though it happened five years ago?

Integrity begins with honesty one day, one moment, one choice at a time.

Making a Lifelong Commitment to Honesty

Lack of honesty poisons our happiness and health. Despite how easy and logical it sounds to get away with things, lies and secrets keep us awake at night. They gnaw at our insides for days, weeks, or years—until we get an ulcer or migraine, get busted, or do the right thing. They suck the joy out of our days while the rest of the world celebrates life.

To live in integrity, our discerning heart requires a lifelong commitment to honesty, no matter what. You begin such a commitment fresh each moment by saying, "I choose honesty now no matter how scary it feels." It begins with our willingness to choose honesty, despite our shady past choices or current temptation to tell a little white lie again. It continues by knowing and loving ourselves enough to disclose our past lies, regrets, and withholds.

Today is a good day to start a lifelong commitment to honesty.

The power of truth returns happiness, inner peace, and freedom to our lives for no reason that will satisfy the mind. Truth really does set us free. When fear demands that we stay silent to keep our job, marriage, or reputation, we recall our commitment to speaking our truth. When ego seduces us to keep the peace by withholding that little white lie, we choose truth. When doubt keeps us confused and indecisive by weighing all the pros and cons indefinitely, we step into clarity by trusting our truth.

But speaking our truth can feel hard, scary, even terrifying. Whether our truth is "I had an affair," "I hate my job," "I'm pregnant," or "You molested me," our discerning heart gives us the courage to choose truth each moment above all else. Our heart knows truth from lies, right from wrong, good from bad. It recognizes fear's latest story as story. It sees judgment as judgment before any thought finishes its sentence.

When our truth might hurt somebody we love, it takes even more courage to speak the unspeakable: "I cheated on you. I had an affair two years ago" or "I stole money from you." Fear says we'll destroy the family if we tell the truth. Yet, unless we fess up, such secrets haunt us in the night and block closeness.

Perhaps the hardest truth of all is telling someone with whom we have raised children and whom we've loved for ten, twenty, or forty years, "I don't love you anymore." Harsh truths can literally feel like a knife stabbing loved ones in the heart. Yet the pain of not speaking our truth festers deep inside until we find courage.

When the father of three teens announced, "I'm leaving," his wife retorted, "So all those years of 'I love you' in the bedroom meant nothing to you? What a cruel joke." He could say nothing to sooth her grief, though they had lived separate lives for years. It wasn't until two years later, when she fell deeply in love and remarried, that she called and said, "Thank you for leaving. I didn't have the guts to do it myself."

In time wounds heal, forgiveness arrives, and we move on to love again.

We are built to hear and speak the truth, despite our discomfort. Since speaking our truth takes courage, it's vital to commit to three golden rules of relationship: *feel our feelings, speak our truth,* and *keep our agreements.* When push comes to shove, caught between speaking up or staying silent, we can lean into these three commitments to guide us in difficult or challenging times.

For instance, Carrie worked full-time as a stock broker and single-handedly parented four young children while her husband nursed his depression for ten years, firing one therapist after another. Fed up at forty, Carrie entered therapy herself. "I meditate and practice loving-kindness toward Phil's wild mood swings daily, but sometimes I'd rather give him a kick in the butt. I don't know whether to continue compassion or file for divorce."

For one whole week, I encouraged Carrie, at the end of her meditation, to ask her truthful heart, "Is it more compassionate to stay silent or speak my truth?"

Carrie arrived a week later looking years younger. "I've been fearing his reaction, calling it compassion," she said between tears. "I've supported him financially and emotionally all these years, hiring all of the best therapists. But depression is Phil's way of life. I can't keep parenting him like a child or representing this as marriage to our children."

That evening, she said she had something difficult to share and asked Phil to listen. "I love you. On some level, I'll always love you," she said. "But I've reached the end of my rope. It's unhealthy for the kids for me to keep financing your depression. I need an equal partner who supports me and helps me parent. Next week, I'm filing for divorce. You can stay in the spare bedroom until you find a job. And I need both of us to speak highly of each other around the kids, no matter how angry we are."

One year later, I ran into Carrie downtown. "I felt so guilty getting a divorce with four kids," she grinned. "But it's the best thing I could have done for all of us.

"Phil is less depressed with his exciting, new job, and I found a good man who loves coparenting. When the children visit their dad, they don't emulate his depression."

Sometimes our truth makes no logical sense. But when we look back one, two, or five years later, our heart sorted through ego's fears and guided us to the broader, higher truth.

Untainted by ego's fears, doubts, and judgment, our heart beats with integrity; it knows to look for the deeper truth right in the middle of life's daily happenings. When anything happens that we don't like, don't want, don't expect, our truthful heart jumps past ego reactions to ask, "What can I learn from this experience if I stay fully present and awake?"

Over time, repeated truth telling builds courage and confidence. It teaches us that, though fear never stops painting tall stories of gloom and doom, there truly is room for our truth in this world. Try as ego may to shame us into silence, our commitment to honesty shows us how the world has plenty of elbow room for us to be exactly who we are in our work, personal, social, and love lives. In fact, the world welcomes our unique gifts.

While lies can backfire on us down the road, honesty rescues us in challenging situations. If we are filled with resentment about a hurtful thing a loved one said or did, our truthful heart smiles dismissively at ego's acting up.

It helps to adopt the phrase "When you said/did _____, I felt _____, so what I need to heal is _____." This relays our specific feelings and needs free of judgment and blame. Knowing what sensitive, tender beings we humans are, our heart finds the kindest words, and if we listen to it, we can learn to use its language with our loved ones: "I love and appreciate you, and I have some feelings I'm scared to share with you. Last night, when we discussed our summer vacation, I felt hurt and undervalued when you kept interrupting me. This isn't the first time you've interrupted me when I begin to speak, so I need you to relax and sit back and listen to my ideas. When I finish, I need to hear you say my input is important."

Love requires saying things that are hard to say—and even harder to hear.

Honesty takes guts. Skillfully naming our vulnerable feelings and specifically asking for what we need to heal takes even more guts. Luckily, in love relationships with spouses, children, parents, and friends, we often have many years to practice.

Some of us procrastinate days, weeks, or years before telling a loved one, "I'm unhappy, sad, scared, or depressed. I can't shake this hopelessness and despair." By the time we finally tell them, it's old news. Since our body cannot lie, it was acting out our feelings each time we failed to name them. Too often loved ones watch us act out our fear, hurt, depression, jealousy, and anger—and feel attacked by our unnamed feelings—before we give ourselves the chance to own our feelings consciously. Not bothering to know or communicate our deeper truth creates suffering.

Love and honesty stretch us to embrace secret places below our awareness. As our ability to know ourselves matures, speaking our vulnerable truth grows easier.

Deeper Honesty Calms and Matures Us

There is truth, and there is deeper truth. In youthful innocence, a hormonal teen may yell, "I hate you!" to individuate from a controlling parent and find their own voice—and in the moment, they may really believe it. In our twenties and thirties, we may judge and blame our lover because we want them to be different from ourselves. But at some point, in our first, second, or third committed relationship, we tire of indulging ego's anger, which only brings distance and loneliness in the long run. As we mature, we long for tools that quiet defensiveness and reveal our deeper truth.

Presence, curiosity, awareness, and deep honesty rescue us from anger's lonely existence. As we quietly watch our breath in morning meditation and label thoughts "thinking," our growing capacity to stay present helps us discern healthy thoughts from those that feed depression, anxiety, or despair. As our curiosity asks, "Which story am I telling myself now?" we sink below ego's story to name our feelings and needs with ease.

The more we let our truthful heart speak our vulnerable feelings, the more we invite loved ones to share theirs. Ego swears such honesty scares love away, but in truth it creates greater closeness. By voicing our tender feelings and core beliefs again and again, asking for what we need to feel loved, we bring healing to the fear, hurt, sadness, and shame that has waited our whole lives to be seen and loved. And we identify with *awareness* of those core wounds—not the wounds themselves.

From such tender awareness, we recognize, "I am my wise, truthful heart noticing which core feeling and belief buttons are being pushed. In this moment, I choose to speak about my wound from awareness rather than act it out." The more our heart discerns between deep truth and reactivity, the more lightness and humor replace heavy conflict. Soon we replace an overdramatic "You never loved me!" with "Let me tell you the outrageous story my abandonment wound is projecting on you right now."

Clear, open, deep honesty between lovers simply takes practice and self-awareness. Disappointment, resentment, or frustration may spill out in a moment of anger. But seconds later, as tears stream down the face of the one we love, our heart softens and forgives. We remember that we always have a choice: between responsible truth telling, naming our feelings and needs clearly, or indulging anger once again.

Mary and Ron described their stalemate in therapy. "We love each other very much," Ron said. "But closeness stays just out of our grasp, eluding us. I'll never leave her, but I'm frustrated as hell with this eddy we've circled in for years."

Mary jumped in. "Ron avoids conflict like the plague. He stays silent to keep the peace. Later, when I find out from my son how he said nothing when someone flirted with him, I'm furious. I unleash my wrath on him. I want closeness, dammit. I want Ron to share everything with me. I want to feel important enough to fight for."

"Before this escalates into your usual argument, allow me to intervene," I said. "Right now, this very argument can bring you closeness, if you're both willing."

They nodded. "But we've been playing this movie for years," Ron said.

"As long as you stay on the surface, identified with your ego reactions, you go round and round with no resolution. You stay stuck. But the second you spend a few meditative moments with your honest heart, you can uncover the childhood feelings and beliefs that refuel your arguments."

Mary and Ron closed their eyes, took a handful of deep breaths and, as instructed, noticed what feelings were present in their bellies at that moment. Then I asked them to name out loud which feelings were present without identifying or merging with the feelings.

"I feel afraid of getting hurt or abandoned," Mary shared.

"I feel shame for messing up again and disappointing Mary," Ron added.

"Now that you made your core feelings conscious," I told them, "you can teach each other about those feelings when they're up for you rather than arguing unconsciously."

I instructed the couple to take a few more deep breaths, focusing on their heart centers and asking their hearts which core belief activates their raw childhood fear and shame during verbal arguments. I encouraged them to breathe deeply and patiently listen for simple phrases such as "I'm unlovable, unimportant, unworthy, or unable to get my needs met."

"Once you name your core belief," I went on, "pause to gently ask your heart, 'What would I love to hear to heal my younger self?'"

After a few minutes, they both looked soft and vulnerable while opening their eyes.

"Now teach each other your core childhood belief and what you need to hear to heal."

"I never thought this affected my adult life," Mary said, "but as you know, Ron, my biological dad left when I was five. And Mom was so young she was never there for me. So I put on a good show, but I'm terrified to trust anyone," as she brushed tears from her cheek. "I keep pointing out your every mistake so I don't have to trust you either."

Mary held her head and sobbed. "I'm so sorry for pushing you away all these years. It's silly, but my 'Don't trust anyone' belief needs daily reassurance that I can trust you."

Ron held her. "You can totally trust me, babe. I love you, and I'm committed to us." He kept repeating the phrases until Mary took a big breath and let herself receive it.

After a long pause, Ron taught Mary what he needs around his core belief.

"Growing up in the seventies, Mom was always stoned. She never gave a rat's ass what I did or didn't do," he said. "As a teenager, when my buddy and I got caught breaking into a store, she barely said a word. But I carried shame about it. I still do.

"Every time you give me feedback, you push my shame button," he said. "This triggers my belief that I'm a shameful person unworthy of love. What I need to hear from you, every day for a while, is that I'm important and what I do is important to you."

Ron hung his head as Mary reached for his hand. "You're so important to me, hon. And when you show your love by sharing your feelings and needs, I feel our connection."

They left the office arm in arm, both knowing something important had shifted inside that day. They practiced speaking their truth at home, stumbling through arguments until one of them invited both of them to start over and name their core feelings and beliefs. Over time, meeting each other's needs grew easier as emotional blowups happened less often.

By speaking our deeper truth, we slowly realize that our tender heart doesn't need as much protecting and defending as we thought. When we communicate from a place of knowing, naming core feelings and beliefs to loved ones, we draw compassion rather than defensiveness from others. This brings freedom and inner peace.

Our truthful heart has a huge capacity to respond to all the ups and downs of life from a spacious pool of loving compassion and kindness. Honesty derived from this wise pool is more accepting of what is—and closer to our deeper truth.

For instance, Connie is a bright, confident businesswoman pushing forty. After two divorces and twenty years working in medicine, she is taking a sabbatical to keep closer tabs on her growing teenagers at home, which definitely has its ups and downs.

"My sixteen-year-old crashed my car into a tree!" she blurted out while sitting down in my therapy office. "She was talking on her cell phone, something I gave her strict instructions never to do while driving, and she missed a turn. Can you believe it? I borrowed my neighbor's car to come here today, because mine is in the shop. Of course, as my luck goes, I just raised my insurance deductible last week! I'm so angry…"

"Is your daughter okay?" I asked.

"Yes, yes, she's with her friends. As usual, Mom's left to clean up the mess."

"You sound angry," I said. "But with your commitment to deepen your awareness, let's have you close your eyes and ask which core feelings are fueling that anger."

Connie focused on her breathing, eyes closed, and peeked underneath. "I'm terrified," she said between tears. "What if it had been worse? What if one of her friends had been killed? What if she had been killed or paralyzed?"

Connie collapsed in her lap and grieved as only a mother can, for some time.

Later I asked, "Are you willing to share your vulnerable feelings with your daughter?"

"Yes," she agreed. "I've never shared my vulnerability with anybody, let alone one of my children. But she's sixteen now, and I've always hidden behind my anger—at least, that's what both my ex-husbands said. When I see her with eyes of compassion, I see how she's beating herself up enough. She doesn't need me tearing her down. I'm scared, but instead of punishing her, I can tell her how scared I am. I can invite softness."

The next week, a humble Connie arrived to therapy. "That night, we talked until midnight about the accident," she said. "We hugged and cried together, something that hasn't happened for at least three years. Seeing me vulnerable, she shared how scared she was. I did lecture her about never talking on her cell phone again while driving, but I did it with a kind voice, not anger. Since that night, we're different—kinder, sweeter, more loving. For years, compassion has evaded me. Here it is. I like it."

With minor self-reflection, Connie's renewed commitment to integrity helped her realize that bitterness and anger toward her daughter would only bring more suffering. Her truthful heart led her deep inside to the root of her own suffering and ultimately to a new closeness with her daughter.

Deep honesty with loved ones begins now as we greet life with compassion.

Living in Integrity with Our Truthful Heart

Too often, we live our lives with a narrow concept of integrity. We confuse integrity as synonymous with being a good Christian, Muslim, Jew, or Buddhist. We swallow society's pressure to hush those aspects of ourselves that don't fit nicely into today's social rules. In such terrain, the truthful heart is dismissed as silly, impractical, and unreasonable.

But living in integrity is much more difficult than following the rules. It is pausing to ask, "What do I truly believe in my heart, no matter how it looks to others?" Integrity means speaking up when a spouse, parent, teacher, or authority figure violates our personal beliefs on human rights, civil rights, environmental rights, and animal rights.

Integrity is speaking out publicly against injustice.

It follows principles of fairness and respect but never black-and-white rules set in cement for generations. Rather than hard rules like "stay married" or "be loyal to the death," integrity trusts our heart's truth in just this present moment. In simple terms, integrity is never having to hide any part of ourselves, because we accept and love all aspects of who we are.

For Jennifer, at thirty-eight, integrity meant leaving a controlling sergeant of a husband to marry her high school sweetheart, who wanted a baby with her. For Dan, reeling from his wife's suicide, integrity meant leaving the Catholic church of his boyhood and finding respite in the Buddhist teachings his parents had ridiculed for years. For Nancy, integrity meant opening her home to friends during her last year of life. For Jim, a successful surgeon, it meant moving his wife and children to Africa to tend the medical needs of poor Kenyan families. For Ann, raised black in the South where whites were the enemy in her family, it meant marrying a nice Jewish man she met in college.

Like learning any new skill, stepping into integrity takes commitment and practice. Some days we stay calm, dodging potential integrity dilemmas easily. Other days, we know the right thing to do but cannot stop the waterfall of bad habits. Be patient. Seeing our lack of integrity without being able to address it is a painful but necessary step in the process. When we pay attention to our internal conflicts, such as a tight belly or chest or headache, these inner signs tell us which issues need our inner compass. With practice integrity becomes easier.

Integrity looks different for different people at different times. But it all comes from the same place: unconditional love for our own and others' pain, tears, and confusion, no exceptions. Integrity nudges us to meet each new challenge with more kindness, patience, acceptance, and compassion. It invites us to respond with compassionate acceptance when others exhibit personal reactions. When we feel upset, scared, or hopeless, it reminds us to place one hand over our heart and whisper, "No worries. Nothing is wrong."

Integrity comes with a discerning heart. It slips into place each time we align with our true values. It gives us courage to live in truth with our highest values, even when our truth looks different than anyone else's in the world. And now that we label thoughts "thinking" and ask, "Which part of me is afraid?" meeting life with integrity comes easier.

Integrity answers our young self's persistent question, "But is there enough elbow room for *me* to be all of who I am in this world?" with a resounding, "Yes, yes, and yes again." Whether knocked down by loss, illness, divorce, or despair, integrity scoops us up off the floor in one fell swoop. It bestows on us the courage to follow our dreams, voice our truth, and pursue our soul's purpose unabashedly.

When Craig said he wanted a divorce, Suzie swung as hard as she could and gave him a bloody nose. She spent several sleepless nights commiserating with her best friend about the ten years she and Craig spent building their dream home—the mansion where his young girlfriend now sleeps in the bed in the room she and Craig built together.

"I wish I were dead," Suzie said in therapy. "After years of living the high life on Craig's dime, I can't imagine supporting myself on a nurse's salary again.

"On the other hand, I gave up everything I believed in to marry Craig—my career, my politics, my integrity. He's such a staunch conservative—against abortion rights and women's equality—that I was embarrassed to introduce him to my friends. I may be poor now, but at least I won't keep suffering the pain of living outside of my values."

That night, Suzie's truthful heart spoke to her in a loving dream.

"I dreamed a firing squad hauled me to my execution," she said. "I went limp, accepting my fate; I closed my eyes and was ready to take a bullet in the head. But then the men said it was late, and they would postpone the execution until morning. I headed to bed in my prison cell, totally accepting that I would die in the morning. But friends surrounded me in the night and said, 'This is your chance! We'll help you escape now!' The whole group of us ran away unharmed with little effort. In the final scene, I was hiking through a grassy meadow, happy."

Her discerning heart's dream woke Suzie up to how controlling Craig was—and how she had abandoned her integrity. By the next week she had hired a lawyer, and she rented a room from two friends, a couple who owned forty acres outside of town with a large, green meadow.

Living in integrity embraces all of our earlier heart qualities: being trusting, wise, curious, aware, resourceful, compassionate, kind, grateful, and forgiving. It happens inside a moment at work when someone cracks a racist joke, and we choose not to laugh, or we speak up. It happens at the dinner table when our child jokes about a classmate who learns slowly, and we pause to say, "It's more kind to accept, not judge, others' differences." Or in the middle of lovemaking when we interrupt the process to say, "I feel scared and need to slow down." Like shifting channels, we shift seamlessly in our day-to-day lives into choosing integrity.

On a balmy April Monday, I hiked alone for hours. Usually I write for three or four hours on Monday. But that day my heart begged me to put on my hiking boots right after breakfast and be "off leash." I hiked and hiked for hours without stopping, winding up on top of a mountain I had not visited since November, when the snow arrived. I found a warm grassy spot out of the wind and lay-watching clouds for over an hour. I hiked home smiling, feeling refreshed.

That Monday, my heart knew I needed a change of pace. It needed me to spend hours feeling my patient, grateful, generous heart, away from the business of life. I'd been pushing hard, seeing more than my usual number of weekly clients and handling too much business for too long. My nerves were shot, my adrenals exhausted. My very soul felt spent. But my heart knew the answer, if only I would listen more often.

The next day, I was back in balance, ready to write and see clients.

Integrity Dilemmas Cut Us Off from Our Heart

The truth is, as innocent children we all sacrifice our integrity to survive. We have to. We cannot survive on our own. As young, helpless beings in dependent bodies, we need nurturing and love to survive. Our integrity, which means nothing to us at two, five, or ten, feels like a tiny price to pay compared with a chance to live and receive love.

Despite good intentions, our parents succumbed to their own unconscious conditioning while caring for us as best they could. In moments of their own anger, frustration, or fear, our parents required that we abandon the integrity of our own being to obey, accept, follow, or please them. Desperate to earn love and approval, and intent on sidestepping possible abuse from the very people our life depends on, we acquiesced. As children, we stepped out of integrity with our deepest truth without knowing it or realizing that it will lead to future problems.

Abandoning our wholeness, the integrity of our sovereign being, is called an *integrity dilemma*. Without yet knowing we are born lovable and worthy, and that nobody can ever take these natural birthrights away from us, we fall into unconscious habits of "earning self-worth" by pleasing, caretaking, flirting, being super responsible, and winning accolades from the external world. Integrity dilemmas split our mind off from our heart-felt truth and wisdom, convincing us to rely on ego's thoughts, ideas, and schemes to survive.

This split from our heart, instigated by childhood traumas, allows ego to talk us into all sorts of cheating and lying and schemes that lack integrity. Ego seduces us with false promises, such as "I'll get you what you want and help you avoid what you don't want, if you just do what I say." As children overwhelmed by parents' mixed messages and a world we struggle to understand, we cling to ego's false promises to calm our confusion. But by adulthood, these false ego roles we adopted years earlier to earn love, approval, and self-worth become our total identity. The integrity of our being stays hidden underneath these roles.

Many of us spend decades out of integrity with ourselves, feeling *something is wrong* but unable to put our finger on what. Life may jolt us awake with a serious illness, injury, divorce, or loss that knocks the smug arrogance out of our ego. But lying flat on our back in pain, or curled up crying in a fetal position, doesn't change anything, unless we ask, "How am I out of integrity?" and "How can I choose integrity now?"

Living out of step with integrity is painful. It grows unbearable with time. Postponing, ignoring, or abandoning who we truly are, inside our heart, wages an inner war. It erodes our health, happiness, hope, joy, and sense of well-being. It can lead to ulcers, depression, anxiety, back pain, and serious illness. When we finally step across the threshold—from trusting ego's pleaser or caretaker, drama queen or controller, to trusting our wise heart—we enter the realm of integrity. Perhaps for the first time, we stand ready to question every false belief we swallowed as children. Now we quickly shed those old beliefs to make room for our long lost integrity. After years of sacrificing our integrity for survival, we are safe to be who we are.

At forty-five, Darlene had never known true inner integrity. After years of meditation and talk therapy, she desperately longed for love but had no clue how to find it or keep it. "I'm a savvy client," she said in her first therapy session. "I know Mom was a psycho. I know her inability to tolerate my needs as a dependent infant messed up my life. And I know that feeling numb probably sabotages my ability to find love. But it makes me a great computer nerd.

"I also know I'm sitting on a lot of anger, grief, and fear, but feelings terrify me."

"You describe your childhood pain well from talk therapy," I said, "but let's try a fresh approach. Since feelings connect you with the integrity of your heart, let's help you make friends with feelings. Close your eyes and watch your breath in your belly as if you are meditating. But this time, using your breath as an anchor, you can return attention to any feelings that are present and where you feel them in your body."

"I only feel safe when I'm *not* feeling," she chuckled nervously. "But with the breath as my anchor, I'm willing for a few seconds. I notice a tight knot in my belly. When I focus on the knot, I fear my new girlfriend will leave, fear I'll get hurt again… Now I'm sad that nobody is ever here for my feelings and needs."

"Good noticing," I said. "Now return attention to your familiar belly breath and relax. Perhaps while meditating you have watched a younger part of you, someone we'll call 'young Darlene,' who scares easily and never felt safe to feel any feelings, correct?"

She nodded and shrugged.

Speaking to that beautiful meditative awareness she had cultivated for years, I invited Darlene to lean into her wise, loving heart—that place inside capable of holding her young child's scared feelings in compassion. "Just witness the fear and sadness in your belly without getting lost in it," I told her.

Darlene sat quietly several minutes as she held her feelings in compassion.

"For years," she said, tears wetting her cheeks, "I felt terrified to feel the feelings Mom never allowed as a kid. This whole time, I only had to hold them in compassion."

Compassion felt vague for Darlene at first, so she thought about how much she loved her dog Chester and imagined bundling all that love into a bright ball to shine on her belly. For the first time, Darlene felt a tenderness toward her child self she had never known before.

Darlene worked in therapy on healing her childhood pain for several months. But that first taste of reconnecting with her inner compass that day in my office sparked a fire inside to know and speak her truth and live in integrity, no matter what. Recently I heard that Darlene and her girlfriend of the past year and a half got married.

It takes great courage to face the feelings we have avoided for years. It takes more courage to stand in integrity with who we truly are. But each time, another puzzle piece falls into place inside as we feel our feelings and speak our truth. Each time, our tolerance for facing discomfort grows from two to ten to twenty minutes at a time until discomfort stops running our lives. Each time, integrity builds deep trust as it helps us breathe into the next scary feeling and come out the other side, more confident. Each time, we return to the compassion and integrity of our truthful hearts.

Feelings become the golden gateway to joy, inner peace, and freedom. Integrity is that place. The more we put our time and energy into those things our heart values most, the more we honor our heart's rightful place as our true compass.

Aligning Our Actions with Our Heart's Values

Living in integrity is putting our body and voice where our heart lives. It is standing up and voicing our heart's true values. At times, it is missing work to help hurricane, earthquake, or tornado victims because our heart calls us. Other times it is attending city council, state board, or federal meetings to take a stand on critical issues because our heart calls us to. Or as one North Carolina doctor did, it is coming out of retirement to provide free medical care to immigrant workers near home. For author Alice Walker, it was flying to Cuba to stand up for Cuban citizens' rights during political conflicts with the U.S.

For me, in the late seventies, with threats of nuclear war rampant, integrity meant forming a human blockade in front of Livermore Laboratory in Pleasanton, California, at 7:30 one April morning. We blocked workers from getting to their jobs to produce more nuclear weapons. Within an hour, hundreds of protesters were loaded onto school buses, arrested, and jailed. After three days and nights, we were released, free of charges. But our stand was clear.

Inside it can feel scary, even terrifying, to show our true colors to parents, neighbors, customers, and strangers, exposing to the world what we believe in our hearts. Fear threatens: "You'll lose your job! Lose your marriage! Lose your business!" Yet after we speak up, we stand more grounded and solid in our body. Inner strength becomes our new best friend.

Ron appeared like an all-American guy to his neighbors. He worked at a bank and his wife Phyllis played the organ at church on Sundays. Ron coached his son's Little League games, mowed the lawn, and sat on the city council. But inside, Ron suffered from depression.

"I've lived on auto-pilot, sentencing myself to a joyless life for years," he said. "After our son left for college, the pain of being gay in a straight marriage felt as unbearable as hurting my wife by telling her I'm gay. Living out of integrity makes me feel hopeless.

"Since I was fourteen, I knew I was gay. But back in my day, this wasn't something you talked about or pursued as a lifestyle. If I keep living this lie, I don't care to live."

I held Ron in compassion as he held his head in his hands and wept.

Later, I strongly encouraged Ron to step into integrity with himself by telling his wife his truth. That night, when he told Phyllis, she denied it, acting as if Ron had not said a word. She begged him not to tell their friends and to try to fix his problem in inpatient treatment.

But Ron stood by his truth. Slowly over time, his wife and son arrived at acceptance.

"I couldn't live a lie anymore," he said. "It killed my spirit. My body was next. I'm living outside of normal now with my new lover. Phyllis and I mended our differences and are good friends, like we were in our marriage. I take care of her household repairs and she feeds my poodle when Jed and I travel. And my true friends stood by me and have accepted who I really am."

As we surrender into integrity, we meet each new conflict and struggle with more spaciousness, kindness, acceptance, and compassion. We find ourselves less at war with ourselves and the world. In finding the inner strength and courage to be who we truly are in life, we allow others more breathing room to be who they really are.

Aligning our actions with our values helps us live from a deeper sense of self—a place of deep integrity. We carve a tunnel past the loud voices of fear, doubt, guilt, and judgment to reach all the way to the loving voice of our truthful heart. Amid tough choices, we find ourselves asking, "How can I choose integrity right now?" We respond to each new difficult conflict and challenge with wisdom, courage, and discernment.

Integrity is doing the right thing. It is quitting smoking, not just talking about it. It is exercising regularly, even if we love to eat and cozy up on the couch. It is getting up a half an hour early to meditate, even if we got to bed late. It is talking to our teenagers about sex when the time comes, even if we feel embarrassed. It is apologizing to those we hurt as many times as it takes for them to forgive us. It is staying monogamous, even when our marriage hits a rough spot and every cell in our body screams to have sex with a hot new thing. It is carving out time to spend with our mate, child, aging parent, and loved ones even if our schedule is full. In short, it is living by our principles.

Integrity is strength of character and courage. It cultivates honesty, compassion, understanding, kindness, and forgiveness. Ultimately we are responsible for how we fill our twenty-four hours each day. At the end of our life, most of the errands and bills and tasks we fill each day with won't matter one bit. So why wait? If we long to paint, draw, write, play guitar, finish a triathlon, or photograph nature someday, let someday be now. We can take that first action step now to align with our values, then keep on going.

Once we embrace a strong commitment to live in integrity, choices become simple. Our truthful heart discerns between right and wrong. It is trustworthy. It leads us through the maze of endless choices. Living in integrity frees us to respond to life from our wise heart.

Living in Truth and Integrity as a Way of Life

When we stand on our own two feet and speak our truth, confidence blooms. When we do the right thing, the thing our truthful heart knows is right, we grow courage. Choosing truth and integrity day after day matures us into trusting life.

Simply stopping is one key to living in truth and integrity. Stopping long enough to ask, "Where is the lie in my life?" Stopping all the doing, thinking, planning, and fantasizing long enough to allow our truthful heart to bask in the here and now. Our heart knows that, when we are truly free, there is nothing to gain or keep that should take us out of step with integrity. Integrity is not something to set on some lofty pedestal to achieve (like ego's other goals); instead, integrity is our natural birthright. It is that pure place inside our heart that lives in the unlimited joy, love, compassion, and inner peace present in each and every moment. In those precious times when we are fully awake, we bask in the still silence of who we truly are.

Resting in the integrity of our being is the source of true happiness. Our wise heart, peaceful with doing the honest thing, is the choiceless choice.

Recently, I joined my heart's integrity in the timeless present. After hiking above 11,000 feet in the San Juan Mountains for two hours, I sat down on a vertical slope of fresh green tundra above tree line. Happiness filled every cell in my body. I couldn't stop smiling. I sat perfectly still. I shed all thoughts momentarily and sat quietly alert, looking and listening and smelling like a wild animal in nature.

I felt so at one with the present, so awake that it brought tears of joy to my eyes.

On this balmy Sunday at 12,500 feet, across from my steep perch, my soul drank in snow-covered peaks wet with melting snow from the warm May sun. For a long time, I lost myself in the cobalt blue sky against the pure white snowy peaks. Uninterested in passing thoughts, my eyes shifted from the spiky grey charcoal mountains to the wide crevices of snow, revealing where huge avalanches had exploded earlier this spring. The silence felt so pure and still that I heard its presence humming in my ears. Far in the distance, rushing waterfalls created from snow melt tumbled ever downward toward Lime Creek miles below. A pica flew over the snow, breaking the silence.

When we stop the busyness, the precious miracles of life unfold at our feet.

The more we pause to witness the magnificence of aspen leaves dancing in the breeze, or hear mourning doves cooing atop a pine tree, the closer we step toward touching our own pure joy of being alive. As our eyes and ears and heart open, eventually we even see what kind, loving, joyful creatures we are.

This pure joy of being alive, shared by all beings, is our basic goodness.

Living in truth and integrity is not about erasing our lives and starting from scratch. We still eat, sleep, love, exercise, commute to work, and act silly. We still change diapers and watch our toddlers take their first step. We still get colds, nurse our body back to health, take vacations, and ride the waves of the stock market. But as we choose honesty and integrity with each challenging dilemma, ego's thoughts, fears, and reactive stories ride in the sidecar of awareness. Our knowing heart, steering our choices, continually points us in the right direction. In the middle of our busy active lives, we step into our wise heart and choose integrity. Like shifting TV channels, we shift seamlessly into the truth of our discerning heart. Inner peace comes from doing the right thing again and again and again.

Choosing truth and integrity spells freedom. They spell the inner peace, gratitude, and joy that come from trusting our truthful heart. As we stand tall in the mountain of being that we are, feeling our deep connection with all living things, we radiate integrity with every cell of our body. We bask in the pure joy of being alive.

Aligning with our values comes down to choosing integrity now and now and now. Luckily, we have the rest of our lives to practice living in integrity.

Heart Tools for Honesty and Integrity

Practice each of these tools for one week before moving on to the next one. But if a specific tool calls you to spend more time with it, give yourself another week, month, or as long as you need in order to heal.

1. Set a Strong Intention to Choose Honesty

Make this intention with yourself and others for at least one week. Notice ego's countless attempts to convince you to avoid conflict, save face, or keep the peace by lying. Choose honesty and see how far ego's fear is from reality. Practice the art of speaking your truth with kindness and respect. See how honesty feels in your body. Notice how others respond to truth. We humans are built to hear and speak the refreshing truth.

2. *Commit to Revealing Deep Honesty*

Do this for at least a week, up to a month. Refrain from acting out ego's initial anger, frustration, or jealousy so that you can uncover your core feelings and beliefs. Ask inside, "Which core feeling—hurt, fear, sadness, or shame—is fueling my reaction?" Take a few deep breaths and patiently wait for a picture, feeling-sense, or word to bubble up into your awareness. When you feel ready to move on, ask, "Which core belief (such as 'I'm undeserving of love' or 'My feelings and needs are unimportant') is feeding my feeling and reaction?" Take some deep breaths and again patiently wait for an image or feeling-sense. Find a good time to consciously share your deeper truth with your mate by saying, "I notice when you said _____, I felt _____. After exploring this, my deeper core feeling of hurt, fear, sadness, or shame was triggered by my core wound belief that 'I'm unlovable.' What I need to hear around this is _____." When we use a kind tone to share our deeper truth, no matter how painful or filled with tears, loved ones can more easily respond with kindness.

3. *Live in Integrity with Your Discerning Heart*

Each morning, for a week or more as needed, call an integrity dilemma into your awareness. Once you have it, place both hands over your heart and ask, "What agreements have I broken, with myself or loved ones, in reacting to this situation? Where have I lied, through omission or half-truths? What about this have I not fully accepted?" After each question, pause to hear your heart's response. Once you accept the situation fully, carve out some time with that loved one to speak your truth and step into integrity. Reassure yourself with "I am safe to speak my truth."

4. *Aligning Daily Actions with Your Values*

At the end of a quiet time or meditation, take a few minutes to notice how you spend your time. Throughout the day ask, "How is my time being used or misused today? Where am I out of integrity with those things I value most?" Notice without judgment. For one week, spend an hour each day doing something your heart values, such as spending time with loved ones, riding your bike, hiking, painting, or calling a friend. Notice how it feels in your body to include things you value in your daily life. Give this gift to yourself and watch integrity return. If you have postponed a lifelong dream, ask your heart, "What is my first action step to bring this to fruition?" Take this step. Ask again and take the next step. Set a strong intention to live in integrity with your heart, aligned with your values, even if you have no clue how. Keep your promise to yourself.

10. Your Peaceful Heart

The Power of Surrender

If you will take a moment to recognize the peace that is
already alive within you, you then actually have the choice
to trust it in all your endeavors, in all your relationships,
in every circumstance of your life.
—GANGAJI

I nner peace comes in knowing and trusting the freedom
of who we are inside.

Spring is altering the Colorado Rockies landscape. Those six-foot tall snow piles lining driveways this winter have disappeared, allowing brown frozen grass to green in the late afternoon sun. Aspen trees, naked for months, hide tiny buds in their branches, promising a plethora of green leaves by May. Rushing creeks and rivers overflowing with snowmelt tumble down hills, reminding us of the great January storms.

Daffodils and crocuses push up through the ground. Hundreds of Canadian geese, headed north, honk overhead before dipping down onto barely thawed reservoirs. Yesterday, a flock of twenty-five grosbeaks descended on the backyard bird feeder, squawking wildly of their grueling migration. Black bears sleeping in the mountains wake up starving after months of hibernation. And elk herds savor fresh green sprouted grass as they head up to 11,000 feet for the summer.

While we complained of the late spring snow, which created cold temperatures and slick roads, the wildlife went quietly about their business. They appeared flexible, open, adaptable, playful, and accepting. They took it all in stride—completely trusting life, as if they remembered some secret to inner peace we had long forgotten:

Stop arguing with reality. Surrender and accept life as it comes.

Inner Peace Is Always Here, Underneath Thought

Most of us have a ways to go before we can live in a state of peaceful surrender. Though inner peace is always present inside, accessing it is not our automatic response. When we feel uncomfortable or don't get our way, we flail and kick and scream. When our spouse blurts out their truth, "I need to move near my parents," our reaction is not even close to peaceful. When we overhear that our lover is painfully unhappy in our relationship, we want to ignore their concern, talk them out of it, discount it—anything but acknowledge their pain.

As we now know, ego's like/dislike reactions to every little thing cover up our innate capacity for meeting life with loving-kindness, compassion, and inner peace. These instant reactions also hide the unlimited joy we are all born with. Through awareness, we now hold in the palm of our hands our free pass to exit ego's runaway train of reactions: the ability to simply stop.

Stop thinking. Stop doing. Stop staying busy. Stop our frenetic habit of chasing happiness by getting more and more things. Stop our ego's attachment to how this moment *should* look and feel. Stop listening to ego's silly belief that some future moment is more important than this one. And when we finally stop, we sink down into the simple profound peace of being alive, a sanctuary available to us every moment, for the rest of our lives. We don't have to *do* anything. Inner peace is right here where it always is.

Inner peace lives here, inside our peaceful heart. Each time we relate to life from this deeper, wiser, more fearless place, we cultivate inner peace. Each moment we pause to remember the conscious awareness that we really are—remembering that thoughts, fears, and feelings are not our identity—we relax into what is. Suddenly the peace we long for is right here, awaiting our focused attention.

Suffering comes from resisting what is true now. If we still experience suffering in our daily life, we can guarantee that, somehow, we are still running a victim story.

Inside, when nobody is watching, even the best of us can sometimes be drama queens. After our morning meditation, prayer, Pilates, or yoga, we sometimes devote the rest of our waking hours to "me and my story," obsessed with how yesterday should have happened differently and how tomorrow should go if "nothing goes wrong."

Our drama-queen minds muse on these juicy thoughts all day. We adapt today's dilemma to our favorite victim story reruns—feeling rejected, misunderstood, betrayed, or hurt—and call it our life. But this story is a cheap dime-store imitation. Rather than experience life directly, we interpret, judge, and compare how we could be happy—if only this moment were somehow more in our favor.

To regain inner peace, we must see our victim stories as stories, not truth. We must stop taking life so personally, so seriously.

I am no exception. Last Thursday, I felt happy and peaceful. It was the end of my workweek. Spring cherry blossoms filled the air. Life felt good—until my last client was about to walk out the front door. I mentioned I was flying to Maui in late July for my summer vacation. She asked, "Which airline do you take to Maui?"

"ATA. I love ATA—it's half the price of other airlines."

"That's unfortunate," she frowned. "This morning I heard on the radio that ATA filed for bankruptcy today. It cancelled all future flights and is going out of business."

I met her shocking news with denial. "ATA?" I mumbled, convinced I would wake up from this bad dream any minute now. "I'm sure they'll fix it by late July."

My client shrugged and left. I walked into the bedroom dazed, donning my bathrobe to soak in the hot tub and contemplate this devastating news. Inside, disbelief turned to rage. "This can't be happening to me. I deserve a vacation. I need a vacation. How could my favorite airline die before my vacation? There must be a big mistake."

My jaw clenched as righteous indignation swelled in my chest.

I was ready to scream bloody murder—until I remembered my intention.

For several weeks now, in my morning meditation, I have been cultivating inner peace. Though none of the ancient Buddhist teachings I read mentioned how to cope with your favorite airline dying before vacation, I gulped and muttered my intention to myself: "I am willing to choose inner peace, even now."

Nothing in me believed inner peace was possible, given the circumstances. My inner skeptic continued to rant bloody murder in my head. And yet, by saying my intention out loud, by choosing inner peace, I felt a little space inside—as if something shifted, lifted, lightened. The more I scratched below the anger and repeated my intention, the more this spacious feeling grew. I still heard my anger inside. But I also heard the soft, quiet voice of my peaceful heart whispering in my ear:

"You have a choice now. You can choose suffering and keep listening to the story or spend two seconds naming it 'thinking' and letting it go. Even though it feels impossible, repeat 'I choose peace' over and over until you feel peacefulness awaken inside.

Rather than stay lost in that victim story for hours, relax. Trust life. Notice the meadowlark. Ask, 'Which will I choose to practice— suffering or inner peace?'"

Put that way, I took a deep breath and made the obvious choice: inner peace.

This freed me to check online for alternate flights, call US Airways, and book a new reservation. Three weeks later, ATA refunded my money on the canceled flight. Even if everything hadn't worked out, I would have made it through that summer okay; each time fear thoughts arose, I kept surrendering to inner peace.

Intentions are powerful antidotes to ego's victim habit of taking life personally. When we say, "I choose peace," we wake up out of ego's stupor and return to the present, where all the power lives. We are free to consciously choose how to respond.

Our job is to remember that inner peace is at our fingertips. Anger, fear, doubt, judgment, and other states of mind do cover it up. Ego still has a like/dislike reaction to every life event. But inner peace is a choice we have every moment. No matter what gift life brings us, or what feelings it triggers, we can choose to perpetuate suffering by indulging our reactions—or reconnect with inner peace.

See inner peace as a mountain of stillness living deep inside every heart. It is like a big brother or sister holding our hand, reminding us: "Take several deep breaths. Take several more deep breaths. Come back into present. Be amused by ego's latest fear, then let it go. Now love yourself for whatever you are feeling."

Inner Peace Flows from the Power of Surrender

When the power of surrender helps us accept what is, inner peace soothes us. It softens any chaos, conflict, disappointment, or fear visiting us today. It brings courage (which is originally from the French word *coeur*, meaning "heart") to meet life on life's terms.

As our eyes open wide to embrace both suffering and joy as integral parts of life, we relax into what is. This spacious acceptance is deeply peaceful. We spent years overlooking the gift of inner peace by protecting ourselves from possible hurt. The whole time, our ego lied, convincing us that our heart needed insulation from the world.

As we drop down into our heart and see the world through the eyes of compassion, we can look back on the pain in our lives as teachers helping us open our own hearts to the jewels of suffering. Without realizing we needed this lesson, pain somehow brought us closer to understanding this mysterious human experience—our own and others—and holding it all in loving compassion. Surrendering to the innate wisdom of life at this deeper level changes us forever. Inner peace comes from this.

Ted was blessed with good health, success, and children who loved him. From this pinnacle Ted felt tortured by his wife's chronic depression. "I tuned Karen out when she spoke of her depression," he said. "I felt sick of hearing about something I couldn't fix." But last November when Ted rolled his Toyota into a ravine, his perspective on Karen's suffering changed. After weeks of traction and therapy, he still suffers back pain.

"I hate the back pain every day," he admitted. "I can't imagine how Karen coped with her depression coming and going all those years. Now, when Karen sits on the edge of our bed to connect and share her feelings, I'm hearing her for the first time. All those years, I was so caught up in how her feelings impacted *me*—how she made me into a victim—but now I look into those beautiful blue eyes I fell in love with years ago and just listen to her. I feel such compassion for her lifelong struggle with depression—and for all people suffering depression and back pain. We're such vulnerable things."

Inner peace comes when we stop running away and accept pain and joy equally. From this fresh vantage point, we start to watch the whole victim story that humanity unconsciously acts out every day as a world story. We do not go so far as to diminish or belittle our own pain. But we realize that a particular predicament that feels so heavy and unusual in the moment is common, shared, and simply part of universal suffering. In short, it is life. Soon we begin to feel compassion for all human struggles, including our own. When we stop chasing after the next great strategy to avoid pain, when we stop believing ego's lie that we have to control life, we can settle in and enjoy the whole wild and crazy journey of being alive. In this place, we meet inner peace.

By meeting our suffering consciously and choosing to let it go, inner peace welcomes all pain and suffering as visiting scholars with something precious to teach.

Inner Peace Lives in Our Deeper Sense of Self

We can sink down into inner peace any moment. Like the bottom of the ocean, the unlimited peace deep inside remains quiet and still while huge waves of fear, doubt, anxiety, and despair come and go, rippling across the surface of our daily life. Inner peace reminds us that those waves of stress and worry that pretend to matter so much are just visitors, not who we are. In fact, any thoughts or feelings that come and go are not who we are in our deep sense of self. It is our conscious, loving heart, noticing the waves—and noticing ego's reactions to these waves—that is our real self.

The unlimited peace inside our heart forms a loving backdrop on this stage called life. It holds all our day-to-day comings and goings in compassion and joy. Just as a loving grandmother treasures each moment with her grandchild, knowing it will all change in a blink, inner peace counsels us not to take anything—not thoughts or feelings, pain or fears—too seriously. It urges us, moment to moment, to savor each life experience, even those we don't like or expect. Tapping into inner peace helps us remember the following:

- To stop reacting with anger and fear—or reacting at all.
- To be entertained—not consumed—by ego's "me and my story."
- That inner peace comes by accepting what is, including ourselves.
- That we are spacious, loving awareness noticing our victim story.
- That we are compassionate awareness letting unconscious habits go.
- That there is nothing we need right now to feel inner peace.

For example, Chris struggled with indecision his whole adult life. At thirty-eight, unable to decide whether to marry his girlfriend, Robin, and have a child, he entered therapy. The surface waves sounded like "What if I marry the wrong person, like Dad did?" or "What if we have a baby and I'm a lousy father?" He chalked his indecision up to being a Libra, always weighing the pros and cons. But by bringing curiosity and compassion to his indecisive habit, he uncovered his deeper self and stumbled upon inner peace.

"At thirteen, when my parents divorced and Mom told us she was gay," he said, "my world as I knew it fell apart. Instead of feeling special to belong to this cool family, I felt ashamed. I started drinking and drugging and stopped caring about my future."

Rather than spend the whole session discussing his childhood story, I invited Chris to lie down, breathe deeply, and notice where he was carrying this trauma and loss in his body. "I feel heavy and numb at the base of my torso," he described.

I invited Chris to breathe into the heavy numbness. "Oh my god, I'm so afraid of the world. Afraid to speak up, afraid to pour myself into anything for fear it will disappear, like my family did." With this came a flood of tears. "I've always felt not good enough, like I never belonged. But I didn't know until now where it came from."

Like most beliefs, his deep unconscious fear of the world wanted to keep proving itself right—at the expense of Chris feeling love and the joy of parenting. Over the next few weeks, he surrendered into the deep grief of how his early teen trauma thwarted his ability to trust and receive love. He shared with friends his struggle with indecision. He even told his mother at Christmastime how she'd impacted his tender teens.

Each morning for a few weeks, Chris put both hands over his heart and loved his shame as it was, without needing it to go away. His issues remain in process, as life goes most of the time. He has not married yet. But after releasing those stuck tears and making his fears conscious, he carries more confidence and a peaceful heart into his daily life. "My heart is more open than ever to receiving Robin's love."

Whenever we focus in this moment, we do have to face whatever grief and despair we have been avoiding. But each time we set aside ego's reactions and step into *this* moment, whatever we find is held in the unlimited compassion and inner peace of our heart.

After breathing into feelings and releasing them, we rest in what is always here: the conscious life force streaming through our bones and veins in the present—the same life force that connects us with all living things. This force maintains inner balance. It helps us not get so thrown off course when unexpected and unfamiliar events land in our lap. It responds to life like an aikido master: "Let it in. Let it be. Let it go."

Like Chris, when we surrender into our deeper sense of self, we remember that who we really are, in our core, has nothing to do with feeling happy or sad, excited or lonely in any given moment. These ripples on the surface, passing through, no longer threaten us. If they take away our inner peace, it is because we let them.

Inner peace prods us to look up at the clouds appearing and disappearing across the sky, to pause and hear the crickets chirping on a summer evening, or to let in our loved one's tears of unhappiness without taking any of it personally. Inner peace lets us watch our own thoughts and feelings move through our awareness, like clouds, without fixating on what every word or action means about us.

As we identify less with the surface waves, we bask in the inner peace of who we are: a loving presence grounded in unlimited joy, loving-kindness, inner peace, and freedom.

Consciously Choosing Peace Over Problems

Every moment of every day, we choose between peace and problems. When we choose peace, problems come and go. When we choose problems, the voice of inner peace is muted into the background. Unfortunately, most of the time, we unconsciously choose problems out of habit. We wake up in the morning, abandon the peace percolating inside, and dredge up yesterday's unresolved problems to breathe fresh life into them today. We pretend to have no choice. We claim that problems find us. But in reality, we boost problems onto center stage and breathe life into them. After all, problems help us feel important. They give us passion and purpose and stave off boredom.

As much as we complain, we kind of like our problems; we cling to them, insisting they are the biggest of all. Ego loves a good, meaty problem to gnaw on all day, or all year.

But few of us realize that problems demand our constant time, effort, and energy to stay afloat. They exhaust us. Whether we are parents or teenagers, professionals or prisoners, problems are mesmerizing. Problems can knock us offbalance and make us prey to ego's One Big Story: "Who wronged me, and how I will get even?" Every time this catchall story snags us, ego chews over and over on what happened that should never have happened—and who is to blame? As soon as we lose ourselves in today's problem, or in resisting that problem, we abandon the joy and inner peace that are also present.

Of course, we can't simply get rid of problems—and working too hard to avoid them is exhausting and fruitless. When they visit, we do need to pay them some bare attention, sticking only to the facts without embellishing. The trick is resting in our inner peace and putting space around each problem—without letting it take over.

Though problems arrive in all shapes and sizes, the *big problem*—the repeated issue we overreact to—is usually linked to a childhood wound imprinted on our life years earlier.

As dependent children, we survive overwhelming feelings or loss by making up a story about the cause of the trauma, such as "It's Mom's fault Dad left." When we decide that we are the cause— "Dad wouldn't have left if I hadn't been so annoying"—such stories later translate into "I'm unlovable, I'm unimportant, something is wrong with me, nobody understands me," and other core beliefs, as we learned earlier.

Such stories and beliefs, though they feel very personal, initiate us into the universal story of what struggles we face as a human being in a body. Our personal story gives us a specific lens to filter life experiences through—and taints how we see the past, the present, and the future. If we grow up feeling unimportant to a parent or sibling, we can perpetuate this unimportance in our interactions with lovers, friends, and mates, then blame them for not treating us with more respect and importance. We continue to suffer at the hands of this trauma filter—until we use this "unimportance" to wake up.

For example, when Bill places both hands over his heart each morning and loves the painful belief that joined his life as an infant, "Something is wrong with me," the heaviness in his heart lightens. When Chris whispers to himself at the end of his morning meditation, "I'm here for you, and I love you for being indecisive," his childhood belief, "I'm unlovable," melts into inner peaceful-ness. When Martha slows down and asks her heart, "What do I need today?" her childhood trauma of nobody caring about her needs softens. Loving our childhood trauma and core beliefs opens our heart's compassion.

Inner peace expands our capacity for meeting whatever appears a hundredfold.

We are free to suffer, or free to stop suffering. Now it is our con-scious choice.

Replacing Childhood Stories and Core Beliefs with Who We Are

Earlier, we already established how much we love stories. It's fun to share ones about our childhood, our love life, our family life, and our weekend adventures. It shoots pizzazz into our daily work grind. We may even hone the art of storytelling. But unless we notice when we cross over into playing victim and proving our childhood story right for the thousandth time, we pay a high price.

When we resent our husband for years for a silly blunder on our honeymoon, or we spend decades tossing out potential mates at the first whiff of disappointment, we close our heart to love. We get so lost in our fear of hurt, discouragement, or rejection that we grow afraid to care, afraid to trust, afraid to believe in life, and in love, and in our dreams. But from this point forward, when hurt arrives (which it always does, as part of being human), we can fall back on conscious choice—we can either give in to despair, prov-ing our "misunderstood" story right again, or hold our suffering in peaceful compassion.

Repeated conflicts with a spouse offer more than just sleepless nights. Kathy and Craig were sick of dragging themselves through the same bitter argument with no resolution. So they experimented with speaking from their deeper sense of self. Craig asked for a time out. He invited them both to close their eyes and ask, "What story or belief is fueling my strong personal reaction, and what do I need right now around it?"

Kathy answered first. "I'm running my childhood belief that nobody cares about my feelings. What I need from you first, Craig, is a big hug. Then I need reassurance that it's okay for me to be scared." After he offered her affection and the reassurance she asked for, Kathy breathed a loud sigh as she came back into the present.

Craig took longer to answer. "I had to wait for my defensiveness to quiet down before I could hear my truth. But I see now that your fear has triggered my fear of not being good enough. I'd love to hear that you love me exactly as I am." Kathy made a habit over the next days and weeks of gently repeating this phrase to her husband. With time, Craig could hear Kathy's fear without taking it personally. Teaching each other which healing phrases sooth our trigger points helps us heal these old wounds.

When we stop letting our childhood stories bully us around, commanding center stage, we teach them to relax and share the same space with inner peace. When we recognize the "story of me" as just a story, we discover open space to explore our deeper sense of self inside. Problems still come, and stories still accompany them. But when we stop buying our childhood story as truth and ask for what we need directly, our hearts see loved ones and strangers as struggling human beings like us, in need of compassion.

I hold deep compassion in my heart for all of our human stories. As a therapist and workshop leader, I have witnessed firsthand the devastating effects that abuse, loss, despair, fear, anger, neglect, and addiction have on us as innocent children. And whether we are perpetrators, victims, or both, we all began as innocent children. Compassion sees us all as walking wounded, wearing the scars of being human. But even these deep scars, like our childhood stories and beliefs, are not all of who we are.

Our life history—our ethnicity, place of birth, parents, childhood joys, and sorrows, and our career and life goals—all shaped our character. But if we cannot look beyond our history to see all of who we are, we keep freedom at arm's length.

We are conscious presence in this body, noticing how past traumas shaped us. We are unlimited joy and compassion, delighting in the joy of being alive. We are spacious stillness, holding the good and bad of life in kindness.

Calming the Fear of Opening to Who We Are

At first, we open slowly to embracing this new sense of self. After all, we spent our entire lives believing that thoughts, feelings, beliefs, accomplishments, and history defined who we are. In this transition, we are not throwing these former identities away. We will still think, feel, believe, and accomplish for the rest of our lives. But we are expanding to include a new reality—the inner wisdom and freedom of our peaceful heart.

This surrender to a new sense of ourselves takes courage and commitment. The truth is, our deeper sense of self can feel threatening at first. The very thought that "I am not the person I've known myself to be for years" threatens our ego to the core. But we seldom realize at first that it is our ego that is threatened. Instead, our strong identity as the parent, professional, hard worker, or athlete we worked so hard to become all these years feels deeply threatened. Survival instincts kick in with this new threat looming. Soon our guard is up, ready to fight, freeze, or flee.

When I first opened to the possibility of my deeper sense of self, I felt threatened. As the first college graduate in my family, I devoted my adult life to getting a master's degree in psychology and being a successful licensed therapist, writer, and teacher. Simultaneously I pursued consciousness with a passion through meditation, body-centered therapy, Buddhism, and spiritual growth. And in my playtime, I trained and ran several marathons, half-marathons, and 10Ks before my knees forced me to limit myself to hiking.

But when my first spiritual teacher, Tarthang Tulku Rinpoche, said I was more than who I thought I was all these years, I felt indignant. All my hard effort to put myself through college and graduate school and be this independent, accomplished woman felt erased by eight simple words emanating from this Tibetan Buddhist master. For a month I stopped attending meditation class and meditating. On long runs, I would ruminate over the prospect of a different "me" for hours, until one day a door opened in my heart. My teacher had handed me the keys to my own freedom.

Instead of feeling like a part of me has been taken or deducted, knowing the conscious awareness that I really am infuses my daily choices with joy and inner peace.

A close friend, now in her sixties, also felt threatened when she first learned this deeper truth. "I was at a meditation retreat," she said, "seven days into silent sitting and walking, feeling calm and peaceful, when my teacher suggested I sit with the question: 'Who am I?' After ten days of labeling fears, judgments, and doubts 'thinking,' my mind jumped excitedly on this question, but I wasn't prepared for how my heart answered: 'You are awake, aware, loving presence in a body. You are nothing and everything.'

"My eyes flew open halfway into a forty-five minute seated meditation," she said. "I could not sit still. I stood up to walk, but by now, my skin was crawling. My mind raced with doubt, 'but but but...' trying to discount this truth and cling to that high-achiever person I thought I was all these years. What would happen to my personality, my tastes, my preferences, my style of being? I walked briskly, then jogged to burn off all the anxiety surrounding this new awareness. Later, when I called my meditation teacher back home, she reaffirmed the deeper truth that my heart told me. She invited me to take several breaths and walk often to integrate this deep truth into my awareness."

Now twenty years later she says, "I'm glad I asked myself 'who am I?' I'm so grateful to have lived two decades in the freedom and inner peace this truth brings."

Most of us welcome the truth of who we are—only after much resistance.

When my client Claudia—a strong-willed, young California lesbian —reached the point in therapy when I encouraged her to see past her childhood story to who she really is, she resisted. She was open to self-awareness, even meditation if it reduced stress. But she never let anyone tell her what to do.

"I worked damn hard to earn my rightful place on the highway union, despite my father's urgings to be a man's wife," she explained. "Sheer willpower and lots of cussing made me successful in this man's field. I'm not about to let anyone take that away."

"You sound threatened and angry," I said with a grin.

"Damn right!" she said. "I'm the first female in my family to work outside the home, and I'm not letting any guru steal my identity. Anyone who tries to tell me I'm not what I feel and believe is wasting their breath. I've found peace in my life with a steady paycheck. But if I'm not the woman I fought hard to become, then who the hell am I?"

"Slow down," I said. "Nobody is trying to take anything away from you. But what if there was room for even more of you inside? What if you get to stay that feisty, highly opinionated achiever that you are and feel much more light-hearted, joyful, peaceful, and free every day by connecting to a deeper sense of self?"

She looked quizzical. "Okay, you've got my attention. Keep talking."

"I know this is outside your comfort zone," I said. "But let's couch it in terms you understand. In therapy, you have grown less angry by labeling your personal reactions 'reacting' and letting them go, right? And when you name thoughts 'thinking' without buying into them, you've told me you feel calmer. In simple terms, this is meditation.

"But have you ever wondered which part of you inside is doing the labeling? It's not young Claudia, because we've both seen how her trauma needs lots of reassurance. And it's not your reactive ego that dredges up stories to hold you captive in the past.

"So I wonder who the you is inside who notices thoughts and feelings come and go? Who is the you that remains aware, after you let thoughts and fears go?"

Claudia looked down pensively. "I never thought of it that way. But since you ask, I guess it's a part of me I've never recognized before. She sure is capable, though, the way she notices everything but is never bothered by anything."

"Yes," I said. "This is your deeper self, your peaceful heart capable of holding all your feelings, thoughts, and experiences in loving compassion. She is always present."

Claudia laughed. "So I'm adding a whole new dimension to myself—not taking anything away. How do I get to know this inner wise me? I'm eager to meet her."

"By being fully present in this moment, where your heart always lives."

Like Claudia, we all need to discover who we are when the time is right. In our own timing, we need to find the courage to ask, "If I'm more than my thoughts, feelings, and reactions, then who am I?" This huge leap in awareness takes patience and courage.

Gradually, with our new tools of awareness, curiosity, kindness, and forgiveness in our back pocket, we step closer to meeting life from our deeper sense of self. Inside our peaceful heart, there is still plenty of room for the one we worked so hard to become *and* for the wise one we have always been.

As we wear this new, wiser, more compassionate self every day, we feel more relaxed, spacious, and peaceful. We give ourselves permission to step off the treadmill and be present in this moment as it is. What peace. What joy. What freedom. Finally we can take some deep breaths and really hear the doves cooing, the crickets chirping, and our hearts whispering loving, reassuring words of wisdom in our ear.

Inner peace comes from choices. Where decisions were once agonies, now they are as natural as the seasons, following their own innate knowledge. When we choose to set down our angry, hurt feelings and listen, to ourselves and others, we plant the seed for inner peace. When we choose again and again to let thoughts and fears flow through us, we nurture inner peace. When we choose to slow down and open our heart, we water the inner peace that is always here, inside our heart. When we choose to notice our judgments and resentments, peace flourishes in our inner garden.

Inner peace grows inside us like a spring tulip. At first, it remains underground, invisible to the naked eye. All we can see is the fear, doubt, judgment, anger, and shame that routinely fill our awareness. But secretly inside our hearts, it is preparing to bloom. And when the frozen ground of old habits thaw, allowing our minds to grow flexible and playful, the first shoots of inner peace appear in our awareness. Over time, as we keep choosing inner peace in the most raucous of settings, it blossoms like a bright red tulip, bringing a smile to our lips and hearts when we least expect it.

Heart Tools for Inner Peace

Practice each of these tools for one week before moving on to the next one. But if a specific tool calls you to spend more time with it, give yourself another week, month, or as long as you need in order to heal.

1. *Set an Intention For Inner Peace*

   Try to do this each morning. When you first wake, before getting out of bed, place both hands over your heart. With eyes closed, repeat five times: "I'm willing to choose inner peace all day." During your day, whenever you think of it, ask, "What am I practicing right now—suffering or inner peace? Fear or presence?" Without even letting a story finish its sentence, accept what is true and remind your self, "Inner peace is always right here."

2. *Drop into Your Deeper Sense of Self*

   View thoughts, reactions, fears, and feelings as waves coming and going on the surface of your awareness. Focus below these surface waves by taking ten deep breaths, then imagine breathing space around each thought, feeling, fear, or reaction. In this spacious present, locate the unlimited inner peace awaiting your arrival in your heart. Remind yourself of your deeper self by repeating, "I am conscious awareness, spacious stillness, and loving presence holding all surface waves in loving compassion." With each breath, relax into what is.

3. *Choose Inner Peace Over Problems*

   Identify a problem you are having and set it aside right now to take ten deep belly breaths. When you notice obsessive thoughts about the problem, name them "thinking" and let them go. Focus on your heart, whispering, "I'm willing to be fully present and tap into my unlimited inner peace." When you locate a smidgeon of inner peace, expand this by breathing directly into the feeling until it fills your whole body. From this place of inner peace, ask your heart, "What is my highest choice for resolving this problem?" Ask, breathe deeply, and listen patiently for a hunch, feeling-sense, or image to enter your awareness.

4. *Identify and Move Past Your Childhood Trauma and Core Beliefs*
Notice a repeated issue that you strongly react to and ask your-self, "Which childhood story is fueling my strong reaction?" Ask, breathe deeply, and patiently listen for the heart to reply.

Whether your childhood story and belief is feeling misunder-stood, unloved, unimportant, unworthy, or not good enough to get your needs addressed, take fifteen minutes to lie down, close your eyes, place both hands over your heart, and love the childhood belief just as it is. When it feels soothed, repeat inside, "In my peaceful heart I am totally joyful, totally loving and accepting, totally grateful and free." Keep repeating this inside until you feel the spaciousness that is deeply peaceful.

Remember that many stories and beliefs will stay with us one way or another for the rest of our lives. Never ignore a repeated feeling, no matter how familiar it is to you, no matter how much you may have worked with it previously. Loving our young self for feeling unlovable, unworthy, or unimportant in this moment heals early trauma.

Conclusion:
Coming Home to Freedom

Although you appear in earthly form,
your essence is pure Consciousness.
You are the fearless guardian
of Divine Light.
So come, return to the root of the root
of your own soul.
—RUMI

As our heart opens and we see ourselves and life through the kind, loving eyes of compassion, freedom becomes our daily companion. We lean into the spacious freedom that holds frustration, confusion, and trauma in its warm, loving embrace. In this real place, underneath ego's reactive anger, resentment, worry, and despair, which initially grab our attention, our wise heart beckons us back again and again into the present, into this peaceful moment where freedom lives right here, right now, always.

Our moment-to-moment task day after day, year after year, is to choose freedom more than anything else—more than the false happiness of money, sex, electronic toys, and fame, and more than chasing pleasure and avoiding pain, as ego promises is possible.

Freedom is the truth of who we are. Freedom is our birthright, our essential core, our true nature. We are always free, no matter what is happening around us or what feelings are moving through us. No longer lost for hours or days in ego's latest greatest thoughts, fears, regrets, and judgments, we freely come back to our breath and rest our awareness in the magic of this moment. We free ourselves when we label all thoughts "thinking" and refocus on what we are seeing, hearing, and touching in this moment.

Awareness brings conscious choice. No longer naive about the unconscious human conditioning we inherited at birth—those ego reactions that ran our ancestors' lives for years—we freely choose between fear and love, suffering and joy, resistance and freedom, reaction and presence. At any moment we possess the freedom to pause and feel the joy of being alive—or chase the false happiness ego promises at some future time. We can surrender, let go, and trust the ancient wisdom of our heart—or allow ego to drain the unlimited joy out of this precious moment.

Freedom evolves as we step into the present and totally accept life as it is.

Nonresistance is the first key. When we find the courage to say "yes" to every paradox life brings, "yes" to sorrow *and* joy, "yes" to loss *and* love, "yes" to illness *and* health, "yes" to disappointment *and* ecstasy, "yes" to resistance *and* acceptance of what is, then we rest in the freedom and inner peace that are our natural birthright.

Nonjudgment is a second key. Shedding our loyalty to ego's life-long habit of finding something wrong with the present returns our childlike wonder and curiosity for life's gifts. Each time we catch ego distracting us from the now with its favorite tactic, judgment, we take a deep breath and return to the unlimited joy, kindness, compassion, and inner peace that brings us home to the freedom inside our wise heart.

Nonattachment is a third key. When we stop needing life to be different than it is, when we let go of our personal attachment to events turning out in our favor, we choose freedom from suffering as our higher priority. We may not immediately welcome the return of back pain or understand the sudden betrayal of our lover leaving us for another. But with patience and awareness, compassion and clarity, as we keep choosing freedom, and keep accepting this paradox of human life as it is, we find spacious freedom and inner peace surrounding our pain and loss with compassion in the present.

Over the past ten months or so, bringing one heart power to every life situation each month, we have collected an inner toolbox filled with ten powerful heart choices, all leading to freedom: trust, curiosity, awareness, resourcefulness, compassion, kindness, gratitude, forgiveness, truthfulness, and peacefulness. Tucked inside each heart power are practical tools reminding us to choose freedom again and again and again.

It is important to remind ourselves, as often as we think of them, that these ten new heart powers will guide, protect, and love us through all sorts of sticky situations. Whenever we notice thoughts as thoughts, feelings as feelings, and reactions as reactions, we embrace the *power of conscious choice*: any moment we can decide to stay lost in ego's thoughts, fears, and reactions—or label them "thinking" and come back to stay in the present. The instant we awaken out of the illusion in our head, the *power of simple questions* deflates it with "Which story am I telling myself now?"

When awareness hears ego's favorite concerto convincing us to feel unlovable, misunderstood, or unworthy for the millionth time, we call upon *the power of responsibility* to ask, "What is my part in perpetuating this victim role?" The *power of fearless love* channels daily the approval, acceptance, and love we have waited a lifetime to receive; its reassuring words soothe our pain, heal our sadness, and love our fears unconditionally. If illness, pain, loss, or suffering arrive unexpectedly, the *power of acceptance* puts space around all unwelcome guests by holding them in warm, loving compassion.

These first five heart powers cultivate an open, loving, accepting relationship with ourselves, and they prepare us to respond differently to loved ones, strangers, problems, and the world—with more kindness, gratitude, honesty, forgiveness, and inner peace. This new, hard-won capacity to replace ego's incessant reactions with compassion—for our own pain and others'—changes how we respond to life forever.

Conscious awareness brings choice. Conscious choice brings freedom.

When loved ones fall back into old unconscious habits, we melt their anger, resentment, indifference, or fear with the *power of generosity*. When we recall the *power of appreciation*, we replace complaining with gratitude; we pause a moment to genuinely acknowledge loved ones daily for the small and not-so-small things they do to help us. This, along with compassionate listening, helps those we love feel seen, heard, valued, and respected. Countless times, we forgive our loved ones' humanness through the *power of letting go*. Despite past histories of lying through omission and half-truths, we commit to the *power of integrity* by speaking our truth and living in integrity with ourselves, loved ones, and the world. Meeting life with these heart powers again and again brings us to a deep place of inner peace through the *power of surrender*.

Now is the time to reconnect with the freedom living inside our wise heart.

When we set an intention in the morning, such as "I choose kindness," we find ourselves hours later meeting another's anger with kind words rather than aggression. Each time we start our day with "I choose compassion," the power of acceptance pops up just at that moment when our mate is plagued with unconscious doubt. We shift both of us into conscious awareness by gently asking, "Is your doubt button pushed? Let's both take a couple deep breaths and love you for getting momentarily lost in doubt."

If disappointment strikes unexpectedly, we can reach into our power tools and quickly address it with "I am free, even now. I choose fearless love." Immediately disappointment yields to the reassuring voice loving ourselves exactly as we are.

Throughout this book I have shared stories about the joy and freedom I feel hiking and skiing in Colorado. But freedom doesn't live only above 11,000 feet. Nor does it only exist on evenings, weekends, vacations, and retirement. It lives inside our heart in the present, beyond the memories, thoughts, and feelings that come and go. We never need to do or get or have or keep anything in order to be free. We simply need to come back into the present, moment to moment.

Freedom is such a basic tenet of democracy and living in the developed world that millions have defended it to the death. Yet freedom eludes us so much of the time. Why does it seem to always live somewhere in the future, just outside our reach?

Finding Freedom Where We Forget to Look

Like love, joy, happiness, and peace, we all want freedom. And freedom is always here. Yet we spend most of our waking hours telling ourselves that we are not free.

We dream about *someday*: "When I finally find love, make my first million, or retire, then I'll be free." But as long as we chase pleasure and convince ourselves that freedom lives in some future moment, not now, it evades us. As long as we buy ego's lie that freedom comes from avoiding pain, illness, loss, and conflict, freedom remains out of reach. Anyone who has graduated college, scored that great job or promotion, or found love knows that the freedom of achieving goals lasts but a fleeting second. Soon we are back in the trenches, facing fear and pain and life again.

We postpone freedom whenever we tell ourselves, "I can't possibly feel free now. I'm too sad, too jealous, too angry, too depressed to feel free." We quickly forget that all thoughts, feelings, and reactions occur *inside* the spacious, living truth of freedom.

We bypass freedom when we treat it like a final destination point. We buy into ego's myth that, once we achieve freedom, we'll never feel sad, angry, or depressed again—only peaceful and happy forever. Any thought or belief that holds us out of the present holds freedom away too. Such detours deny the real truth—that freedom is the truth of daily life. It shares the same vast inner space with all of life's ups and downs.

One morning, in meditation, I felt filled with freedom. I stood up from my meditation pillow, made breakfast, turned my computer on, and sat down to write—only to find a technological glitch that took two hours to fix. My clarity for writing was eaten alive by frustration, irritation, resentment, and impatience. Some days, this is how it goes.

On such days we wake up feeling fresh, open, and energetic, ready for the day—until something happens. Most days, something does happen. Freedom lives above, around, underneath, and right in the middle of what happens. Taking full responsibility for how our ego reacts to what happens each precious moment helps us reconnect with the warm, peaceful, spacious freedom surrounding life's daily events.

The naive belief that thinking will end once we label and let go of thoughts through meditation postpones freedom. Thoughts can sound so important and appear to matter so much. They constantly tell us what to say, how to say it, and what to do or not do. And too often we obey, no questions asked. But thoughts are not always our friend.

No matter how many years we meditate or how aware we become, we never stop thinking. And thoughts keep our calendar straight, keep us on task in our routine, and keep us boarding the right plane, bus, or train at the right time. Thoughts sort through a zillion details and dole them out to us as needed, so we are not perpetually overwhelmed by too much stimulus. Thoughts help us drive seventy miles per hour or more down the freeway with hundreds of other cars without hitting someone (hopefully). They remind us when to drive the kids to soccer or where we left the car keys.

The problem is when thoughts get top billing and control our lives. Instead, we need to hand control over to our heart, which is much better equipped to make wise, loving, compassionate choices. Rather than try to stop thinking, we need to remember, "I am not my thoughts, ego reactions, or childhood beliefs." This is when freedom comes.

As a therapist I have watched depression thoughts chew up a man's hard-earned retirement years. I have witnessed thoughts shrink and shrivel the kindest, most loving heart with self-loathing. I have seen doubt destroy countless creative ideas and business ventures before they enter the starting gate. I have witnessed fear cripple a cancer patient's hope far more than the disease itself. And more times than I wish to count, I have watched unacknowledged resentment kill perfectly good marriages.

Bringing Freedom into Love Relationships

In love relationships especially, we hold freedom away. We fall in love and create the dream relationship with a perfect someone we can share everything with—someone who adores us, accepts us, understands us, and loves us. But within some months or years, after we feel hurt or rejected by our perfect someone, we shift loyalties and adopt ego's fear: "If they really loved me, I'd never feel hurt, rejected, or abandoned."

What changed? That person who loved and adored us might have changed very little. But the victim story ego tells us inside our head—how we feel misunderstood, mistrustful, rejected, abandoned, unlovable, or hopeless—has a heyday demolishing our relationship. After months of hearing our childhood story and core beliefs rather than seeing our lover clearly daily, our willingness to trust love changes. And we begin the long, downhill slide into sabotaging the love we cocreated together, blaming the other person the whole time for destroying our relationship.

We compromise freedom. We paint a false picture in our head of *how love should look*, then compare how love is to this image. Real love never measures up. Ego prefers our picture of how love should be to how love is because this keeps ego in the driver's seat, manufacturing past and future possibilities. This prevents us from feeling love.

Freedom returns when we accept how love looks and feels right here, right now in this moment, even if our mind never expected love to look this way.

We must move beyond thought and reactivity into conscious awareness. Presence allows us to be still and open, to just look and listen, to be free to see the gifts that each moment of ordinary life brings. It allows us to relax and flow through life with ease. To surrender to what is. Freedom is like a trustworthy friend that brings many gifts:

- Freedom is seeing the sacred importance of this moment exactly as it is.
- Freedom is the inner peace and joy that come from loving compassion.
- Freedom is totally loving and accepting ourselves exactly as we are.
- Freedom is totally loving and accepting others exactly as they are.
- Freedom is finding gratitude for *everything* in life exactly as it is.
- Freedom is trusting ourselves, trusting life, and trusting who we are.
- Freedom comes from stepping into the present, again and again and again.

Freedom to Be Who We Really Are

We have the freedom to meet each moment with the joy, love, kindness, compassion, and inner peace that abound inside our heart, or we can keep letting fear drag us around by the nose another five years. It is always our choice.

Which will we choose today, now, in this moment? The time has arrived to gift ourselves with the freedom that is our true nature. With thoughts, stories, fears, and feelings taking up much less time, we feel more spacious inside, rich with time and ideas.

Freedom is this simple. So simple, mind often overlooks it.

Freedom fills us with the pure joy of being alive as we see the deeper truth: *We are the conscious awareness, the awake, loving presence animating our body.* And as conscious presence, we embody an unlimited capacity for joy, kindness, compassion, and inner peace. Knowing this brings constant delight in the process of life unfolding.

Freedom is open and trusting, graciously receiving this moment, each moment, while it leans back to rest in our deep, deep connection with all living things.

Freedom is the truth of life, including who we are in our heart.

Freedom is everywhere every moment, alive in all living things.

Freedom is the gift of this moment. Unwrap it now.

Selected Bibliography

Almaas, A. H. *Essence.* York Beach, ME: Samuel Weiser, 1986.

_____. *The Pearl Beyond Price.* Berkeley, CA: Diamond Books, 1988.

_____. *Diamond Heart, Book Four.* Berkeley, CA: Diamond Books, 1997.

Baraz, James, and Shoshana Alexander. *Awakening Joy.* New York: Bantam Publications, 2010.

Brach, Tara. *Radical Acceptance.* New York: Bantam-Dell Publishing, 2003.

_____. *True Refuge.* New York: Bantam Publications, 2012.

Chah, Ajahn. *Food for the Heart.* Boston: Wisdom Publications, 2002.

Chodron, Pema. *When Things Fall Apart.* Boston: Shambhala Publications, 1997.

_____. *The Places That Scare You.* Boston: Shambhala Publications, 2001.

_____. *Comfortable with Uncertainty.* Boston: Shambhala Publications, 2002.

_____. *Living Beautifully with Uncertainty and Change.* Boston: Shambhala, 2012.

Choquette, Sonia. *Your Heart's Desire.* New York: Three Rivers Press, 1997.

Gangaji. *The Diamond in Your Pocket.* Boulder, CO: Sounds True, 2005 and 2007.

Goldstein, Joseph. *Mindfulness: A Practical Guide.* Boulder, CO: Sounds True, 2013.

_____, and Jack Kornfield. *Seeking the Heart of Wisdom.* Boston: Shambhala Publications, 1987.

Friedman, Lenore, and Susan Moon. *Being Bodies.* Boston: Shambhala Publications, 1997.

Hendricks, Gay. *Learning To Love Yourself.* New York: Prentice Hall Press, 1987.

Hendricks, Gay and Kathlyn. *Conscious Loving.* New York: Bantam Books, 1990.

_____. *At The Speed Of Life.* New York: Bantam Books, 1993.

_____. *The Conscious Heart.* New York: Bantam Books, 1997.

His Holiness The Dalai Lama. *An Open Heart.* Boston: Little, Brown & Co., 2001.

Ingram, Catherine. *Passionate Presence.* Portland, OR: Diamond Books, 2003.

Jung, Carl G. *Memories, Dreams, Reflections.* New York: Random House, 1963.

Kornfield, Jack. *A Path with Heart.* New York: Bantam Books, 1993.

_____. *After the Ecstasy, the Laundry.* New York: Bantam Books, 2000.

_____. *The Art of Forgiveness, Lovingkindness, and Peace.* New York: Bantam, 2004.

_____. *The Wise Heart.* New York: Bantam Books: 2008.

_____. *The Buddha Is Still Teaching.* Boston: Shambhala Publications, 2010.

_____. *A Lamp in the Darkness.* Boulder, CO: Sounds True, 2011.

Ladinsky, Daniel. *I Heard God Laughing.* New York: Penguin Books, 2006.

Lesser, Elizabeth. *Broken Open.* New York: Random House & Villard, 2005.

Lowen, Alexander. *Bioenergetics.* New York: Penguin Books, 1975.

_____. *The Language of the Body.* New York: Collier Books, 1971.

Mindell, Arnold. *Working with the Dreaming Body*. New York: Viking Penguin, 1985.

Mindell, Arnold, and Amy Mindell. *Riding the Horse Backwards*. New York: Penguin Books, 1992.

Pierrakos, John C. *Core Energetics*. Mendocino, CA: LifeRhythm Publication, 1987.

Poonja, H. W. L. *Wake Up and Roar*. Kula, HI: Pacific Center Publishing, 1992.

_____. *Wake Up And Roar, Vol. 2*. Kula, HI: Pacific Center Publishing, 1993.

Richo, David. *How to Be an Adult in Relationships*. Boston: Shambhala, 2002.

Rodegast, Pat, and Judith Stanton. *Emmanuel's Book II: The Choice for Love*. New York: Bantam Books, 1989.

_____. *Emmanuel's Book III: What Is an Angel Doing Here?* New York: Bantam Books, 1994.

Salzberg, Sharon. *Lovingkindness*. Boston: Shambhala Publications, 1995.

Sewell, Marilyn. *Cries of the Spirit*. Boston: Beacon Press, 1991.

Tolle, Eckhart. *Stillness Speaks*. Novato, CA: Namaste Publications and New World Library. 2003

_____. *A New Earth*. New York: Dutton/Penguin Group, 2005.

_____. *Oneness with All Life*. New York: Dutton/Penguin Group, 2008.

Tsoknyi Rinpoche. *Carefree Dignity*. Hong Kong: Rangjung Yeshe Publications 1998.

_____. *Fearless Simplicity*. Hong Kong: Rangjung Yeshe Publications, 2003.

Tulku, Tarthang. *Gesture of Balance*. Berkeley, CA: Dharma Publishing, 1977.

_____. *Kum Nye Relaxation, Part I and II*. Berkeley, CA: Dharma Publishing, 1978.

_____. *Knowledge of Freedom*. Berkeley, CA: Dharma Publishing, 1984.

_____. *Hidden Mind of Freedom*. Berkeley, CA: Dharma Publishing, 1981.

Walker, Alice. *We Are the Ones We Have Been Waiting For*. New York: The New Press, 2006.

_____. *Hard Times Require Furious Dancing*. Novato, CA: New World Library, 2010.

Williams, Terry Tempest. *An Unspoken Hunger*. New York: Pantheon Books, 1994.

_____. *When Women Were Birds*. New York: Sarah Crichton Books, 2012.

Woodman, Marion. *The Pregnant Virgin*. Toronto, Canada: Inner City Books, 1985.

_____. *Conscious Femininity*. Toronto, Canada: Inner City Books, 1993.

Woodman, Marion, with K. Danson, M. Hamilton, and R. Allen. *Leaving My Father's House*. Boston: Shambhala Publications, 1992.

Woodman, Marion, and Elinor Dickson. *Dancing in the Flames*. Boston: Shambhala Publications, 1996.

Woodman, Marion, and Jill Mellick. *Coming Home to Myself*. Berkeley, CA: Conari Press, 1998.

Acknowledgments

I express deep gratitude to Susan Schulman, my literary agent, for supporting my books internationally, and to my editor, Shoshana Alexander, for refocusing twenty-six formative chapters into ten clear chapters. At Wisdom Publications, I thank Josh Bartok for envisioning the global value of *Free Yourself* and I thank editors Maura Gaughan and Laura Cunningham for helping the writing sing with their wise, skillful editing eyes. And I am forever indebted to Eleanor Greenlee, LMFT and International Bioenergetic Trainer, and to Tarthang Tulku, founder of Nyingma Institute in Berkeley, CA, who first opened the gateways to self-love and Buddhist wisdom simultaneously to me at age twenty-three.

Every day I feel grateful for my spiritual heart family of lifelong friends, whose personal commitments to meditation and cultivating presence, awareness, kindness, compassion, forgiveness, and integrity inspire my path to awakening: I thank my spouse Jo Alexander, whose generous heart and awake presence help me choose conscious loving daily; I thank my mentor, spirit sister, poet, and beloved friend Devi Weisenberg for her unconditional love, deep life wisdom, and willingness to hold my body, feelings, and heart in tender compassion whenever I am lost in suffering; I thank my beloved friend Debra Chamberlin-Taylor, a core teacher at Spirit Rock Meditation Center, whose fierce commitment to waking up into truth, compassion, and love shines like a guiding star to remind me and her students that we are always safe and loved enough to live in truth; and I thank Pamela Polland, whose generosity redefines the boundaries of friendship as she opened her Maui home and heart to us each August for twenty years to share the sheer joy of friendship and swimming with dolphins, sea turtles, and eagle rays. I thank my beloved friend Stan Weisenberg, whose healing hands and joyful heart constantly remind me that healing our past wounds is so worth the effort; I thank my dear friends Jen Behn and Joan Lohman, whose devotion to meditation and heart-felt political acts inspire me daily; and I thank my sister Carole Wampole, whose loving support and family gatherings fill me with family love and a true sense of belonging.

I thank Bill Ernst, who lovingly shared his Maui home and computer savvy with me for years. I thank my chiropractor Dr. Jim Forleo for healing my back, hips, and knees after hours of writing. And I thank longtime friend, poet, and fellow therapist George Taylor, for his great humor, poetry, and loving commitment to healing fellow brothers on the awakening path.

Professionally, I am deeply grateful for international trainers Gay and Kathlyn Hendricks, authors of *Conscious Loving* and *Conscious Heart*, whose body-centered therapy trainings taught me to unquestionably trust the body's wisdom and fearlessly surrender into the deepest realms of consciousness in my body. This helped me open this door for hundreds of clients. I deeply appreciate Jack Kornfield, Pema Chodron, Tarthang Tulku, Poonjaji, Gangaji, Eckhart Tolle, James Baraz, and now countless teachers around the world for making the spiritual teachings and Buddhist wisdom so available to everyone at this time. Locally, I appreciate Katherine Barr, Erin Treat, Maureen Fallon-Cyr, Bill Ball, and the Durango Dharma Center for all the ways they offer Buddhist teachings. And I honor Marion Woodman, whose lifelong passion for feminine consciousness inspired me. I also thank Mother Nature, whose eternal silence and unconditional loving acceptance nurtured my awakening as I walked her quiet meadows, hiked her mountainsides, and lay under her pine trees, asking, "What wants to be included?" in writing *Free Yourself*.

Index

Note: Page numbers followed by "q" indicate quotations. Page numbers in italics indicate heart tools.

About the Author

 As author, therapist, teacher, and work-shop leader, Carolyn Hobbs has used the heart tools outlined in this book with clients, couples, and workshop students for over thirty years. A licensed marriage and family therapist with a master's degree in humanistic psychology, Hobbs blends her two lifelong passions—Buddhist meditative wisdom and body-centered therapy—into her work, which draws from studies in Bioenergetics, Feldenkrais work and Breathwork, as well as Buddhism.

Based on her first book, *JOY, No Matter What* (2005), Hobbs began in 2004 teaching Everyday Joy workshops each spring at Spirit Rock Meditation Center in the San Francisco Bay Area and lecturing to professional therapists at U.S. Journal's annual conferences in Seattle, WA, and Santa Fe, NM. Prior to this, she was a visiting professor at Naropa Institute in Boulder, CO, and Ft. Lewis College in Durango, CO. In 2014, she began teaching at Omega Institute in Rhinebeck, NY. Excerpts and reviews of her first book appeared in such magazines and professional journals as *Woman's World*, *Woman's Day*, *Shambhala Sun*, *AHP Perspective*, *Imagine*, and *Essence*.

Certified since 1992 as a body-centered therapist by Gay and Kathlyn Hendricks, she works with clients nationally from her home base in Durango, CO. She's available for phone sessions with remote clients; please contact her through www.carolyn-hobbs.com.

About Wisdom Publications

Wisdom Publications is the leading publisher of classic and contemporary Buddhist books and practical works on mindfulness. Publishing books from all major Buddhist traditions, Wisdom is a nonprofit charitable organization dedicated to cultivating Buddhist voices the world over, advancing critical scholarship, and preserving and sharing Buddhist literary culture.

To learn more about us or to explore our other books, please visit our website at www.wisdompubs.org. You can subscribe to our eNewsletter, request a print catalog, and find out how you can help support Wisdom's mission either online or by writing to:

Wisdom Publications
199 Elm Street
Somerville, Massachusetts 02144 USA

You can also contact us at 617-776-7416, or info@wisdompubs.org.

Wisdom is a 501(c)(3) organization, and donations in support of our mission are tax deductible.

Wisdom Publications is affiliated with the Foundation for the Preservation of the Mahayana Tradition (FPMT).

Also from Wisdom Publications

Selfless Love
Beyond the Boundaries of Self and Other
Ellen Birx
248 pages | $15.95 | ebook $11.99

"Love is the common element that all of humanity strives for.
Ellen's exposition of selfless love shows how we can attain this. A
wonderful book. I heartily recommend it."
— Bernie Glassman, cofounder of the Zen Peacemaker Order
and author of *The Dude and the Zen Master*

How to Wake Up
Toni Bernhard
240 pages | $16.95 | ebook $12.35

"This is a book for everyone."
—Alida Brill, author of *Dancing at the River's Edge*

The Wisdom of Listening
Edited by Mark Brady
320 pages | $16.95 | ebook $12.35

"This collection of essays raises listening to a spiritual art."
—*Sacred Pathways*

The Grace in Aging
Awaken as You Grow Older
Kathleen Dowling-Singh
240 pages | $17.95 | ebook $11.99

"Don't grow old without it."
—Rachel Naomi Remen, MD, author of *Kitchen Table Wisdom*

Awakening through Love
Unveiling Your Deepest Goodness
John Makransky
Foreword by Lama Surya Das
280 pages | $16.95 | ebook $12.35

"A rare combination of fine Buddhist scholarship and deep meditative understanding. John Makransky has done us all a great service."
—Joseph Goldstein, author of *A Heart Full of Peace*

NOW!
The Art of Being Truly Present
Jean Smith
208 pages | $14.00

"Every saying in this book is a good tool for meditation."
—*Eastern Horizon*